THE 100 MOST INFLUENTIAL
PHILOSOPHERS
OF ALL TIME

THE BRITANNICA GUIDE TO THE WORLD'S MOST INFLUENTIAL PEOPLE

THE 100 MOST INFLUENTIAL PHILOSOPHERS OF ALL TIME

EDITED BY BRIAN DUIGNAN, SENIOR EDITOR, RELIGION AND PHILOSOPHY

Britannica®
Educational Publishing

IN ASSOCIATION WITH

ROSEN
EDUCATIONAL SERVICES

Published in 2010 by Britannica Educational Publishing
(a trademark of Encyclopædia Britannica, Inc.)
in association with Rosen Educational Services, LLC
29 East 21st Street, New York, NY 10010.

First Edition

Britannica Educational Publishing
Michael I. Levy: Executive Editor
Marilyn L. Barton: Senior Coordinator, Production Control
Steven Bosco: Director, Editorial Technologies
Lisa S. Braucher: Senior Producer and Data Editor
Yvette Charboneau: Senior Copy Editor
Kathy Nakamura: Manager, Media Acquisition
Brian Duignan: Senior Editor, Religion and Philosophy

Rosen Educational Services
Jeanne Nagle: Senior Editor
Nelson Sa: Art Director
Nicole Russo: Designer
Introduction by Stephanie Watson

Library of Congress Cataloging-in-Publication Data

The 100 most influential philosophers of all time / edited by Brian Duignan. — 1st ed.
    p. cm. — (The Britannica guide to the world's most influential people)
"In association with Britannica Educational Publishing, Rosen Educational Services."
Includes Index.
ISBN 978-1-61530-009-9 (library binding)
1. Philosophy. 2. Philosophers. I. Duignan, Brian. II. Title: One hundred most influential
philosophers of all time.
B72.A15 2010
109.2 — dc22

                                                              2009029773

Manufactured in the United States of America

Cover credit: Real Academia de Bellas Artes de San Fernando, Madrid, Spain/The Bridgeman Art Library/Getty Images

CONTENTS

Introduction	9
Pythagoras	17
Confucius	19
Heracleitus	25
Parmenides	26
Zeno of Elea	27
Socrates	28
Democritus	35
Plato	37
Aristotle	47
Mencius	54
Zhuangzi	55
Pyrrhon of Elis	57
Epicurus	57
Zeno of Citium	60
Philo Judaeus	62
Epictetus	65
Marcus Aurelius	66
Nagarjuna	69
Plotinus	71
Sextus Empiricus	72
Saint Augustine	74
Hypatia	79
Anicius Manlius Severinus Boethius	80
Śaṅkara	83
Yaqūb ibn Isḥāq aṣ-Ṣabāḥ al-Kindī	85
Al-Fārābī	86
Avicenna	89
Rāmānuja	92
Ibn Gabirol	95
Saint Anselm of Canterbury	96
al-Ghazālī	98
Peter Abelard	100
Averroës	103
Zhu Xi	105
Moses Maimonides	108
Ibn al-'Arabī	112

Shinran	114
Saint Thomas Aquinas	117
John Duns Scotus	122
William of Ockham	125
Niccolò Machiavelli	128
Wang Yangming	133
Francis Bacon, Viscount Saint Alban (or Albans), Baron of Verulam	134
Thomas Hobbes	139
René Descartes	143
John Locke	150
Benedict de Spinoza	160
Gottfried Wilhelm Leibniz	165
Giambattista Vico	168
George Berkeley	171
Charles-Louis de Secondat, baron de La Brède et de Montesquieu	175
David Hume	179
Jean-Jacques Rousseau	182
Immanuel Kant	188
Moses Mendelssohn	194
Marie-Jean-Antoine-Nicolas de Caritat, marquis de Condorcet	197
Jeremy Bentham	199
Georg Wilhelm Friedrich Hegel	200
Arthur Schopenhauer	206
Auguste Comte	209
John Stuart Mill	211
Søren Kierkegaard	214
Karl Marx	218
Herbert Spencer	223
Wilhelm Dilthey	226
William James	227
Friedrich Nietzsche	230
Friedrich Ludwig Gottlob Frege	236
Edmund Husserl	238

131

208

Henri Bergson   241
John Dewey   244
Alfred North Whitehead   247
Benedetto Croce   250
Nishida Kitarō   252
Bertrand Russell   254
G.E. Moore   263
Martin Buber   264
Ludwig Wittgenstein   269
Martin Heidegger   275
Rudolf Carnap   279
Sir Karl Popper   285
Theodor Wiesengrund Adorno   286
Jean-Paul Sartre   287
Hannah Arendt   292
Simone de Beauvoir   295
Willard Van Orman Quine   297
Sir A.J. Ayer   299
Wilfrid Sellars   303
John Rawls   305
Thomas S. Kuhn   308
Michel Foucault   309
Noam Chomsky   314
Jürgen Habermas   317
Sir Bernard Williams   320
Jacques Derrida   327
Richard Rorty   330
Robert Nozick   332
Saul Kripke   336
David Kellogg Lewis   339
Peter (Albert David) Singer   341
Glossary   345
Further Reading   347
Index   349

INTRODUCTION

Life doesn't come with an instruction manual. Each person is released into the world in the same way, naked and unaware, left to find his or her own way to some sort of understanding about the mysteries of their own existence. Once people grow and learn enough, they naturally start asking questions. How did the world—and universe—come to exist? Why am I here? What is my purpose in life? What happens after I die? People began their search for meaning very early on in the course of human history. The ancient Greeks developed an entire mythology of gods and goddesses to answer many of life's most fundamental questions.

Yet there were some who were not satisfied with the explanation that every major human event, from birth to death, was dictated by the whims of the gods. Men like Plato (429–347 BCE), Socrates (469–399 BCE), and Aristotle (384–322 BCE) preferred a more rational approach. Long before the age of modern science, they used reason to understand why things happened as they did, and to find some sort of order and security in what was an often chaotic and dangerous world. They questioned, probed, and refused to accept commonly held beliefs. Through their teachings, they became the towering figures of ancient Greek philosophy.

Theories of existence, knowledge, and ethics have been advanced and argued since the time of the ancient Greeks. Travelling through the pages of this book, you will discover the ideas that shaped the history of philosophy, and the men—and women—who gave birth to those ideas. In addition to Plato and Socrates, Aristotle, Thomas Aquinas, René Descartes, Arthur Schopenhauer, Jean-Paul Sartre, and Simone de Beauvoir are just a few of the philosophic luminaries profiled in this title.

In the simplest terms, philosophy is about thinking. French philosopher René Descartes (1596–1650) defined his entire existence in those terms. "I think, therefore I am," he famously proclaimed. The concept of a philosopher practicing his craft might bring to mind the famous Auguste Rodin sculpture, *The Thinker*, which depicts a man with chin on hand in deep contemplation. Yet philosophers do much more than sit around thinking and asking questions. They engage in fundamental discussions about nature, society, science, psychology, and ethics. They develop critical ideas about the way people live, and the way they should live.

There are three major fields of philosophical investigation. The first is ontology, which is the study of existence—what applies neutrally to everything that is real. Some of the earliest philosophers attributed human existence to the natural elements: earth, air, fire, and water. The Greek philosopher Heracleitus (lived around 500 BCE) thought it was fire that was the essential material uniting all things. The opposing forces of igniting and extinguishing fire gave balance and order to an otherwise random and disordered world.

The Greek scholar Democritus (c. 460–c. 370 BCE) found the basis of life in an element of a different kind—the atom. He believed not only that atoms made up everything in the universe, but also that the movement of atoms was responsible for every change or event that occurred (he had unknowingly discovered the foundation of modern physics). Democritus assumed that because atoms cannot be created or destroyed, nothing (and no one) can die in the absolute sense.

Other philosophers have claimed that the basis of all things is not elements, but mathematics. Pythagoras (c. 570–c. 490 BCE), familiar to high school math students for the theorem of right triangles ($a^2 + b^2 = c^2$) that's associated with his name, surmised that numbers gave an underlying harmony and order to everything in existence.

When it came to answering the question of existence, philosophy and religion often overlap. Some philosophers believed firmly in the religious ideal of God as the creator of all things. They have even used philosophy to prove the existence of God. The Archbishop St. Anselm of Canterbury (1033–1109 CE) argued that God must exist because it is impossible for humans to conceive of the greatest possible being as not existing. St. Augustine (354–430 CE) claimed that it is only through the contemplation of, and connection with, God that humans can find real happiness.

Other thinkers used philosophy for the opposite purpose—to dispute the ideas of religion and God. Danish philosopher and theologian Søren Kierkegaard (1813–1855) believed that the highest task of human existence was to become oneself in an ethical and religious sense. In part, he called faith irrational, and said people should take personal responsibility for their own destinies rather than simply follow the flock.

Philosophy and religion also have many differences of opinion when it comes to another theme in the search for the origins of human existence—the soul. Some religious belief holds that the body is just a container of sorts, which temporarily holds the essence of a person, which is deemed his or her soul. After death (if the person has behaved well in life), the soul supposedly goes on to a better place, which the Judeo-Christian religion has termed "heaven." Philosophers have had their own conceptions of the soul's purpose and journey. Plato saw it as immortal, while Baruch Spinoza (1632–1677) said that once the body died, the soul was gone too. French Existentialist Jean-Paul Sartre (1905–1980) held that there is no God, and therefore human beings were not designed for any particular purpose. The only thing that truly exists, he said, is the way things appear to us, or our perception of things.

The second field of philosophical investigation, epistemology, involves the study of knowledge—how we know what we know. It might seem as though people who sit around thinking all the time would know a great deal. However, the more philosophers pondered, the more they realized how little they actually understood. This led to questioning about the very origins of knowledge.

Socrates was a firm believer that people didn't know as much as they claimed they did. He was masterful at putting his students on the spot. Socrates' technique, called the Socratic method, was to ask his students a question, such as "What is knowledge?" or "What is virtue?" Then he would proceed to poke holes in their responses until they questioned their own understanding of the topic. In one conversation captured in Plato's *Republic*, Socrates relentlessly challenged the dramatist Agathon over the ideas of desire and love, until Agathon finally conceded his position, saying, "It turns out, Socrates, I didn't know what I was talking about in that speech."

How we obtain knowledge also has been the subject of some debate among philosophers. While Plato believed that people are born with some knowledge of an ideal reality (and it is the philosophers' job to show them how to live in accordance with that reality), John Locke (1632–1704) felt that babies are merely blank slates, waiting to be filled with the knowledge gained from experience and observation. Francis Bacon (1561–1626) agreed with the importance of observation. In fact, he suggested that every philosopher who had come before him had been wrong by focusing on words rather than on experimentation. Bacon's empirical approach to knowledge formed the foundation of the modern scientific method.

Yet there were some philosophers who questioned the validity of observation, arguing that people couldn't always trust their senses. Pyrrhon of Elis (360 – 270 BCE) and his fellow Skeptics believed that truth is unknowable, therefore nothing is as it seems. If we can't trust what we see, hear, smell, and feel, how can we be sure of anything? What we think we are experiencing in life might be nothing more than a dream.

The final of these three fields of investigation is ethics, also known as the study of values, or put simply, deciding what is right and what is wrong. The fundamental nature of humankind has long challenged the great philosophers. Are people born inherently good, evil, or somewhere in between? Is human nature predetermined by a supernatural being or self-directed? These ethical questions are crucial to systems of government and justice, determining the way people should live together in society, and when and how punishment should be meted out to those who don't follow what is considered the "right" way to behave.

The Scottish philosopher David Hume (1711–1776) said that good and evil can be derived from pleasure or pain. People's actions are not morally good or evil. It's how they are perceived that makes them that way. So if someone commits murder, the act itself has no significance other than that society views it as evil. German Existentialist Friedrich Nietzsche (1844–1900), who felt the idea of morality was something invented by the "herd" (society, community, family, the church), said people should throw out the ideas of good and evil as mere conventions, and instead create their own individual value systems.

Some philosophers, among them a member of the French Enlightenment named Jean-Jacques Rousseau (1712–1778), felt that human nature is inherently good, but people become corrupted when they stifle their natural desires to fit within the confines of society's rules and order. This repression is what ultimately leads to bad behaviour.

Are there ultimate rewards for following the rules, and punishments for failing to behave according to society's dictates? In the Judeo-Christian tradition, heaven awaits those who are "good," while hell lies below to capture those who are "bad." In Indian religion and philosophy, the idea of karma dictates that every action people take—good or bad—will determine what happens to them down the road. According to this idea, if you help an old woman cross the road, supposedly good things will be coming your way, either in this lifetime or the next (reincarnation is part of this belief). Steal money from a friend, and you might be coming back in the next life as a dung beetle.

The ideas of right and wrong extend to the political systems that govern people, and the way in which they should be ruled. Philosophers such as Niccolo Machiavelli (1469–1527) felt that people are inherently weak, and therefore need strong, even despotic leaders who rule by fear and intimidation. (The term "Machiavellian" has come to refer to unscrupulous or deceptive behaviours.) In contrast to these ideas are the teachings of Chinese philosopher Confucius (551–479 BCE), who believed that those in power should treat their subjects kindly in order to earn their respect.

These and the other great thinkers whose lives and beliefs are detailed in these pages have helped give shape and depth to human existence. And yet philosophy is a constantly evolving science. Just as some questions are addressed, new questions emerge. Expect the list of influential philosophers to grow over the years as people continue to probe and wonder about the great mysteries of the universe and human existence.

PYTHAGORAS

(b. c. 580, Samos, Ionia [now in Greece]—d. c. 500 BCE, Metapontum, Lucania [now in Italy])

Pythagoras was a Greek philosopher and mathematician. Born in what is modern-day Greece, Pythagoras migrated to southern Italy about 532 BCE, apparently in an effort to escape the merchant and territorial ruler Samos's tyrannical ways. After he arrived in southern Italy, Pythagoras proceeded to establish his ethical and political academy at Croton (now Crotone, Italy). At this academy, he founded the Pythagorean brotherhood, which, although religious in nature, formulated principles that influenced the thought of Greek philosophers Plato and Aristotle. In addition, it contributed to the development of mathematics and Western rational philosophy. Pythagoreans followed a very structured way of life. They believed that the human soul resided in a new human or animal body after a person died.

It is difficult to distinguish Pythagoras's teachings from those of his disciples. None of his writings have survived, and Pythagoreans invariably supported their doctrines by indiscriminately citing their master's authority. Pythagoras, however, is generally credited with the theory of the functional significance of numbers in the objective world and in music. Other discoveries often attributed to him (e.g., the incommensurability of the side and diagonal of a square, and the Pythagorean theorem for right triangles) were probably developed only later by the Pythagorean school. More probably the bulk of the intellectual tradition originating with Pythagoras himself belongs to mystical wisdom rather than to scientific scholarship.

Pythagoras demonstrating his Pythagorean theorem in the sand using a stick.
© Photos.com/Jupiterimages

CONFUCIUS

(b. 551, Qufu, state of Lu [now in Shandong province, China]—d. 479 BCE, Lu)

Confucius was China's most famous teacher, philosopher, and political theorist. His ideas have exerted an enormous influence on China and other civilizations of East Asia.

Confucius's life, in contrast to his tremendous importance, seems starkly undramatic—or, as a Chinese expression has it, "plain and real."

Although the facts about Confucius's life are scanty, they do establish a precise time frame and historical context. Confucius was born in the 22nd year of the reign of Duke Xiang of Lu (551 BCE). The traditional claim that he was born on the 27th day of the eighth lunar month has been questioned by historians, but September 28 is still widely observed in East Asia as Confucius's birthday. It is an official holiday, "Teachers' Day," in Taiwan.

Confucius's family name was Kong and his personal name Qiu, but he is referred to as either Kongzi or Kongfuzi (Master Kong) throughout Chinese history. The adjectival "Confucian," derived from the Latinized Confucius, is not a meaningful term in Chinese, nor is the term Confucianism, which was coined in Europe as recently as the 18th century.

Confucius's ancestors were probably members of the aristocracy who had become virtual poverty-stricken commoners by the time of his birth. His father died when Confucius was only three years old. Instructed first by his mother, Confucius then distinguished himself as an indefatigable learner in his teens.

Confucius had served in minor government posts managing stables and keeping books for granaries before he married a woman of similar background when he was

19. It is not known who Confucius's teachers were, but he made a conscientious effort to find the right masters to teach him, among other things, ritual and music. His mastery of the six arts—ritual, music, archery, charioteering, calligraphy, and arithmetic—and his familiarity with the classical traditions, notably poetry and history, enabled him to start a brilliant teaching career in his 30s.

In his late 40s and early 50s Confucius served first as a magistrate, then as an assistant minister of public works, and eventually as minister of justice in the state of Lu. It is likely that he accompanied King Lu as his chief minister on one of the diplomatic missions. Confucius's political career was, however, short-lived. At 56, when he realized that his superiors were uninterested in his policies, Confucius left the country in an attempt to find another feudal state to which he could render his service. Despite his political frustration he was accompanied by an expanding circle of students during this self-imposed exile of almost 12 years. His reputation as a man of vision and mission spread. Indeed, Confucius was perceived as the heroic conscience who knew realistically that he might not succeed but, fired by a righteous passion, continuously did the best he could. At the age of 67 he returned home to teach and to preserve his

Painting of Chinese philosopher Confucius, c. 500 BCE. Hulton Archive/Getty Images

cherished classical traditions by writing and editing. He died in 479 BCE, at the age of 73. According to the *Records of the Historian*, 72 of his students mastered the "six arts," and those who claimed to be his followers numbered 3,000.

THE *ANALECTS*

The story of Confucianism does not begin with Confucius. Nor was Confucius the founder of Confucianism in the sense that Buddha was the founder of Buddhism and Christ the founder of Christianity. Rather Confucius considered himself a transmitter who consciously tried to reanimate the old in order to attain the new. He proposed revitalizing the meaning of the past by advocating a ritualized life. Confucius' love of antiquity was motivated by his strong desire to understand why certain life forms and institutions, such as reverence for ancestors, human-centred religious practices, and mourning ceremonies, had survived for centuries. His journey into the past was a search for roots, which he perceived as grounded in humanity's deepest needs for belonging and communicating. He had faith in the cumulative power of culture. The fact that traditional ways had lost vitality did not, for him, diminish their potential for regeneration in the future. In fact, Confucius' sense of history was so strong that he saw himself as a conservationist responsible for the continuity of the cultural values and the social norms that had worked so well for the idealized civilization of the Western Zhou dynasty.

The *Lunyu* (*Analects*), the most revered sacred scripture in the Confucian tradition, was probably compiled by the succeeding generations of Confucius' disciples. Based primarily on the Master's sayings, preserved in both oral and written transmissions, it captures the Confucian spirit in form and content in the same way that the Platonic dialogues embody the pedagogy of Socrates.

The purpose of compiling these distilled statements centring on Confucius seems not to have been to present an argument or to record an event but to offer an invitation to readers to take part in an ongoing conversation with the Master.

Confucius' life as a student and teacher exemplified his idea that education was a ceaseless process of self-realization. When one of his students reportedly had difficulty describing him, Confucius came to his aid:

> *"Why did you not simply say something to this effect: he is the sort of man who forgets to eat when he engages himself in vigorous pursuit of learning, who is so full of joy that he forgets his worries, and who does not notice that old age is coming on?"*

Confucius was deeply concerned that the culture (*wen*) he cherished was not being transmitted and that the learning (*xue*) he propounded was not being taught. His strong sense of mission, however, never interfered with his ability to remember what had been imparted to him, to learn without flagging, and to teach without growing weary.

The community that Confucius created was a scholarly fellowship of like-minded men of different ages and different backgrounds from different states. They were attracted to Confucius because they shared his vision and to varying degrees took part in his mission to bring moral order to an increasingly fragmented world. This mission was difficult and even dangerous. Confucius himself suffered from joblessness, homelessness, starvation, and occasionally life-threatening violence. Yet his faith in the survivability of the culture that he cherished and the workability of the approach to teaching that he propounded was so steadfast that he convinced his followers as well as himself that heaven was on their side.

As a teacher of humanity Confucius stated his ambition in terms of concern for human beings: "To bring comfort to the old, to have trust in friends, and to cherish the young". Confucius' vision of the way to develop a moral community began with a holistic reflection on the human condition. Instead of dwelling on abstract speculations such as man's condition in the state of nature, Confucius sought to understand the actual situation of a given time and to use that as his point of departure. His aim was to restore trust in government and to transform society into a flourishing moral community by cultivating a sense of humanity in politics and society. To achieve that aim, the creation of a scholarly community, the fellowship of *junzi* (exemplary people), was essential.

The fellowship of *junzi* as moral vanguards of society, however, did not seek to establish a radically different order. Its mission was to redefine and revitalize those institutions that for centuries were believed to have maintained social solidarity and enabled people to live in harmony and prosperity. An obvious example of such an institution was the family.

It is related in the *Analects* that Confucius, when asked why he did not take part in government, responded by citing a passage from the ancient *Shujing* ("Classic of History"), "Simply by being a good son and friendly to his brothers a man can exert an influence upon government!" to show that what a person does in the confines of his home is politically significant. This maxim is based on the Confucian conviction that cultivation of the self is the root of social order and that social order is the basis for political stability and enduring peace.

The assertion that family ethics is politically efficacious must be seen in the context of the Confucian conception of politics as "rectification" (*zheng*). Rulers should begin by rectifying their own conduct; that is, they are to be examples who govern by moral leadership and exemplary teaching rather than by force. Government's responsibility is not only to provide food and security but also to educate the people. Law and punishment are the minimum requirements for order; the higher goal of social harmony, however, can only be attained by virtue expressed through ritual performance. To perform rituals, then, is to take part in a communal act to promote mutual understanding.

One of the fundamental Confucian values that ensures the integrity of ritual performance is *xiao* (filial piety). Indeed, Confucius saw filial piety as the first step toward moral excellence, which he believed lay in the attainment of the cardinal virtue, *ren* (humanity). To learn to embody the family in the mind and heart is to become able to move beyond self-centredness or, to borrow from modern psychology, to transform the enclosed private ego into an open self. Filial piety, however, does not demand unconditional submissiveness to parental authority but recognition of and reverence for the source of life. The purpose of filial piety, as the ancient Greeks expressed it, is to enable both parent and child to flourish. Confucians see it as an essential way of learning to be human.

Confucius defined the process of becoming human as being able to "discipline yourself and return to ritual." The dual focus on the transformation of the self (Confucius is said to have freed himself from four things: "opinionatedness, dogmatism, obstinacy, and egoism") and on social participation enabled Confucius to be loyal (*zhong*) to himself and considerate (*shu*) of others. It is easy to understand why the Confucian "golden rule" is "Do not do unto others what you would not want others to do unto you!" Confucius' legacy, laden with profound ethical implications, is captured by his "plain and real" appreciation that learning to be human is a communal enterprise.

HERACLEITUS

(b. *c.* 540, Ephesus, Anatolia [now Selćuk, Turk.]—d. 480 BCE)

Heracleitus was a Greek philosopher known for his cosmology, in which fire forms the basic material principle of an orderly universe. Little is known about his life, and the one book he apparently wrote is lost. His views survive in the short fragments quoted and attributed to him by later authors.

Though primarily concerned with explanations of the world around him, Heracleitus also stressed the need for people to live together in social harmony. He complained that most people failed to comprehend the Logos (Greek: "reason"), the universal principle through which all things are interrelated and all natural events occur, and thus lived like dreamers with a false view of the world. A significant manifestation of the logos, Heracleitus claimed, is the underlying connection between opposites. For example, health and disease define each other. Good and evil, hot and cold, and other opposites are similarly related. In addition, he noted that a single substance may be perceived in varied ways—seawater is both harmful (for human beings) and beneficial (for fishes). His understanding of the relation of opposites to each other enabled him to overcome the chaotic and divergent nature of the world, and he asserted that the world exists as a coherent system in which a change in one direction is ultimately balanced by a corresponding change in another. Between all things there is a hidden connection, so that those that are apparently "tending apart" are actually "being brought together."

Viewing fire as the essential material uniting all things, Heracleitus wrote that the world order is an "ever-living fire kindling in measures and being extinguished in measures." He extended the manifestations of fire to include not only fuel, flame, and smoke but also the ether in the upper atmosphere. Part of this air, or pure fire, "turns to" ocean, presumably as rain, and part of the ocean turns to earth. Simultaneously, equal masses of earth and sea everywhere are returning to the respective aspects of sea and fire. The resulting dynamic equilibrium maintains an orderly balance in the world. This persistence of unity despite change is illustrated by Heracleitus' famous analogy of life to a river: "Upon those who step into the same rivers different and ever different waters flow down." Plato later took this doctrine to mean that all things are in constant flux, regardless of how they appear to the senses.

Heracleitus was unpopular in his time and was frequently scorned by later biographers. His primary contribution lies in his apprehension of the formal unity of the world of experience.

PARMENIDES

(b. *c.* 515 BCE)

Parmenides was a Greek philosopher from Elea (in southern Italy) who founded Eleaticism, one of the leading schools of Greek thought before Socrates. His general teaching has been diligently reconstructed from the few surviving fragments of his principal work, a lengthy three-part verse composition titled *On Nature*.

Parmenides held that the multiplicity of existing things, their changing forms and motion, are but an appearance of a single eternal reality ("Being"), thus giving rise to the Parmenidean principle that "all is one." From this concept of Being, he went on to say that all claims of change or of non-Being are illogical. Because he introduced the method of basing claims about appearances on a logical concept of Being, he is considered one of the founders of metaphysics.

In Plato's dialogue the *Parmenides*, the character Parmenides, in conversation with Socrates, demonstrates that the latter's metaphysics of forms (ideal properties of things) is not viable.

ZENO OF ELEA

(b. *c.* 495—d. *c.* 430 BCE)

Zeno of Elea was a Greek philosopher and mathematician, whom Aristotle called the inventor of dialectic (a technique of logical argumentation and analysis). He is especially known for his paradoxes, which contributed to the development of logical and mathematical rigour and were insoluble until the development of precise concepts of continuity and infinity.

Zeno was the pupil and friend of Parmenides. In Plato's *Parmenides*, Socrates, "then very young," converses with Parmenides and Zeno, "a man of about forty"; but it may be doubted whether such a meeting was chronologically possible. Plato's account of Zeno's purpose (*Parmenides*), however, is presumably accurate. In order to recommend the Parmenidean doctrine of the existence of "the one" (i.e., indivisible reality), Zeno sought to controvert the commonsense belief in the existence of "the many" (i.e., distinguishable qualities and things capable of motion). In reply to those who thought that Parmenides' theory of the existence of "the one" involved inconsistencies, Zeno tried to show that the assumption of the existence of a plurality of things in time and space carried with it more serious inconsistencies. In early youth he collected his arguments in a book, which, according to Plato, was put into circulation without his knowledge.

Zeno made use of three premises: first, that any unit has magnitude; second, that it is infinitely divisible; and third, that it is indivisible. Yet he incorporated arguments for each. For the first premise, he argued that that which, added to or subtracted from something else, does not increase or decrease the second unit is nothing. For the second, he argued that a unit, being one, is homogeneous and that therefore, if divisible, it cannot be divisible at one point rather than another. His argument for the third premise was that a unit, if divisible, is divisible either into extended minima, which contradicts the second premise or, because of the first premise, into nothing. He had in his hands a very powerful complex argument in the form of a dilemma, one horn of which supposed indivisibility, the other infinite divisibility, both leading to a contradiction of the original hypothesis. His method had great influence and may be summarized as follows: he continued Parmenides' abstract, analytic manner but started from his opponents' theses and refuted them by *reductio ad absurdum*. It was probably the two latter characteristics which Aristotle had in mind when he called him the inventor of dialectic.

That Zeno was arguing against actual opponents, Pythagoreans who believed in a plurality composed of numbers that were thought of as extended units, is a matter of controversy. It is not likely that any mathematical implications received attention in his lifetime. But in fact the logical problems which his paradoxes raise about a mathematical continuum are serious, fundamental, and inadequately solved by Aristotle.

SOCRATES

(b. *c.* 470, Athens, Greece—d. 399 BCE, Athens)

Socrates was a Greek philosopher whose way of life, character, and thought exerted a profound influence on ancient and modern philosophy. Although Socrates himself wrote nothing, he is portrayed in conversation in compositions by a small circle of his admirers, the most important of whom was his student Plato. In Plato's dialogues, Socrates appears as a man of great insight, integrity, self-mastery, and argumentative skill.

LIFE AND PERSONALITY

Although the sources provide only a small amount of information about the life and personality of Socrates, a unique and vivid picture of him shines through, particularly in some of the works of Plato. We know the names of his father, Sophroniscus (probably a stonemason), his mother, Phaenarete, and his wife, Xanthippe, and we know that he had three sons. (In Plato's *Theaetetus*, Socrates likens his way of philosophizing to the occupation of his mother, who was a midwife: not pregnant with ideas himself, he assists others with the delivery of their ideas, though they are often stillborn.) With a snub nose and bulging eyes, which made him always appear to be staring, he was unattractive by conventional standards. He served as a hoplite (a heavily armed soldier) in the Athenian army and fought bravely in several important battles. Unlike many of the thinkers of his time, he did not travel to other cities in order to pursue his intellectual interests.

Socrates' personality was in some ways closely connected to his philosophical outlook. He was remarkable for the absolute command he maintained over his emotions and his apparent indifference to physical hardships. Corresponding to these personal qualities was his commitment to the doctrine that reason, properly cultivated, can and ought to be the all-controlling factor in human life. Thus he has no fear of death, he says in Plato's *Apology*, because he has no knowledge of what comes after it, and he holds that, if anyone does fear death, his fear can be based only on a pretense of knowledge. The assumption

An artist's representation of Socrates' (centre) *enforced suicide.* Hulton Archive/Getty Images

underlying this claim is that, once one has given sufficient thought to some matter, one's emotions will follow suit. Fear will be dispelled by intellectual clarity. Similarly, according to Socrates, if one believes, upon reflection, that one should act in a particular way, then, necessarily, one's feelings about the act in question will accommodate themselves to one's belief—one will desire to act in that way. It follows that, once one knows what virtue is, it is impossible not to act virtuously. Anyone who fails to act virtuously does so because he incorrectly identifies virtue with something it is not.

Socrates' conception of virtue as a form of knowledge explains why he takes it to be of the greatest importance to seek answers to questions such as "What is courage?" and "What is piety?" If we could just discover the answers to these questions, we would have all we need to live our lives well.

Another prominent feature of the personality of Socrates, one that often creates problems about how best to interpret him, is (to use the ancient Greek term) his *eirôneia*. Although this is the term from which the English word *irony* is derived, there is a difference between the two. To speak ironically is to use words to mean the opposite of what they normally convey, but it is not necessarily to aim at deception, for the speaker may expect and even want the audience to recognize this reversal. In contrast, for the ancient Greeks *eirôneia* meant "dissembling" — a user of *eirôneia* is trying to hide something. This is the accusation that is made against Socrates several times in Plato's works (though never in Xenophon's). His *eirôneia* may even have lent support to one of the accusations made against him, that he corrupted the young. For if Socrates really did engage in *eirôneia*, and if his youthful followers delighted in and imitated this aspect of his character, then to that extent he encouraged them to become dissembling and untrustworthy, just like himself.

SOCRATES IN THE DIALOGUES OF PLATO

Most scholars do not believe that every Socratic discourse of Plato was intended as a historical report of what the real Socrates said, word-for-word, on some occasion. What can reasonably be claimed about at least some of these dialogues is that they convey the gist of the questions Socrates asked, the ways in which he typically responded to the answers he received, and the general philosophical orientation that emerged from these conversations.

There is a broad consensus among scholars, however, that in Plato's early dialogues, in which Socrates insists that he does not have satisfactory answers to the questions he poses—questions such as "What is courage?," "What is self-control?," and "What is piety?"—Plato was attempting to convey the views of the historical Socrates. In the middle and late dialogues, in which Socrates does offer systematic answers to such questions, Plato was using the character of Socrates to present views that were largely his own, though they were inspired by his encounter with the historical Socrates and were developed using Socratic methods of inquiry.

The portrait of Socrates in all of the dialogues in which he appears (the *Laws* is the single exception) is fully consonant with that given in the *Apology*, a dialogue purported to be Socrates' speech at his trial for impiety in 399 BCE. In that work, Socrates insists that he devotes his life to one question only: how he and others can become good human beings, or as good as possible. The questions he asks others, and discovers that they cannot answer, are posed in the hope that he might acquire greater wisdom about just this subject.

"Socratic method" in modern usage is a name for any educational strategy that involves cross-examination of students by their teacher. However, in the method used by Socrates in the conversations re-created by Plato, Socrates describes himself not as a teacher but as an ignorant inquirer, and the series of questions he asks are designed to show that the principal question he raises (for example, "What is piety?") is one to which his interlocutor has no adequate answer. Typically, the interlocutor is led, by a series of supplementary questions, to see that he must withdraw the answer he at first gave to the principal question, because that answer falls afoul of the other answers he has given. This method employed by Socrates is a strategy for showing that the interlocutor's several answers do not fit together as a group, thus revealing the interlocutor's poor grasp of the concepts under discussion.

The interlocutor, having been refuted by means of premises he himself has agreed to, is free to propose a new answer to Socrates' principal question. But although the new answers avoid the errors revealed in the preceding cross-examination, fresh difficulties are uncovered, and in the end the "ignorance" of Socrates is revealed as a kind of wisdom, whereas the interlocutors are implicitly criticized for failing to recognize their ignorance.

It would be a mistake, however, to suppose that Socrates suspends judgment about all matters whatsoever. On the contrary, he has some ethical convictions about which he is completely confident: human wisdom begins with the recognition of one's own ignorance; the unexamined life is not worth living; ethical virtue is the only thing that matters; and a good human being cannot be harmed (because whatever misfortune he may suffer, including poverty, physical injury, and even death, his virtue will remain intact).

PLATO'S *APOLOGY*

Scholars generally agree about certain historical details of the trial depicted in Plato's *Apology*. They agree about what the charges against Socrates were: failing to acknowledge the gods recognized by the city, introducing other new divinities, and corrupting the young. They also agree that, having been found guilty, Socrates refused to propose a punishment that the jury would find acceptable; and that, after the jury voted in favour of the death penalty, he once again addressed the jury and expressed no regrets for his manner of living or the course of his trial.

Socrates spends a large part of his speech trying to persuade his fellow citizens that he is indeed a pious man, because his philosophical mission has been carried out in obedience to the god who presides at Delphi. But the two modes of religiosity he observes—serving the god by cross-examining one's fellow citizens and accepting the guidance of a divine voice—are nothing like the conventional forms of piety in ancient Athens. The Athenians expressed their piety by participating in festivals, making sacrifices, visiting shrines, and the like. They assumed that it was the better part of caution to show one's devotion to the gods in these public and conventional ways because, if the gods were not honoured, they could easily harm or destroy even the best of men and women and their families and cities as well.

If Plato's account of his philosophy is accurate, then Socrates lacked the typical Athenian's motives for participating in conventional forms of piety. He cannot believe that the gods might harm him, because he is confident that he is a good man and that a good man cannot be harmed. In effect, then, Socrates admits that his understanding of piety is radically different from the conventional conception. But not only does Socrates have an unorthodox conception of piety and of what the gods want from the citizens of the city, he also claims to receive infallible guidance from a voice that does not hesitate to speak to him about public matters.

If there is any doubt that the unorthodox form of piety Socrates embodies could have brought him into direct conflict with the popular will, one need only think of the portion of Plato's *Apology* in which Socrates tells the jurors that he would obey the god rather than them. Imagining the possibility that he is acquitted on the condition that he cease philosophizing in the marketplace, he unequivocally rejects the terms of this hypothetical offer, precisely because he believes that his religious duty to call his fellow citizens to the examined life cannot be made secondary to any other consideration. It is characteristic of his entire speech that he brings into the open how contemptuous he is of Athenian civic life and his fellow citizens. Here, as in so many parts of his speech, he treats his day in court as an opportunity to accuse his accusers, as well as his fellow citizens, for the way they lead their lives.

In effect, Socrates uses the occasion of his trial to put his accusers and the jurors on trial. But this was a natural role for him, because he had done the same thing, day after day, to everyone he met. The impact of his life was all the greater because of the way in which it ended. Following his trial, he was sentenced to death by poisoning (the poison probably being hemlock). He died at age 70.

DEMOCRITUS

(b. *c.* 460 — d. *c.* 370 BCE)

D emocritus was a Greek philosopher and a central figure in the development of the atomic theory of the universe.

Knowledge of Democritus' life is largely limited to untrustworthy tradition. It seems that he was a wealthy citizen of Abdera, in Thrace, he travelled widely in the East, and he lived to a great age. According to Diogenes Laërtius, an author noted for his history of Greek philosophy, Democritus' his works numbered 73. Only a few hundred fragments have survived, mostly from his treatises on ethics.

Democritus' physical and cosmological doctrines were an elaborated and systematized version of those of his teacher, Leucippus. To account for the world's changing physical phenomena, Democritus asserted that space, or the Void, had an equal right with reality, or Being, to be considered existent. He conceived of the Void as a vacuum, an infinite space in which moved an infinite number of atoms that made up Being (i.e., the physical world). These atoms are eternal and invisible; absolutely small, so small that their size cannot be diminished (hence the name *atomon*, or "indivisible"); absolutely full and incompressible, as they are without pores and entirely fill the space they occupy; and homogeneous, differing only in shape, arrangement, position, and magnitude. But while atoms thus differ in quantity, differences of quality are only apparent, owing to the impressions caused on our senses by different configurations and combinations of atoms. A thing is hot or cold, sweet or bitter, or hard or soft only by convention; the only things that exist in reality are atoms and the Void. Thus, the atoms of water and iron are the same, but those of water, being smooth and round and therefore unable to hook onto one another, roll over and over like small globes, whereas those of iron, being rough, jagged, and uneven, cling together and form a solid body. Because all phenomena are composed of the same eternal atoms, it may be said that nothing comes into being or perishes in the absolute sense of the words, although the compounds made out of the atoms are liable to increase and decrease, explaining a thing's appearance and disappearance, or "birth" and "death."

Just as the atoms are uncaused and eternal, so too, according to Democritus, is motion. Democritus posited the fixed and "necessary" laws of a purely mechanical system, in which there was no room for an intelligent cause working with a view to an end. He explained the origin of the universe as follows. The original motion of the atoms was in all directions—it was a sort of "vibration"; hence there resulted collisions and, in particular, a whirling movement, whereby similar atoms were brought together and united to form larger bodies and worlds. This happened not as the result of any purpose or design but rather merely as the result of "necessity"; i.e., it is the normal manifestation of the nature of the atoms themselves. Atoms and

Void being infinite in number and extent, and motion having always existed, there must always have been an infinite number of worlds, all consisting of similar atoms in various stages of growth and decay.

Democritus devoted considerable attention to perception and knowledge. He asserted, for example, that sensations are changes produced in the soul by atoms emitted from other objects that impinge on it; the atoms of the soul can be affected only by the contact of other atoms. But sensations such as sweet and bitter are not as such inherent in the emitted atoms, for they result from effects caused merely by the size and shape of the atoms; e.g., sweet taste is due to round and not excessively small atoms. Democritus also was the first to attempt to explain colour, which he thought was due to the "position" (which he differentiated from shape) of the constituent atoms of compounds. The sensation of white, for instance, is caused by atoms that are smooth and flat so as to cast no shadow; the sensation of black is caused by rough, uneven atoms.

Democritus attributed popular belief in the gods to a desire to explain extraordinary phenomena (thunder, lightning, earthquakes) by reference to superhuman agency. His ethical system, founded on a practical basis, posited an ultimate good ("cheerfulness") that was "a state in which the soul lives peacefully and tranquilly, undisturbed by fear or superstition or any other feeling."

PLATO

(b. 428/427, Athens, Greece—d. 348/347 BCE, Athens)

Plato was the most famous student of Socrates (c. 470–399 BCE), the teacher of Aristotle (384–322 BCE), and the founder of the Academy. He is best known as the author of philosophical works of unparalleled influence.

The son of Ariston (his father) and Perictione (his mother), Plato was born in the year after the death of the great Athenian statesman Pericles. His brothers Glaucon and Adeimantus are portrayed as interlocutors in Plato's masterpiece the *Republic*, and his half brother Antiphon figures in the *Parmenides*. Plato's family was aristocratic and distinguished: his father's side claimed descent from the god Poseidon, and his mother's side was related to the lawgiver Solon (*c.* 630–560 BCE). Less creditably, his mother's close relatives Critias and Charmides were among the Thirty Tyrants who seized power in Athens and ruled briefly until the restoration of democracy in 403.

Plato as a young man was a member of the circle around Socrates. Since the latter wrote nothing, what is known of his characteristic activity of engaging his fellow citizens (and the occasional itinerant celebrity) in conversation derives wholly from the writings of others, most notably Plato himself. The works of Plato commonly referred to as "Socratic" represent the sort of thing the historical Socrates was doing.

Plato was profoundly affected by both the life and the death of Socrates. The activity of the older man provided the starting point of Plato's philosophizing. In fact, his classic *Apology* purports to be the speech Socrates gave at his trial in response to the accusations made against him (Greek *apologia* means "defense"). Its powerful advocacy of the examined life and its condemnation of Athenian democracy have made it one of the central documents of Western thought and culture.

Plato's motives in writing the *Apology* are likely to have been complex. One of them, no doubt, was to defend and praise Socrates by making use of many of the points Socrates himself had offered in his speech. But Plato is at the same time using the trial and death of Socrates to condemn Athens, to call upon his readers to reject the conventional life that Athens would have preferred Socrates to lead, and to choose instead the life of a Socratic philosopher. In the 4th century BCE Athens had no norm of accurate reportage or faithful biography, and so Plato would have felt free to shape his material in whatever way suited his mulitple aims. Because it was Socrates he wished to praise, he had no choice but to make the Socrates of the *Apology* close to the original. But he would not have felt bound merely to reproduce, as best he could, the speech that Socrates delivered.

Plato's Academy, founded in the 380s, was the ultimate ancestor of the modern university (hence the English term *academic*); an influential centre of research and learning, it attracted many men of outstanding ability. For 20 years Aristotle was also a member of the Academy. He started his own school, the Lyceum, only after Plato's death, when he was passed over as Plato's successor at the Academy, probably because of his connections to the court of Macedonia.

HAPPINESS AND VIRTUE

The characteristic question of ancient ethics is "How can I be happy?" and the basic answer is "by means of virtue." But in the relevant sense of the word, happiness—the conventional English translation of the ancient Greek *eudaimonia*—is not a matter of mood or emotional state. Rather, as in a slightly archaic English usage, it is a matter of having things go well. Being happy in this sense is living a life of what some scholars call "human flourishing." Thus, the question "How can I be happy?" is equivalent to "How can I live a good life?"

Whereas the notion of happiness in Greek philosophy applies at most to living things, that of *arete*—"virtue" or "excellence"—applies much more widely. Anything that

The artist Raphael portrayed a meeting between Plato (left) *and Aristotle in the fresco* School of Athens. Hulton Archive/Getty Images

has a characteristic use, function, or activity has a virtue or excellence, which is whatever disposition enables things of that kind to perform well. The excellence of a race horse is whatever enables it to run well; the excellence of a knife is whatever enables it to cut well; and the excellence of an eye is whatever enables it to see well. Human virtue, accordingly, is whatever enables human beings to live good lives. Thus the notions of happiness and virtue are linked.

But it is far from obvious what a good life consists of, and so it is difficult to say what virtue, the condition that makes it possible, might be. Already by Plato's time a conventional set of virtues had come to be recognized by the larger culture; they included courage, justice, piety, modesty or temperance, and wisdom. Socrates and Plato undertook to discover what these virtues really amount to. A truly satisfactory account of any virtue would identify what it is, show how possessing it enables one to live well, and indicate how it is best acquired.

In Plato's representation of the activity of the historical Socrates, the interlocutors are examined in a search for definitions of the virtues. It is important to understand, however, that the definition sought for is not lexical, merely specifying what a speaker of the language would understand the term to mean as a matter of linguistic competence. Rather, the definition is one that gives an account of the real nature of the thing named by the term; accordingly, it is sometimes called a "real" definition. The real definition of *water*, for example, is H_2O, though speakers in most historical eras did not know this.

THE REPUBLIC

In *The Republic*, a Socratic dialogue that is considered one of the most influential works of philosophical thought,

Plato develops a unique view of happiness and virtue. According to Plato, there are three parts of the soul, each with its own object of desire. Reason desires truth and the good of the whole individual, spirit is preoccupied with honour and competitive values, and appetite has the traditional low tastes for food, drink, and sex. Because the soul is complex, erroneous calculation is not the only way it can go wrong. The three parts can pull in different directions, and the low element, in a soul in which it is overdeveloped, can win out. Correspondingly, the good condition of the soul involves more than just cognitive excellence. In the terms of *The Republic*, the healthy or just soul has psychic harmony—the condition in which each of the three parts does its job properly.

Although the dialogue starts from the question "Why should I be just?," Socrates proposes that this inquiry can be advanced by examining justice "writ large" in an ideal city. Thus, the political discussion is undertaken to aid the ethical one. One early hint of the existence of the three parts of the soul in the individual is the existence of three classes in the well-functioning state: rulers, guardians, and producers. The wise state is the one in which the rulers understand the good; the courageous state is that in which the guardians can retain in the heat of battle the judgments handed down by the rulers about what is to be feared; the temperate state is that in which all citizens agree about who is to rule; and the just state is that in which each of the three classes does its own work properly.

Justice as conceived in *The Republic* is so comprehensive that a person who possessed it would also possess all the other virtues, thereby achieving "the health of that whereby we live [the soul]." Yet, lest it be thought that habituation and correct instruction in human affairs alone can lead to this condition, one must keep in view that *The*

Republic also develops the famous doctrine according to which reason cannot properly understand the human good or anything else without grasping the form of the Good itself. Thus the original inquiry, whose starting point was a motivation each individual is presumed to have (to learn how to live well), leads to a highly ambitious educational program. Starting with exposure only to salutary stories, poetry, and music from childhood and continuing with supervised habituation to good action and years of training in a series of mathematical disciplines, this program—and so virtue—would be complete only in the person who was able to grasp the first principle, the Good, and to proceed on that basis to secure accounts of the other realities. There are hints in *The Republic*, as well as in the tradition concerning Plato's lecture *On the Good* and in several of the more technical dialogues, that this first principle is identical with Unity, or the One.

THE THEORY OF FORMS

Plato is both famous and infamous for his theory of forms. Just what the theory is, and whether it was ever viable, are matters of extreme controversy. To readers who approach Plato in English, the relationship between forms and sensible particulars, called in translation "participation," seems purposely mysterious. Moreover, the claim that the sensible realm is not fully real, and that it contrasts in this respect with the "pure being" of the forms, is perplexing. A satisfactory interpretation of the theory must rely on both historical knowledge and philosophical imagination.

FORMS AS PERFECT EXEMPLARS

According to a view that some scholars have attributed to Plato's middle dialogues, participation is imitation or resemblance. Each form is approximated by the sensible particulars that display the property in question. Thus, Achilles and Helen are imperfect imitations of the Beautiful, which itself is maximally beautiful. On this interpretation, the "pure being" of the forms consists of their being perfect exemplars of themselves and not exemplars of anything else. Unlike Helen, the form of the Beautiful cannot be said to be both beautiful and not beautiful— similarly for Justice, Equality, and all the other forms.

This "super-exemplification" interpretation of participation provides a natural way of understanding the notion of the pure being of the forms and such self-predication sentences as "the Beautiful is beautiful." Yet it is absurd. In Plato's theory, forms play the functional role of universals, and most universals, such as greenness, generosity, and largeness, are not exemplars of themselves. (Greenness does not exhibit hue; generosity has no one to whom to give; largeness is not a gigantic object.) Moreover, it is problematic to require forms to exemplify only themselves, because there are properties, such as being and unity, that all things, including all forms, must exhibit. (So Largeness must have a share of Being to be anything at all, and it must have a share of Unity to be a single form.) Plato was not unaware of the severe difficulties inherent in the super-exemplification view; indeed, in the *Parmenides* and the *Sophist* he became the first philosopher to demonstrate these problems.

The first part of the *Parmenides* depicts the failure of the young Socrates to maintain the super-exemplification view of the forms against the critical examination of the older philosopher Parmenides. Since what Socrates there says about forms is reminiscent of the assertions of the character Socrates in the middle dialogues *Symposium*, *Phaedo*, and *Republic*, the exchange is usually interpreted as a negative assessment by Plato of the adequacy of his earlier presentation. Those who consider the first part of the *Parmenides* in isolation tend to suppose that Plato had heroically come to grips with the unviability of his theory, so that by his late period he was left with only dry and uninspiring exercises, divorced from the exciting program of the great masterpieces. Those who consider the dialogue as a whole, however, are encouraged by Parmenides' praise for the young Socrates and by his assertion that the exercise constituting the second part of the dialogue will help Socrates to get things right in the future. This suggests that Plato believed that the theory of forms could be developed in a way that would make it immune to the objections raised against the super-exemplification view.

FORMS AS GENERA AND SPECIES

Successful development of the theory of forms depended upon the development of a distinction between two kinds of predication. Plato held that a sentence making a predication about a sensible particular, "A is B," must be understood as stating that the particular in question, A, displays a certain property, B. There are ordinary predications about the forms, which also state that the forms in question display properties. Crucially, however, there is also a special kind of predication that can be used to express a form's nature. Since Plato envisaged that these natures could be given in terms of genus-species trees, a special predication about a form, "A is B," is true if B appears above A in its correct tree as a differentia or genus. Equivalently, "A is B" has the force that being a B is (part of) what it is to be an A. This special predication is closely approximated in modern classifications of animals and plants according to a biological taxonomy. "The wolf is a canis," for example, states that "wolf" appears below "canis" in a genus-species classification of the animals, or equivalently that being a canis is part of what it is to be a wolf (*Canis lupus*).

Plato's distinction can be illustrated by examples such as the following. The ordinary predication "Socrates is just" is true, because the individual in question displays the property of being just. Understood as a special predication, however, the assertion is false, because it is false that being just is part of what it is to be Socrates (there is no such thing as what it is to be Socrates). "Man is a vertebrate," understood as an ordinary predication, is false, since the form Man does not have a backbone. But when treated as a special predication it is true, since part of what it is to be a human is to be a vertebrate. Self-predication sentences are now revealed as trivial but true: "the Beautiful is beautiful" asserts only that being beautiful is (part of) what it is to be beautiful. In general one must be careful not to assume that Plato's self-predication sentences involve ordinary predication, which would in many cases involve problematic self-exemplification issues.

By means of special predication it is possible to provide an account of each fundamental nature. Such accounts, moreover, provide a way of understanding the "pure being" of the forms: it consists of the fact that there cannot be a true special predication of the form "A is both B and not-B." In other words, special predication sentences do not exhibit the phenomenon of rolling around between being and not being. This is because it must be the case that either B appears above A in a correct genus-species classification or it does not. Moreover, since forms do not function by being exemplars of themselves only, there is nothing to prevent their having other properties, such as being and unity, as appropriate. As Plato expresses it, all forms must participate in Being and Unity.

Because the special predications serve to give (in whole or in part) the real definitions that Socrates had been searching for, this interpretation of the forms connects Plato's most technical dialogues to the literary master-pieces and to the earlier Socratic dialogues. The technical works develop a schema that, with modifications of course, went on to be productive in the work of Aristotle and many later researchers. In this way, Plato's late theory of the forms grows out of the program of his teacher and leads forward to the research of his students and well beyond.

ARISTOTLE

(b. 384, Stagira, Chalcidice, Greece—d. 322 BCE, Chalcis, Euboea)

Aristotle, a Greek philosopher and scientist, was one of the greatest intellectual figures of Western history. He was the author of a philosophical and scientific system that became the framework and vehicle for both Christian Scholasticism and medieval Islamic philosophy. Even after the intellectual revolutions of the Renaissance, the Reformation, and the Enlightenment, Aristotelian concepts remained embedded in Western thinking.

Aristotle was born on the Chalcidic peninsula of Macedonia, in northern Greece. His father, Nicomachus, was the physician of Amyntas III (reigned *c.* 393–*c.* 370 BCE), king of Macedonia and grandfather of Alexander the Great (reigned 336–323 BCE). After his father's death in 367, Aristotle migrated to Athens, where he joined the Academy of Plato (*c.* 428–*c.* 348 BCE). He remained there for 20 years as Plato's pupil and colleague.

When Plato died about 348, his nephew Speusippus became head of the Academy, and Aristotle left Athens. He migrated to Assus, a city on the northwestern coast of Anatolia (in present-day Turkey), where Hermias, a graduate of the Academy, was ruler. Aristotle became a close friend of Hermias and eventually married his ward Pythias.

About eight years after the death of Hermias, in 343 or 342, Aristotle was summoned by Philip II to the Macedonian capital at Pella to act as tutor to Philip's 13-year-old son, the future Alexander the Great. Little is known of the content of Aristotle's instruction. By 326 Alexander had made himself master of an empire that stretched from the Danube to the Indus and included Libya and Egypt.

In about 334, Aristotle, now 50 years old, established his own school, called the Lyceum, just outside Athens.

When Alexander died in 323, democratic Athens became uncomfortable for Macedonians. Saying that he did not wish the city that had executed Socrates "to sin twice against philosophy," Aristotle fled to Chalcis, where he died the following year.

DOCTRINES

Aristotle rightly claimed to be the founder of logic. His chief works in this field are the *Categories*, the *De interpretatione*, and the *Prior Analytics*, which deal respectively with words, propositions, and syllogisms.

The syllogism, a central method of inference, can be illustrated by familiar examples such as the following:

Every Greek is human. Every human is mortal. Therefore, every Greek is mortal.

Aristotle discusses the various forms that syllogisms can take and identifies which forms constitute reliable inferences. The example above contains three "propositions," the third of which Aristotle calls the "conclusion." The other two propositions may be called "premises," though

Aristotle does not consistently use any particular technical term to distinguish them.

The propositions in the example above begin with the word *every*; Aristotle calls such propositions "universal." Universal propositions may be affirmative, as in this example, or negative, as in *No Greek is a horse*. Universal propositions differ from "particular" propositions, such as *Some Greek is bearded* (a particular affirmative) and *Some Greek is not bearded* (a particular negative). In the Middle Ages it became customary to call the difference between universal and particular propositions a difference of "quantity" and the difference between affirmative and negative propositions a difference of "quality."

In propositions of all these kinds, Aristotle says, something is predicated of something else. The items that enter into predications Aristotle calls "terms." It is a feature of terms that they can figure either as predicates or as subjects of predication. This means that they can play three distinct roles in a syllogism. The term that is the predicate of the conclusion is the "major" term; the term of which the major term is predicated in the conclusion is the "minor" term; and the term that appears in each of the premises is the "middle" term.

Aristotle also introduced the practice of using schematic letters to identify particular patterns of argument. Thus, the pattern of argument exhibited in the example above can be represented in the schematic proposition:

If A belongs to every B, and B belongs to every C, A belongs to every C.

Because propositions may differ in quantity and quality, and because the middle term may occupy several different places in the premises, many different patterns of syllogistic inference are possible.

From late antiquity, these different patterns were called "moods" of the syllogism. Importantly, some moods correspond to valid arguments and some to invalid ones (an argument is valid if it is impossible for its premises to be true while its conclusion is false). Aristotle sought to determine which moods result in valid inferences, and he set out a number of rules giving necessary conditions for the validity of a syllogism.

Physics and Metaphysics

Aristotle understood physics as equivalent to what would now be called "natural philosophy," or the study of nature (*physis*); in this sense it encompasses not only the modern field of physics but also biology, chemistry, geology, psychology, and even meteorology. Although Aristotle never uses the word "metaphysics"—it first appeared in the posthumous catalog of his writings as a name for the works listed after the *Physics*—he does recognize the branch of philosophy now called metaphysics, which he calls it "first philosophy."

Forms

Although Aristotle's system makes room for forms, they differ significantly from forms as Plato conceived them. For Aristotle, the form of a particular thing is not separate (*chorista*) from the thing itself—any form is the form of some thing. In Aristotle's physics, form is always paired with matter, and the paradigm examples of forms are those of material substances.

When a thing comes into being, neither its matter nor its form is created. But the fact that the forms of things are not created does not mean that they must exist independently of matter, outside space and time, as Plato maintained. The bronze sphere derives its shape not from an ideal Sphere but from its maker, who introduces form into the appropriate matter in the process of his work. Likewise, Socrates' humanity derives not from an ideal Human but from his parents, who introduce form into the appropriate matter when they conceive him.

CAUSATION

In several places Aristotle distinguishes four types of cause, or explanation. First, he says, there is that of which and out of which a thing is made, such as the bronze of a statue. This is called the material cause. Second, there is the form or pattern of a thing, which may be expressed in its definition; Aristotle's example is the proportion of the length of two strings in a lyre, which is the formal cause of one note's being the octave of another. The third type of cause is the origin of a change or state of rest in something; this is often called the "efficient cause." Aristotle gives as examples a person reaching a decision, a father begetting a child, a sculptor carving a statue, and a doctor healing a patient. The fourth and last type of cause is the end or goal of a thing—that for the sake of which a thing is done. This is known as the "final cause."

The way in which Aristotle seeks to show that the universe is a single causal system is through an examination of the notion of movement, which finds its culmination in Book XI of the *Metaphysics*. Motion, for Aristotle, refers to change in any of several different categories. Aristotle's fundamental principle is that everything that is in motion is moved by something else, and he offers a number of (unconvincing) arguments to this effect. He then argues that there cannot be an infinite series of moved movers. If it is true that when A is in motion, there must be some B that moves A; then if B is itself in motion, there must be some C moving B, and so on. This series cannot go on forever, and so it must come to a halt in some X that is a cause of motion but does not move itself—an unmoved mover. Aristotle is prepared to call this unmoved mover "God."

ETHICS

The surviving works of Aristotle include three treatises on moral philosophy: the *Nicomachean Ethics* in 10 books, the *Eudemian Ethics* in 7 books, and the *Magna moralia* (Latin: "Great Ethics").

Aristotle's approach to ethics is teleological. If life is to be worth living, he argues, it must surely be for the sake of something that is an end in itself—i.e., desirable for its own sake. If there is any single thing that is the highest human good, therefore, it must be desirable for its own sake, and all other goods must be desirable for the sake of it.

The term that Aristotle uses to designate the highest human good is "happiness," by which he means well-being or flourishing, not a feeling of contentment. Aristotle argues that human beings must have a function, because particular types of humans (e.g., sculptors) do, as do the parts and organs of individual human beings. This function must be unique to humans; it must therefore involve the peculiarly human faculty of reason. The highest human good, happiness, is the same as good human functioning, and good human functioning is the same as the good exercise of the faculty of reason—that is to say, the activity of the rational soul in accordance with virtue. There are two kinds of virtue: moral and intellectual. Moral virtues are exemplified by courage, temperance, and liberality; the key intellectual virtues are wisdom, which governs ethical behaviour, and understanding, which is expressed in scientific endeavour and contemplation.

People's virtues are a subset of their good qualities. Moral virtue is expressed in actions that avoid both excess and defect. A temperate person, for example, will avoid eating or drinking too much, but he will also avoid eating or drinking too little. Virtue chooses the mean, or middle ground, between excess and defect. Besides purpose and action, virtue is also concerned with feeling. One may, for example, be excessively concerned with sex or insufficiently interested in it.

While all the moral virtues are means of action and passion, it is not the case that every kind of action and passion is capable of a virtuous mean. There are some actions of which there is no right amount, because any amount of them is too much; Aristotle gives murder and adultery as examples. The virtues, besides being concerned with means of action and passion, are themselves means in the sense that they occupy a middle ground between two contrary vices. Thus, the virtue of courage is flanked on one side by foolhardiness and on the other by cowardice.

The intellectual virtue of wisdom is inseparably linked with the moral virtues of the affective part of the soul. Only if an agent possesses moral virtue will he endorse an appropriate recipe for a good life. Only if he is gifted with intelligence will he make an accurate assessment of the circumstances in which his decision is to be made. It is impossible, Aristotle says, to be really good without wisdom or to be really wise without moral virtue. Only when correct reasoning and right desire come together does truly virtuous action result.

ACTION AND CONTEMPLATION

Plato had posed the question of whether the best life consists in the pursuit of pleasure or the exercise of the intellectual virtues. Aristotle's answer is that, properly understood, the two are not in competition with each other. The exercise of the highest form of virtue is the very same thing as the truest form of pleasure; each is identical with the other and with happiness. The highest virtues are the intellectual ones, wisdom and understanding. To the question of whether happiness is to be identified with the pleasure of wisdom or with the pleasure of understanding, Aristotle gives different answers in his main ethical treatises. In the *Nicomachean Ethics* perfect happiness, though it presupposes the moral virtues, is constituted solely by the activity of philosophical contemplation, whereas in the *Eudemian Ethics* it consists in the harmonious exercise of all the virtues, intellectual and moral.

MENCIUS

(b. *c.* 371, ancient state of Zou, China—d. *c.* 289 BCE, China)

Mencius was an early Chinese philosopher who developed orthodox Confucianism and thereby earned the title "second sage."

Of noble origin, the Meng family settled in Zou, a minor state in the present province of Shantung. Mencius was born there about 372 BCE. Like Confucius, Mencius was only three when he lost his father. As a young scholar Mencius had for his mentor a pupil of Zisi, who was himself the grandson of Confucius. In due time Mencius became a teacher himself and for a brief period served as an official in the state of Qi. He spent much time travelling, offering his advice and counsel to the various princes on government by *ren* ("human-heartedness"), or humane government. The effort was doomed, however, because the times were chaotic and the contending princes were interested not in humane government but in power.

DOCTRINE OF HUMAN NATURE

The philosophical ideas of Mencius might be regarded as an amplification of the teachings of Confucius. Confucius taught the concept of *ren*, love or human-heartedness, as the basic virtue of manhood. Mencius made the original goodness of human nature (*xing*) the keynote to his system. That the four beginnings (*siduan*)—the feeling of commiseration, the feeling of shame, the feeling of courtesy, and the feeling of right and wrong—are all inborn in humans was a self-evident truth to Mencius; and the "four beginnings," when properly cultivated, will develop into the four cardinal virtues of *ren*, righteousness (*yi*), decorum (*li*), and wisdom (*zhi*). This doctrine of the goodness of human nature on the part of Mencius has become an enduring topic for debate among the Chinese thinkers throughout the ages.

Mencius went further and taught that humans possess intuitive knowledge and intuitive ability and that personal cultivation consisted in developing one's mind. Mencius said: "Persons who have developed their hearts and minds to the utmost, know their nature. Knowing their nature, they know Heaven." Hence, all people can become like the great sage-kings Yao and Shun, the legendary heroes of the archaic past, according to Mencius.

While Mencius has always been regarded as a major philosopher, special importance was attributed to him and his work by the neo-Confucians of the Song dynasty (960–1279). For the last 1,000 years, Mencius has been revered among the Chinese people as the cofounder of Confucianism, second only to Confucius himself.

ZHUANGZI

(b. *c.* 369, Meng [now Shangqiu, Henan province], China—d. 286 BCE)

Zhuangzi was the most significant of China's early interpreters of Daoism.

In spite of his importance, details of Zhuangzi's life, apart from the many anecdotes about him in the *Zhuangzi* itself, are unknown. The biographical sketch by the "Grand

Historian" of the Han dynasty, Sima Qian (died *c.* 87 BCE), indicates that Zhuangzi was a native of the state of Meng, that his personal name was Zhou, and that he was a minor official at Qiyuan in his home state.

PHILOSOPHY

Zhuangzi is best known through the book that bears his name, the *Zhuangzi*, also known as *Nanhua zhenjing* ("The Pure Classic of Nanhua"). It is composed of 33 chapters, and evidence suggests that there may have been as many as 53 chapters in copies of the book circulated in the 4th century. It is generally agreed that the first seven chapters, the "inner books," are for the most part from the hand of Zhuangzi himself, whereas the "outer books" (chapters 8–22) and the miscellany (chapters 23–33) are largely the product of his later followers.

Zhuangzi taught that what can be known or said of the Dao is not the Dao. It has neither initial beginning nor final end, nor limitations or demarcations. Life is the ongoing transformation of the Dao, in which there is no better or worse, no good or evil. Things should be allowed to follow their own course, and men should not value one situation over another. A truly virtuous man is free from the bondage of circumstance, personal attachments, tradition, and the need to reform his world. Zhuangzi declined an offer to be prime minister of the state of Chu because he did not want the entanglements of a court career.

The relativity of all experience is in constant tension in the *Zhuangzi* with the unity of all things. When asked where the Dao was, Zhuangzi replied that it was everywhere. When pushed to be more specific, he declared that it was in ants and, still lower, in weeds and potsherds; furthermore, it was also in excrement and urine. This forceful statement of the omnipresence of the Dao had its parallels in later Chinese

Buddhism, in which a similar figure of speech was used to describe the ever-present Buddha (Buddhist scholars, especially those of the Chan [Zen] school, also drew heavily on Zhuangzi's works). Zhuangzi was par excellence the philosopher of the unattached man who is at one with the Dao.

PYRRHON OF ELIS

(b. c. 360—d. c. 272 BCE)

Pyrrhon of Elis was an ancient Greek philosopher who is generally accepted as the father of Skepticism. The philosophical school of Pyrrhonism takes its name from him.

Pyrrhon was a pupil of Anaxarchus of Abdera and in about 330 established himself as a teacher at Elis. Believing that equal arguments can be offered on both sides of any proposition, he dismissed the search for truth as a vain endeavour. While travelling with an expedition under Alexander the Great, Pyrrhon saw in the fakirs of India an example of happiness flowing from indifference to circumstances. He concluded that humans must suspend judgment (practice *epochē*) on the reliability of sense perceptions and simply live according to reality as it appears. Pyrrhonism permeated the Middle and New Academy of Athens and strongly influenced philosophical thought in 17th-century Europe with the republication of the Skeptical works of Sextus Empiricus, who had codified Greek Skepticism in the 3rd century CE. Pyrrhon's teaching was preserved in the poems of Timon of Phlius, who studied with him.

EPICURUS

(b. 341, Samos, Greece—d. 270 BCE, Athens)

Epicurus was an ancient Greek philosopher who developed the ethics of simple pleasure, friendship,

The strong features of philosopher Epicurus are forever captured in a bust sculpted c. 281 BCE. Hulton Archive/Getty Images

and retirement. He founded schools of philosophy that survived directly from the 4th century BCE until the 4th century CE.

Epicurus was born of Athenian parents who had gone to Samos as military settlers. According to his own report, Epicurus began his study of philosophy at the age of 14. He was for three years (327–324) a student in the Ionian city of Teos, where his teacher was Nausiphanes, a disciple of the naturalistic philosopher Democritus. It may have been from this source that Epicurus' atomistic theory came, which he used not as a means of studying physics but as the basis for a philosophical system that ultimately sought ethical ends.

At the age of 18, Epicurus went to Athens to perform the two years of military training required for Athenian citizenship. One year later Epicurus rejoined his parents at Colophon, where they had gone as exiles when, at the close of the Lamian War, Athens lost Samos to the Macedonians. For the next 10 years it seems probable that Epicurus travelled and studied. At the age of 32, he began to teach, first at Mytilene and subsequently at Lampsacus, a period that lasted from 311/310 to 307/306.

Apart from his two years in Athens, Epicurus spent the first 35 years of his life in Asia. His Asiatic ties, which he continued to cultivate intensely all his life (including two or three actual journeys to Asia Minor), seem to have been reflected mainly in his choice of words and style and, more significantly, in the ecumenical scope of his philosophy.

THE SCHOOLS AT ATHENS AND ELSEWHERE

When Epicurus and his followers came to Athens in 306, he bought a house and, in the garden, established a school, which came to be known as Ho Kepos (The Garden).

What Epicurus brought to Athens was more a way of life than a school or a community. Unlike both of the famous schools, it admitted women, and even one of Epicurus' slaves, named Mouse. It taught the avoidance of political activity and of public life.

Quite different from the usual connotations borne by the term *epicurean* today, life in the house and garden was simple. There was no communal property, as was the case in Pythagorean schools. Epicurus wrote clearly but in no highly organized way. There was much correspondence with students in Athens and at other schools, some letters being concerned with doctrinal matters but many seeming to be merely social and friendly.

On the day in his 72nd year that Epicurus died painfully of prostatitis, he dictated an affectionate and touching letter to Idomeneus—probably intended, in fact, for all of his friends in Lampsacus—which displayed the spirit in which he had remained true to his philosophy of repose and serenity even in the throes of pain. Epicurus' will left the house, garden, and some funds to trustees of the school. His slaves were freed, and provision was made that the daughter of Metrodorus should be wed to someone in the Athenian school, with the approval of Hermarchus.

ZENO OF CITIUM

(b. *c.* 335, Citium, Cyprus — d. *c.* 263 BCE, Athens)

Zeno of Citium was a Greek thinker who founded the Stoic school of philosophy, which influenced the development of philosophical and ethical thought in Hellenistic and Roman times.

Zeno went to Athens *c.* 312 BCE and attended lectures by the Cynic philosophers Crates of Thebes and Stilpon of Megara, in addition to lectures at the Academy. Arriving at his own philosophy, he began to teach in the Stoa Poikile

(Painted Colonnade), whence the name of his philosophy. None of his many treatises, written in harsh but forceful Greek, has survived save in fragmentary quotations.

Zeno's philosophical system included logic and theory of knowledge, physics, and ethics — the latter being central. He taught that happiness lay in conforming the will to the divine reason, which governs the universe. In logic and the theory of knowledge he was influenced by Antisthenes and Diodorus Cronus, in physics by Heracleitus.

ZENO'S PHILOSOPHY

Zeno showed in his own doctrines the influence of earlier Greek attitudes. He was apparently well versed in Platonic thought, owing to his study at Plato's Academy. He was responsible for the division of philosophy into three parts: logic, physics, and ethics. He also established the central Stoic doctrines in each part, so that later Stoics were to expand rather than to change radically the views of the founder. With some exceptions (in the field of logic), Zeno thus provided the following themes as the essential framework of Stoic philosophy:

- Logic as an instrument and not as an end in itself
- Human happiness as a product of life according to nature
- Physical theory as providing the means by which right actions are to be determined
- Perception as the basis of certain knowledge
- The wise man as the model of human excellence
- Platonic forms as the abstract properties that things of the same genus share — as being unreal

- True knowledge as always accompanied by assent
- The fundamental substance of all existing things as being a divine fire, the universal principles of which are (1) passive (matter) and (2) active (reason inherent in matter)
- Belief in a world conflagration and renewal
- Belief in the corporeality of all things
- Belief in the fated causality that necessarily binds all things
- Cosmopolitanism, or cultural outlook transcending narrower loyalties

Stoics also believed that it was humankind's obligation, or duty, to choose only those acts that are in accord with nature, all other acts being a matter of indifference.

PHILO JUDAEUS

(b. 15–10 BCE, Alexandria, Egypt—d. 45–50 CE, Alexandria)

Philo Judaeus was a Greek-speaking Jewish philosopher and the most important representative of Hellenistic Judaism.

Little is known of the life of Philo. Josephus, the historian of the Jews who also lived in the 1st century, says that Philo's family surpassed all others in the nobility of its lineage. His father had apparently played a prominent role in Palestine before moving to Alexandria.

The Alexandrian Jews were eager to enroll their children of secondary school age in Greek gymnasiums, institutions with religious associations dedicated to the liberal arts and athletics, in which Jews were certainly called upon to make compromises with their traditions. It may be assumed that Philo was a product of such an education. Philo says nothing of his own Jewish education. The only mention of

Jewish education in his work indicates how relatively weak it must have been, because he speaks only of Jewish schools that met on the Sabbath for lectures on ethics.

That Philo experienced some sort of identity crisis is indicated by a passage in his *On the Special Laws*. In this work, he describes his longing to escape from worldly cares to the contemplative life, his joy at having succeeded in doing so, and his renewed pain at being forced once again to participate in civic turmoil. The one identifiable event in Philo's life occurred in the year 39 or 40, when, after a pogrom against the Jews in Alexandria, he headed an embassy to the emperor Caligula asking him to reassert Jewish rights granted by the Ptolemies (rulers of Egypt) and confirmed by the emperor Augustus.

Philo was the first to show the difference between the knowability of God's existence and the unknowability of his essence. Again, in his view of God, Philo was original in insisting on an individual Providence able to suspend the laws of nature in contrast to the prevailing Greek philosophical view of a universal Providence who is himself subject to the unchanging laws of nature.

Philo saw the cosmos as a great chain of being presided over by the Logos, a term going back to pre-Socratic philosophy, which is the mediator between God and the world, though at one point he identifies the Logos as a second God. Philo departed from Plato principally in using the term Logos for the Idea of Ideas and for the Ideas as a whole and in his statement that the Logos is the place of the intelligible world. In anticipation of Christian doctrine he called the Logos the first-begotten Son of God, the man of God, the image of God, and second to God.

Philo was also novel in his exposition of the mystic love of God that God has implanted in man and through which man becomes Godlike. The influence of the mystic notions of Platonism, especially of the *Symposium*, and of the popular mystery cults on Philo's attempt to present Judaism as the one true mystery is hardly superficial; indeed, Philo is a major source of knowledge of the doctrines of these mystery cults, notably that of rebirth.

The purpose of what Philo called mystic "sober intoxication" was to lead one out of the material into the eternal world. Like Plato, Philo regarded the body as the prison house of the soul, and in his dualism of body and soul, as in his description of the flight from the self, the contrast between God and the world, and the yearning for a direct experience of God, he anticipated much of Gnosticism, a dualistic religion that became important in the 2nd century BCE. But unlike all the Greek philosophers, with the exception of the Epicureans, who believed in limited freedom of will, Philo held that man is completely free to act against all the laws of his own nature.

In his ethical theory Philo described two virtues, under the heading of justice, that are otherwise unknown in Greek philosophic literature—religious faith and humanity. Again, for him repentance was a virtue, whereas for other Greek philosophers it was a weakness. Perfect happiness comes, however, not through men's own efforts to achieve virtue but only through the grace of God.

In his political theory Philo often said that the best form of government is democracy; but for him democracy was far from mob rule, which he denounced as the worst of polities, perhaps because he saw the Alexandrian mob in action. For Philo democracy meant not a particular form of government but due order under any form of government in which all men are equal before the law. From this point of view, the Mosaic constitution, which embodies the best elements of all forms of government, is the ideal. Indeed, the ultimate goal of history is that the whole world be a single state under a democratic constitution.

EPICTETUS

(b. 55 CE, probably at Hierapolis, Phrygia [now Pamukkale, Turk.]—d. *c.* 135, Nicopolis, Epirus [Greece])

E pictetus was a Greek philosopher associated with the Stoics. He is remembered for the religious tone of his teachings, which commended him to numerous early Christian thinkers.

His original name is not known; *epiktētos* is the Greek word meaning "acquired." As a boy he was a slave but managed to attend lectures by the Stoic Musonius Rufus. He later became a freedman and lived his life lame and in ill health.

As far as is known, Epictetus wrote nothing. His teachings were transmitted by Arrian, his pupil, in two works: *Discourses*, of which four books are extant; and the *Encheiridion*, or *Manual*, a condensed aphoristic version of the main doctrines. Primarily interested in ethics, Epictetus described philosophy as learning "how it is possible to employ desire and aversion without hindrance." True education, he believed, consists in recognizing that there is only one thing that belongs to an individual fully— his will, or purpose. God, acting as a good king and father, has given each being a will that cannot be compelled or thwarted by anything external. Humans are not responsible for the ideas that present themselves to their consciousness, though they are wholly responsible for the way in which they use them.

"Two maxims," Epictetus said, "we must ever bear in mind—that apart from the will there is nothing good or bad, and that we must not try to anticipate or to direct events, but merely to accept them with intelligence." Man must, that is, believe there is a God whose thought directs the universe.

MARCUS AURELIUS

(b. April 26, 121, Rome [Italy]—d. March 17, 180, Vindobona [Vienna], or Sirmium, Pannonia)

Marcus Aurelius was a Roman emperor (121–180) and the author of the *Meditations*, a work on Stoic philosophy. He has symbolized for many generations in the West the Golden Age of the Roman Empire.

Marcus was born into a wealthy and politically powerful family. Although he was clearly destined for social distinction, how he came to the throne remains a mystery. In 136 the emperor Hadrian inexplicably announced as his eventual successor a certain Lucius Ceionius Commodus. Early in 138, however, Commodus died. Hadrian then adopted Titus Aurelius Antoninus (the husband of Marcus' aunt) to succeed him as the emperor Antoninus Pius, arranging that Antoninus should adopt as his sons two young men, one the son of Commodus and the other Marcus, whose name was then changed to Marcus Aelius Aurelius Verus.

Marcus was consul in 140, 145, and 161. In 145 he married his cousin, the emperor's daughter Annia Galeria Faustina, and in 147 the *imperium* and *tribunicia potestas*, the main formal powers of emperorship, were conferred upon him; henceforth, he was a kind of junior co-emperor.

MARCUS AS ROMAN EMPEROR

On March 7, 161, at a time when the brothers were jointly consuls (for the third and the second time), their father died. The transition was smooth as far as Marcus was concerned. Already possessing the essential constitutional powers, he stepped automatically into the role of full emperor, and his name henceforth was Imperator Caesar Marcus Aurelius Antoninus Augustus. At his own insistence, however, his adoptive brother was made co-emperor with him. For the first time in history the Roman Empire had two joint emperors of formally equal constitutional status and powers.

In 167 or 168, Marcus and Verus together set out on a punitive expedition across the Danube. Behind their backs a horde of German tribes invaded Italy in massive strength and besieged Aquileia, on the crossroads at the head of the Adriatic. Marcus and Verus fought the Germans off with success, but in 169 Verus died suddenly, and doubtless naturally, of a stroke. Three years of fighting were still needed, with Marcus in the thick of it, to restore the Danubian frontier.

In 177 Marcus proclaimed his 16-year-old son, Commodus, joint emperor. Together they resumed the Danubian wars. Marcus was determined to pass from defense to offense and to an expansionist redrawing of Rome's northern boundaries. His determination seemed to be winning success when, in 180, he died at his military headquarters, having just had time to commend Commodus to the chief advisers of the regime.

THE *MEDITATIONS*

To what extent Marcus intended the *Meditations* for eyes other than his own is uncertain. They consist of fragmentary notes, discursive and epigrammatic by turn, of his reflections in the midst of campaigning and administration. Strikingly, though they comprise the innermost thoughts of a Roman, the *Meditations* were written in Greek—to such an extent had the union of cultures become a reality. In many ages these thoughts have been admired. The modern age, however, is more likely to be struck by the pathology of them, their mixture of priggishness and hysteria. Marcus was forever proposing to himself unattainable goals of conduct, forever contemplating the triviality, brutishness, and transience of the physical world and of humanity in general, and himself in particular. Otherworldly, yet believing in no other world, he was therefore tied to duty and service with no hope, even of everlasting fame, to sustain him. More certain and more important is the point that Marcus' anxieties reflect, in an exaggerated manner, the ethos of his age.

Though they were Marcus' own thoughts, the *Meditations* were not original. They are basically the moral tenets of Stoicism, learned from Epictetus: the cosmos is a unity governed by an intelligence, and the human soul is a part of that divine intelligence and can therefore stand, if naked and alone, at least pure and undefiled, amidst chaos and futility. One or two of Marcus' ideas, perhaps more through lack of rigorous understanding than anything else, diverged from Stoic philosophy and approached Platonism, which was

A bust of Marcus Aurelius, commissioned c. 165 CE, by an unknown artist. Hulton Archive/Getty Images

itself then turning into the Neoplatonism—into which all pagan philosophies, except Epicureanism, were destined to merge. But Marcus did not deviate so far as to accept the comfort of any kind of survival after death.

NAGARJUNA

(fl. 2nd century CE)

Nagarjuna was an Indian Buddhist philosopher who articulated the doctrine of emptiness (*sunyata*). He is traditionally regarded as the founder of the Madhyamika school, an important tradition of Mahayana Buddhist philosophy.

Very little can be said concerning Nagarjuna's life. Scholars generally place him in South India during the 2nd century CE. Traditional accounts state that he lived 400 years after the Buddha passed into nirvana (*c.* 5th–4th century BCE). Some biographies also state, however, that he lived for 600 years, apparently identifying him with a second Nagarjuna known for his tantric (esoteric) writings.

PHILOSOPHY

In his first sermon, the Buddha prescribed a "middle way" between the extremes of self-indulgence and self-mortification. Nagarjuna, citing an early sutra, expanded the notion of the middle way into the philosophical sphere, identifying a middle way between existence and non-existence, or between permanence and annihilation. For Nagarjuna, the ignorance that is the source of all suffering is the belief in *svabhava*, a term that literally means "own being" and has been rendered as "intrinsic existence" and "self-nature." It is the belief that things exist autonomously, independently, and permanently. To hold this belief is to succumb to the extreme of permanence. It is equally mistaken, however, to believe that nothing exists; this is the extreme of annihilation. Emptiness, which for Nagarjuna is the true nature of reality, is not the absence of existence but the absence of intrinsic existence.

Nagarjuna developed his doctrine of emptiness in the *Madhyamika-sastra*, a thoroughgoing analysis of a wide range of topics. Examining, among other things, the Buddha, the Four Noble Truths, and nirvana, Nagarjuna demonstrates that each lacks the autonomy and independence that is falsely ascribed to it. His approach generally is to consider the various ways in which a given entity could exist and then to show that none of them is tenable because of the absurdities that would be entailed. In the case of something that is regarded to be the effect of a cause, he shows that it cannot be produced from itself (because an effect is the product of a cause), from something other than itself (because there must be a link between cause and effect), from something that is both the same as and different from itself (because the former two options are not possible), or from something that is neither the same as nor different from itself (because no such thing exists).

Nagarjuna defined emptiness in terms of the doctrine of *pratityasamutpada* ("dependent origination"), which holds that things are not self-arisen but produced in dependence on causes and conditions. Adopting this view allowed him to avoid the charge of nihilism, which he addressed directly in his writings and which his followers would confront over the centuries. Nagarjuna employs the doctrine of the two truths, *paramartha satya* ("ultimate truth") and *samvrti satya* ("conventional truth"), explaining that everything that exists is ultimately empty of any intrinsic nature but does exist conventionally. The conventional is the necessary means for understanding the ultimate, and it is the ultimate that makes the conventional possible.

As Nagarjuna wrote, "For whom emptiness is possible, everything is possible."

PLOTINUS

(b. 205, Lyco, or Lycopolis, Egypt? — d. 270, Campania)

Plotinus was an ancient philosopher who founded the Neoplatonic school of philosophy.

The only important source for the life of Plotinus is the *Enneads*, a biography that his disciple and editor, Porphyry, wrote as a preface to his edition of the writings of his master. Other ancient sources add almost no reliable information to what Porphyry relates. Unfortunately, apart from a few fascinating scraps of information about the earlier parts of the life of Plotinus, Porphyry concentrates on the last six years, when he was with his master in Rome. Thus, a fairly complete picture is available only of the last six years of a man who died at the age of 65. Plotinus' own writings contain no autobiographical information, and they can give no unintentional glimpses of his mind or character when he was young. Nothing is known about his intellectual and spiritual development.

The main activity of Plotinus, to which he devoted most of his time and energy, was his teaching and, after his first 10 years in Rome, his writing. There was nothing academic or highly organized about his "school," though his method of teaching was rather scholastic. He would have passages read from commentaries on Plato or Aristotle by earlier philosophers and then expound his own views. The meetings, however, were friendly and informal, and Plotinus encouraged unlimited discussion. Difficulties, once raised, had to be discussed until they were solved. The school was a loose circle of friends and admirers with no corporate organization. It was for these friends that he wrote the treatises that Porphyry collected and arranged as the *Enneads*.

Some passages in the *Enneads* give an idea of Plotinus' attitude to the religions and superstitions of his intensely religious and superstitious age, an attitude that seems to have been unusually detached. Like all men of his time, he believed in magic and in the possibility of foretelling the future by the stars, though he attacked the more bizarre and immoral beliefs of the astrologers. His interest in the occult was philosophical rather than practical, and there is no definite evidence that he practiced magic. A person called Olympius is reported to have once tried to use magic against Plotinus, but he supposedly found that the malignant forces he had evoked were bouncing back from Plotinus to himself. Plotinus was once taken to the Temple of Isis for a conjuration of his guardian spirit. Porphyry stated that a god appeared instead of an ordinary guardian angel but could not be questioned because of a mishandling of the conjuring process that broke the spell. What Plotinus himself thought of the proceedings is not known, but apparently he was not deeply interested.

In his last years Plotinus, whose health had never been very good, suffered from a painful and repulsive sickness that Porphyry describes so imprecisely that one modern scholar has identified it as tuberculosis and another as a form of leprosy. His last words were either "Try to bring back the god in you to the divine in the All" or "I am trying to bring back the divine in us to the divine in the All." In either case, they express very simply the faith that he shared with all religious philosophers of late antiquity.

SEXTUS EMPIRICUS

(fl. 3rd century CE)

Sextus Empiricus was an ancient Greek philosopher-historian who produced the only extant comprehensive account of Greek Skepticism. The republication of his

Hypotyposes in 1562 had far-reaching effects on European philosophical thought. Indeed, much of the philosophy of the 17th and 18th centuries can be interpreted in terms of diverse efforts to grapple with the ancient Skeptical arguments handed down through Sextus.

Almost all details of his life are conjectural except that he was a medical doctor. As a major exponent of *epochē*, or "suspension of judgment," the central doctrine of the philosophical school of Pyrrhonism (named after Pyrrhon of Elis). In his *Outlines of Pyrrhonism* and *Adversus mathematicos*, Sextus presented the tropes developed by previous Pyrrhonists. The 10 tropes attributed to Aenesidemus showed the difficulties encountered by attempts to ascertain the truth or reliability of judgments based on sense information, owing to the variability and differences of human and animal perceptions. Other arguments raised difficulties in determining whether there are any reliable criteria or standards—logical, rational, or otherwise—for judging whether anything is true or false.

To settle any disagreement, a criterion seems to be required. Any purported criterion, however, would have to be based either on another criterion—thus leading to an infinite regress of criteria—or on itself, which would be circular. Sextus offered arguments to challenge any claims of dogmatic philosophers to know more than what is evident, and in so doing he presented, in one form or another, practically all of the skeptical arguments that have ever appeared in subsequent philosophy.

Sextus said that his arguments were aimed at leading people to a state of *ataraxia* (unperturbability). People who thought that they could know reality were constantly disturbed and frustrated. If they could be led to suspend judgment, however, they would find peace of mind. In this state of suspension they would neither affirm nor deny the possibility of knowledge but would remain peaceful, still waiting to see what might develop. The Pyrrhonist did not become inactive in this state of suspense but lived undogmatically according to appearances, customs, and natural inclinations.

SAINT AUGUSTINE

(b. Nov. 13, 354, Tagaste, Numidia [now Souk Ahras, Alg.]—d. Aug. 28, 430, Hippo Regius [now Annaba, Alg.]; feast day August 28)

St. Augustine is one of the Latin Fathers of the Church, one of the Doctors of the Church, and perhaps the most significant Christian thinker after St. Paul. Augustine's adaptation of classical thought to Christian teaching created a theological system of great power and lasting influence. His numerous written works, the most important of which are *Confessions* and *City of God*, shaped the practice of biblical exegesis and helped lay the foundation for much of medieval and modern Christian thought.

LIFE

Augustine's parents were of the respectable class of Roman society, free to live on the work of others, but their means were sometimes straitened. They managed, sometimes on borrowed money, to acquire a first-class education for Augustine, and, although he had at least one brother and one sister, he seems to have been the only child sent off to be educated.

At the age of 28 Augustine left Africa in 383 to make his career in Rome. He taught there briefly before landing a plum appointment as imperial professor of rhetoric at Milan, the customary residence of the emperor at the time and the de facto capital of the Western Roman Empire. Augustine's career, however, ran aground. After only two years in Milan, he resigned his teaching post and made his way back to Tagaste. There he passed the time as a cultured squire until, at age 36, he was literally pressed into service against his will as a junior clergyman in the coastal city of Hippo, north of Tagaste. Made a "presbyter" (roughly, a priest, but with less authority than modern clergy of that title) at Hippo in 391, Augustine became bishop there in 395 or 396 and spent the rest of his life in that office.

In his years of rustication and early in his time at Hippo, he wrote book after book attacking Manichaeism, a Christian sect he had joined in his late teens and left 10 years later when it became impolitic to remain with them. For the next 20 years, from the 390s until his death, he was preoccupied with the struggle to make his own brand of Christianity prevail over all others in Africa.

CONFESSIONS

Two of Augustine's works stand out above the others for their lasting influence, but they have had very different fates. *City of God* was widely read in Augustine's time and throughout the Middle Ages and still demands attention today, but it is impossible to read without a determined effort to place it in its historical context. The *Confessions* was not much read in the first centuries of the Middle Ages, but from the 12th century onward it has been continuously read as a vivid portrayal of an individual's struggle for self-definition in the presence of a powerful God.

Although autobiographical narrative makes up much of the first nine of the 13 books of Augustine's *Confessiones*, autobiography is incidental to the main purpose of the work. For Augustine, *confessions* is a catchall term for acts of religiously authorized speech, namely praise of God, blame of self, confession of faith. The book is a richly textured meditation by a middle-aged man (Augustine was in his early 40s when he wrote it) on the course and meaning of

Engraving of Saint Augustine, putting thoughts to paper, c. *415 CE.* Hulton Archive/Getty Images

his own life. The dichotomy between past odyssey and present position of authority as bishop is emphasized in numerous ways in the book, not least in that what begins as a narrative of childhood ends with an extended and very churchy discussion of the book of Genesis—the progression is from the beginnings of a man's life to the beginnings of human society. Between those two points the narrative of sin and redemption holds most readers' attention. Those who seek to find in it the memoirs of a great sinner are invariably disappointed, indeed often puzzled at the minutiae of failure that preoccupy the author.

Religion for Augustine, however, was never merely a matter of the intellect. The seventh book of the *Confessions* recounts a perfectly satisfactory intellectual conversion to Christianity, but the extraordinary eighth book takes him one necessary step further. Augustine could not bring himself to seek the ritual purity of baptism without cleansing himself of the desires of the flesh to an extreme degree. For him, baptism required renunciation of sexuality in all its express manifestations. The narrative of the *Confessions* shows Augustine forming the will to renounce sexuality through a reading of the letters of Paul. The decisive scene occurs in a garden in Milan, where a child's voice seems to bid Augustine to "take up and read," whereupon he finds in Paul's writings the inspiration to adopt a life of chastity.

CITY OF GOD

Fifteen years after Augustine wrote the *Confessions*, the Roman world was shaken by news of a military action in Italy. A ragtag army under the leadership of Alaric, a general of Germanic ancestry, had been seeking privileges from the empire for many years, making from time to time extortionate raids against populous and prosperous areas. Finally, in 410, his forces attacked and seized the city of Rome itself, holding it for several days before decamping to the south of Italy. The symbolic effect of seeing the city of Rome taken by outsiders for the first time since the Gauls had done so in 390 BCE shook the secular confidence of many thoughtful people across the Mediterranean. Coming as it did less than 20 years after the decisive edict against "paganism" by the emperor Theodosius I in 391, it was followed by speculation that perhaps the Roman Empire had mistaken its way with the gods. Perhaps the new Christian god was not as powerful as he seemed. Perhaps the old gods had done a better job of protecting their followers.

Augustine saw in the murmured doubts a splendid polemical occasion he had long sought, and so he leapt to the defense of God's ways. During the next 15 years, working meticulously through a lofty architecture of argument, he outlined a new way to understand human society, setting up the City of God over and against the City of Man.

De civitate Dei contra paganos (413–426/427; *City of God*) is divided into 22 books. The first 10 refute the claims to divine power of various pagan communities. The last 12 retell the biblical story of mankind from Genesis to the Last Judgment, offering what Augustine presents as the true history of the City of God against which, and only against which, the history of the City of Man, including the history of Rome, can be properly understood. The work remains impressive as a whole and fascinating in its parts. The stinging attack on paganism in the first books is memorable and effective, the encounter with Platonism in books 8–10 is of great philosophical significance, and the last books (especially book 19, with a vision of true peace) offer a view of human destiny that would be widely persuasive for at least a thousand years.

HYPATIA

(b. *c.* 370, Alexandria, Egypt—d. March 415, Alexandria)

Hypatia was an Egyptian Neoplatonist philosopher who was the first notable woman in mathematics.

The daughter of Theon, also a notable mathematician and philosopher, Hypatia became the recognized head of the Neoplatonist school of philosophy at Alexandria about 400; her eloquence, modesty, and beauty, combined with her remarkable intellectual gifts, attracted a large number of pupils. Among them was Synesius of Cyrene, afterward bishop of Ptolemais (*c.* 410), several of whose letters to her are still extant.

Hypatia lectured on mathematics and on the philosophical teachings of two Neoplatonists: Plotinus, the founder of Neoplatonism, and Iamblichus, the founder of the Syrian branch of Neoplatonism. She symbolized learning and science, which at that time in Western history were largely identified with paganism.

According to the *Suda Lexicon*, a 10th-century encyclopedia, Hypatia wrote commentaries on the *Arithmetica* of Diophantus of Alexandria, on the *Conics* of Apollonius of Perga, and on an astronomical canon (presumably Ptolemy's *Almagest*). We have it on the authority of her father, Theon, that she revised Book III of his commentary on the *Almagest*. All of these works are lost, although some may survive as parts of the extant Arabic versions of the *Arithmetica*. The known titles of her works, combined with the letters of Synesius who consulted her about the construction of an astrolabe and a hydroscope (identified in the 17th century by Pierre de Fermat as a hydrometer), indicate that she devoted herself particularly to astronomy and mathematics. The existence of any strictly philosophical works by her is unknown.

In 380, Theodosius I, Roman emporer in the East from 379 to 392 and then emporer in both the East and West until 395, initiated an official policy of intolerance to paganism and Arianism. In 391, he gave permission to destroy Egyptian religious institutions. Christian mobs obliged by destroying the Library of Alexandria, the Temple of Serapis, and other pagan monuments. Although legislation in 393 sought to curb violence, particularly the looting and destruction of Jewish synagogues, a renewal of disturbances occurred after the accession of Cyril to the patriarchate of Alexandria in 412. Hypatia's philosophy was more scholarly and scientific in its interest and less mystical and intransigently pagan than the Neoplatonism taught in other schools. Nevertheless, statements attributed to her, such as "Reserve your right to think, for even to think wrongly is better than not to think at all" and "To teach superstitions as truth is a most terrible thing," must have incensed Cyril, who in turn incensed the mob.

Tension culminated in the forced, albeit illegal, expulsion of Alexandrian Jews in 414 and the murder of Hypatia, the most prominent Alexandrian pagan, by a fanatical mob of Christians in 415. The departure soon afterward of many scholars marked the beginning of the decline of Alexandria as a major centre of ancient learning.

ANICIUS MANLIUS SEVERINUS BOETHIUS

(b. 470–475?, Rome? [Italy]—d. 524, Pavia?)

Boethius was a Roman scholar, a Christian philosopher, and a statesman. He is best known as the author of *De consolatione philosophiae* (*Consolation of Philosophy*), a largely Neoplatonic work in which the pursuit of wisdom and the love of God are described as the true sources of human happiness.

Boethius belonged to the ancient Roman family of the Anicii, which had been Christian for about a century

Anicius Manlius Severinus Boethius. © Photos.com/Jupiterimages

and of which Emperor Olybrius had been a member. Boethius' father had been consul in 487 but died soon afterward, and Boethius was raised by Quintus Aurelius Memmius Symmachus, whose daughter Rusticiana he married. He became consul in 510 under the Ostrogothic king Theodoric.

It was Boethius' scholarly aim to translate into Latin the complete works of Aristotle with commentary and all the works of Plato "perhaps with commentary," to be followed by a "restoration of their ideas into a single harmony." Boethius' dedicated Hellenism, modeled on Cicero's, supported his long labour of translating Aristotle's *Organon* (six treatises on logic) and the Greek glosses on the work.

About 520 Boethius put his close study of Aristotle to use in four short treatises in letter form on the ecclesiastical doctrines of the Trinity and the nature of Christ; these are basically an attempt to solve disputes that had resulted from the Arian heresy, which denied the divinity of Christ. Using the terminology of the Aristotelian categories, Boethius described the unity of God in terms of substance and the three divine persons in terms of relation. He also tried to solve dilemmas arising from the traditional description of Christ as both human and divine, by deploying precise definitions of "substance," "nature," and "person."

In about 520 Boethius became *magister officiorum* (head of all the government and court services) under Theodoric. His two sons were consuls together in 522.

Eventually Boethius fell out of favour with Theodoric. The *Consolation* contains the main extant evidence of his fall but does not clearly describe the actual accusation against him. After the healing of a schism between Rome and the church of Constantinople in 520, Boethius and other senators may have been suspected of communicating with the Byzantine emperor Justin I, who was orthodox in faith whereas Theodoric was Arian. Boethius openly defended the senator Albinus, who was accused of treason "for having written to the Emperor Justin against the rule of Theodoric." The charge of treason brought against Boethius was aggravated by a further accusation of the practice of magic, or of sacrilege, which the accused was at great pains to reject. Sentence was passed and was ratified by the Senate, probably under duress.

In prison, while he was awaiting execution, Boethius wrote his masterwork, *De consolatione philosophiae*. The *Consolation* is the most personal of Boethius' writings, the crown of his philosophic endeavours. The argument of the *Consolation* is basically Platonic. Philosophy, personified as a woman, converts the prisoner Boethius to the Platonic notion of Good and so nurses him back to the recollection that, despite the apparent injustice of his enforced exile, there does exist a *summum bonum* ("highest good"), which "strongly and sweetly" controls and orders the universe. Fortune and misfortune must be subordinate to that central Providence, and the real existence of evil is excluded. Man has free will, but it is no obstacle to divine order and foreknowledge. Virtue, whatever the appearances, never goes unrewarded. The prisoner is finally consoled by the hope of reparation and reward beyond death.

After his detention, probably at Pavia, Boethius was executed in 524.

ŚANKARA

(b. 700?, Kāladi village?, India—d. 750?, Kedārnāth)

Śankara, an Indian philosopher and theologian, is most renowned as an exponent of the Advaita Vedānta school of philosophy, from whose doctrines the main currents of modern Indian thought are derived. He wrote commentaries on the *Brahma-sūtras* and the principal *Upaniṣad*s, affirming his belief in one eternal unchanging reality (Brahman) and the illusion of plurality and differentiation.

According to one tradition, Śankara was born into a pious Nambūdiri Brahman family in a quiet village called Kāladi on the Cūrṇā (or Pūrṇā, Periyār) River, Kerala, southern India. He is said to have lost his father, Śivaguru, early in his life. He renounced the world and became a *sannyāsin* (ascetic) against his mother's will. He studied under Govinda, who was a pupil of Gauḍapāda. Nothing certain is known about Govinda, but Gauḍapāda is notable as the author of an important Vedānta work, *Māṇḍūkya-*

kārikā, in which the influence of Mahāyāna Buddhism—a form of Buddhism aiming at the salvation of all beings and tending toward nondualistic or monistic thought—is evident and even extreme, especially in its last chapter.

Biographers narrate that Śaṅkara first went to Kāśī (Vārānasi), a city celebrated for learning and spirituality, and then travelled all over India, holding discussions with philosophers of different creeds. His heated debate with Maṇḍana Miśra, a philosopher of the Mīmāṃsā (Investigation) school, whose wife served as an umpire, is perhaps the most interesting episode in his biography and may reflect a historical fact; that is, keen conflict between Śaṅkara, who regarded the knowledge of Brahman as the only means to final release, and followers of the Mīmāṃsā school, which emphasized the performance of ordained duty and the Vedic rituals.

Śaṅkara was active in a politically chaotic age. He would not teach his doctrine to city dwellers. The power of Buddhism was still strong in the cities, though already declining, and Jainism, a nontheistic ascetic faith, prevailed among the merchants and manufacturers. Popular Hinduism occupied the minds of ordinary people, while city dwellers pursued ease and pleasure. There were also epicureans in cities. It was difficult for Śaṅkara to communicate Vedānta philosophy to these people. Consequently, Śaṅkara propagated his teachings chiefly to *sannyāsin*s and intellectuals in the villages, and he gradually won the respect of Brahmans and feudal lords. He enthusiastically endeavoured to restore the orthodox Brahmanical tradition without paying attention to the bhakti (devotional) movement, which had made a deep impression on ordinary Hindus in his age.

Śaṅkara made full use of his knowledge of Buddhism to attack Buddhist doctrines severely or to transmute them into his own Vedāntic nondualism, and he tried with great effort to "vedanticize" the Vedānta philosophy, which had been made extremely Buddhistic by his predecessors. The basic structure of his philosophy is more akin to Sāṅkya, a philosophic system of nontheistic dualism, and the Yoga school than to Buddhism. It is said that Śaṅkara died at Kedārnātha in the Himalayas.

YAQŪB IBN ISHĀQ AS-SĀBAH AL-KINDĪ
(d. c. 870)

A l-Kindī was the first outstanding Islamic philosopher. He is known as "the philosopher of the Arabs."

Although al-Kindī lived during the triumph of the Mu'tazilah of Baghdad and was connected with the 'Abbāsid caliphs who championed the Mu'tazilah and patronized the Hellenistic sciences, there is no clear evidence that he belonged to a theological school. His writings show him to have been a diligent student of Greek and Hellenistic authors in philosophy and point to his familiarity with Indian arithmetic. His conscious, open, and unashamed acknowledgment of earlier contributions to scientific inquiry was foreign to the spirit, method, and purpose of the theologians of the time. His acquaintance with the writings of Plato and Aristotle was still incomplete and technically inadequate. He improved the Arabic translation of the "Theology of Aristotle" but made only a selective and circumspect use of it.

Devoting most of his writings to questions of natural philosophy and mathematics, al-Kindī was particularly concerned with the relation between corporeal things, which are changeable, in constant flux, infinite, and as such unknowable, on the one hand, and the permanent world of forms (spiritual or secondary substances), which are not subject to flux yet to which man has no access except through things of the senses. He insisted that a purely human knowledge of all things is possible, through the use of various scientific devices, learning such things as mathematics and logic, and assimilating the contributions of earlier thinkers. The existence of a "supernatural" way to this knowledge in which all these requirements can be dispensed with was acknowledged by al-Kindī: God may choose to impart it to his prophets by cleansing and illuminating their souls and by giving them his aid, right guidance, and inspiration; and they, in turn, communicate it to ordinary men in an admirably clear, concise, and comprehensible style. This is the prophets' "divine" knowledge, characterized by a special mode of access and style of exposition. In principle, however, this very same knowledge is accessible to man without divine aid, even though "human" knowledge may lack the completeness and consummate logic of the prophets' divine message.

Reflection on the two different kinds of knowledge — the human knowledge bequeathed by the ancients and the revealed knowledge expressed in the Qur'ān — led al-Kindī to pose a number of themes that became central to Islamic philosophy: the rational–metaphorical exegesis of the Qur'ān and the Ḥadīth; the identification of God with the first being and the first cause; creation as the giving of being and as a kind of causation distinct from natural causation and Neoplatonic emanation; and the immortality of the individual soul.

AL-FĀRĀBĪ

(b. *c.* 878, Turkistan — d. *c.* 950, Damascus?)

Al-Fārābī was a Muslim philosopher and one of the preeminent thinkers of medieval Islam. He was regarded in the Arab world as the greatest philosophical authority after Aristotle.

Very little is known of al-Fārābī's life. He was of Turkic origin and is thought to have been brought to Baghdad as a child by his father, who was probably in the Turkish bodyguard of the Caliph (the titular leader of the Islamic community). Al-Fārābī was not a member of the court society, and neither did he work in the administration of the central government. In 942 he took up residence at the court of the prince Sayf ad-Dawlah, where he remained, mostly in Ḥalab (modern Aleppo), until the time of his death.

POLITICAL PHILOSOPHY AND THE STUDY OF RELIGION

Al-Fārābī regarded theology and the juridical study of the law as derivative phenomena that function within a framework set by the prophet as lawgiver and founder of a human community. In this community, revelation defines the opinions the members of the community must hold and the actions they must perform if they are to attain the earthly happiness of this world and the supreme happiness of the other world. Philosophy could not understand this framework of religion as long as it concerned itself almost exclusively with its truth content and confined the study of practical science to individualistic ethics and personal salvation.

In contrast to al-Kindī and ar-Rāzī, al-Fārābī recast philosophy in a new framework analogous to that of the Islamic religion. The sciences were organized within this philosophic framework so that logic, physics, mathematics, and metaphysics culminated in a political science whose subject matter is the investigation of happiness and how it can be realized in cities and nations. The central theme of this political science is the founder of a virtuous or excellent community. Included in this theme are views concerning the supreme rulers who follow the founder, their qualifications, and how the community must be ordered so that its members attain happiness as citizens rather than isolated human beings.

Once this new philosophical framework was established, it became possible to conduct a philosophical investigation of all the elements that constituted the Islamic community: the prophet-lawgiver, the aims of the divine laws, the legislation of beliefs as well as actions, the role of the successors to the founding legislator, the grounds of the interpretation or reform of the law, the classification of human communities according to their doctrines in addition to their size, and the critique of "ignorant" (pagan), "transgressing," "falsifying," and "erring" communities. Philosophical cosmology, psychology, and politics were blended by al-Fārābī into a political theology whose aim was to clarify the foundations of the Islamic community and defend its reform in a direction that would promote scientific inquiry and encourage philosophers to play an active role in practical affairs.

The Analogy of Religion and Philosophy

Al-Fārābī's theological and political writings showed later Muslim philosophers the way to deal with the question of the relation between philosophy and religion and presented them with a complex set of problems that they continued to elaborate, modify, and develop in different directions. Starting with the view that religion is analogous or similar to philosophy, al-Fārābī argued that the idea of the true prophet-lawgiver ought to be the same as that of the true philosopher-king. Thus, he challenged both al-Kindī's view that prophets and philosophers have different and independent ways to the highest truth available to man and ar-Rāzī's view that philosophy is the only way to that knowledge. That a man could combine the functions of prophecy, lawgiving, philosophy, and kingship did not necessarily mean that these functions were identical; it did mean, however, that they all are legitimate subjects of philosophic inquiry. Philosophy must account for the powers, knowledge, and activities of the prophet, lawgiver, and king, which it must distinguish from and relate to those of the philosopher. The public, or political, function of philosophy was emphasized. Unlike Neoplatonism, which had for long limited itself to the Platonic teaching that the function of philosophy is to liberate the soul from the shadowy existence of the cave—in which knowledge can only be imperfectly comprehended as shadows reflecting the light of the truth beyond the cave (the world of senses)—al-Fārābī insisted with Plato that the philosopher must be forced to return to the cave, learn to talk to its inhabitants in a manner they can comprehend, and engage in actions that may improve their lot.

AVICENNA

(b. 980, Bukhara, Iran—d. 1037, Hamadan)

Avicenna was an Islamic philosopher and scientist. Avicenna's versatility, imagination, inventiveness, and prudence shaped philosophy into a powerful force that gradually penetrated Islamic theology and mysticism and Persian poetry in eastern Islam and gave them universality and theoretical depth. His own personal philosophic views, he said, were those of the ancient sages of Greece (including the genuine views of Plato and Aristotle), which he had set forth in the Oriental Philosophy, a book that has not survived and probably was not written or meant to be written. They were not identical with the common Peripatetic (Aristotelian) doctrines and were to be distinguished from the learning of his contemporaries, the Christian "Aristotelians" of Baghdad, which he attacked as vulgar, distorted, and falsified. His most voluminous writing, *Kitāb ash-shifā'* ("The Book of Healing"), was meant to accommodate the doctrines of other philosophers as well as hint at his own personal views, which are elaborated elsewhere in more imaginative and allegorical forms.

THE DOCTRINE OF CREATION

Avicenna had learned from certain hints in al-Fārābī that the exoteric teachings of Plato regarding "forms," "creation," and the immortality of individual souls were closer to revealed doctrines than the genuine views of Aristotle, that the doctrines of Plotinus and later Neoplatonic commentators were useful in harmonizing Aristotle's views with revealed doctrines, and that philosophy must accommodate itself to the divine law on the issue of creation and of reward and punishment in the hereafter, which presupposes some form of individual immortality. Following al-Fārābī's lead, Avicenna initiated a full-fledged inquiry into the question of being, in which he distinguished between essence and existence. He argued that the fact of existence cannot be inferred from or accounted for by the essence of existing things and that form and matter by themselves cannot interact and originate the movement of the universe or the progressive actualization of existing things. Existence must, therefore, be due to an agent-cause that necessitates, imparts, gives, or adds existence to an essence.

To do so, the cause must be an existing thing and coexist with its effect. The universe consists of a chain of actual beings, each giving existence to the one below it and responsible for the existence of the rest of the chain below. Because an actual infinite is deemed impossible by Avicenna, this chain as a whole must terminate in a being that is wholly simple and one, whose essence is its very existence, and therefore is self-sufficient and not in need of something else to give it existence. Because its existence is not contingent on or necessitated by something else but is necessary and eternal in itself, it satisfies the condition of being the necessitating cause of the entire chain that constitutes the eternal world of contingent existing things.

All creation is necessarily and eternally dependent upon God. It consists of the intelligences, souls, and bodies of the heavenly spheres, each of which is eternal, and the sublunary sphere, which is also eternal, undergoing a perpetual process of generation and corruption, of the succession of form over matter, very much in the manner described by Aristotle.

THE IMMORTALITY OF INDIVIDUAL SOULS

There is, however, a significant exception to this general rule—the human rational soul. The individual can affirm the existence of his soul from direct consciousness of his self (what he means when he says "I") and imagine this happening even in the absence of external objects and bodily organs. This proves, according to Avicenna, that the soul is indivisible, immaterial, and incorruptible substance, not imprinted in matter, but created with the body, which it uses as an instrument. Unlike other immaterial substances (the intelligences and souls of the spheres), it is not pre-eternal but is generated, or made to exist, at the same time as the individual body, which can receive it, is formed.

The composition, shape, and disposition of its body and the soul's success or failure in managing and controlling it, the formation of moral habits, and the acquisition of knowledge all contribute to its individuality and difference from other souls. Though the body is not resurrected after its corruption, the soul survives and retains all the individual characteristics, perfections or imperfections, that it achieved in its earthly existence and in this sense is rewarded or punished for its past deeds. Avicenna's claim that he has presented a philosophic proof for the immortality of generated ("created") individual souls no doubt constitutes the high point of his effort to harmonize philosophy and religious beliefs.

RĀMĀNUJA

(b. *c.* 1017, Śrīperumbūdūr, India—d. 1137, Śrīraṅgam)

Rāmānuja, a South Indian Brahman theologian and philosopher, was the single most influential thinker of devotional Hinduism.

Information on the life of Rāmānuja consists only of the accounts given in the legendary biographies about him, in which a pious imagination has embroidered historical details. According to tradition, he was born in southern India, in what is now Tamil Nadu (formerly Madras) state. He became a temple priest at the Varadarāja temple at Kāñcī, where he began to expound the doctrine that the goal of those who aspire to final release from transmigration is not the impersonal Brahman but rather Brahman as identified with the personal god Vishnu.

Like many Hindu thinkers, he made an extended pilgrimage, circumambulating India from Rāmeswaram (part of Adams Bridge), along the west coast to Badrīnāth, the source of the holy river Ganges, and returning along the east coast. He returned after 20 years to Śrīraṅgam, where he organized the temple worship, and, reputedly, he founded 74 centres to disseminate his doctrine. After a life of 120 years, according to the tradition, he passed away in 1137.

PHILOSOPHY AND INFLUENCE

Rāmānuja's chief contribution to philosophy was his emphasis that discursive thought is necessary in man's search for the ultimate verities, that the phenomenal world is real and provides real knowledge, and that the exigencies of daily life are not detrimental or even contrary to the life of the spirit. In this emphasis he is the antithesis of Śaṅkara, of whom he was sharply critical and whose interpretation of the scriptures he disputed. Like other adherents of the Vedānta system, Rāmānuja accepted that any Vedānta system must base itself on the three "points of departure," namely, the *Upaniṣads*, the *Brahma-sūtra*s (brief exposition of the major tenets of the *Upaniṣad*s), and the *Bhagavadgītā*, the colloquy of the god Kṛṣṇa and his friend Arjuna. He wrote no commentary on any single *Upaniṣad* but explained in detail the method of understanding the *Upaniṣad*s in his first major work, the *Vedārtha-saṃgraha* ("Summary of the Meaning of the Veda"). Much of this was incorporated in his commentary on the *Brahma-sūtra*s, the *Śrī-bhāṣya*, which presents his fully developed views. His commentary on the *Bhagavadgītā*, the *Bhagavadgītā-bhāṣya*, dates from a later age.

Although Rāmānuja's contribution to Vedānta thought was highly significant, his influence on the course of Hinduism as a religion has been even greater. By allowing the urge for devotional worship (bhakti) into his doctrine of salvation, he aligned the popular religion with the pursuits of philosophy and gave bhakti an intellectual basis. Ever since, bhakti has remained the major force in the religions of Hinduism. His emphasis on the necessity of religious worship as a means of salvation continued in a more systematic context the devotional effusions of the Āḷvārs, the

7th–10th century poet-mystics of southern India, whose verse became incorporated into temple worship. This bhakti devotionalism, guided by Rāmānuja, made its way into northern India, where its influence on religious thought and practice has been profound.

Rāmānuja's world view accepts the ontological reality of three distinct orders: matter, soul, and God. Like Śaṅkara and earlier Vedānta, he admits that there is nonduality (*advaita*), an ultimate identity of the three orders, but this nonduality for him is asserted of God, who is modified (*viśiṣṭa*) by the orders of matter and soul; hence his doctrine is known as Viśiṣṭādvaita ("modified nonduality") as opposed to the unqualified nonduality of Śaṅkara.

Central to his organic conception of the universe is the analogy of body and soul: just as the body modifies the soul, has no separate existence from it, and yet is different from it, just so the orders of matter and soul constitute God's "body," modifying it, yet having no separate existence from it. The goal of the human soul, therefore, is to serve God just as the body serves the soul. Anything different from God is but a *śeṣa* of him, a spilling from the plenitude of his being. All the phenomenal world is a manifestation of the glory of God (*vibhūti*), and to detract from its reality is to detract from his glory.

Rāmānuja transformed the practice of ritual action into the practice of divine worship and the way of meditation into a continuous loving pondering of God's qualities; both, in turn, a subservient to bhakti, the fully realized devotion that finds God. Thus, release is not merely a shedding of the bonds of transmigration but a positive quest for the contemplation of God, who is pictured as enthroned in his heaven, called Vaikuṇṭha, with his consort and attendants.

IBN GABIROL

(b. *c.* 1022, Málaga, caliphate of Córdoba—d. *c.* 1058/70, Valencia, kingdom of Valencia)

I bn Gabirol (in full Solomon ben Yehuda Ibn Gabirol) was an important Neoplatonic philosopher and one of the outstanding figures of the Hebrew school of religious and secular poetry during the Jewish Golden Age in Moorish Spain.

Born in Málaga about 1022, Ibn Gabirol received his higher education in Saragossa, where he joined the learned circle of other Cordoban refugees established there around famed scholars and the influential courtier Yekutiel ibn Ḥasan. Protected by this patron, whom Ibn Gabirol immortalized in poems of loving praise, the 16-year-old poet became famous for his religious hymns in masterly Hebrew.

Against all warnings by his patron Yekutiel, Ibn Gabirol concentrated on Neoplatonic philosophy. In need of a new patron after the execution of Yekutiel in 1039 by those who had murdered his king and taken over power, Ibn Gabirol secured a position as a court poet with Samuel ha-Nagid, who, becoming the leading statesman of Granada, was in need of the poet's prestige. Ibn Gabirol composed widely resounding poems with a messianic tinge for Samuel and for Jehoseph (Yūsuf), his son and later successor in the vizierate of Granada. All other biographical data about Ibn Gabirol except his place of death, Valencia, must be extrapolated from his writing.

PHILOSOPHY

Ibn Gabriol's *Fountain of Life*, in five treatises, is preserved in toto only in the Latin translation, *Fons vitae*, with the author's name appearing as Avicebron or Avencebrol; it was re-identified as Ibn Gabirol's work in 1846. The work had little influence upon Jewish philosophy other than on León Hebreo (Judah Abrabanel) and Benedict de Spinoza, but it inspired the Kabbalists, the adherents of Jewish esoteric mysticism. Its influence upon Christian Scholasticism was marked, although it was attacked by St. Thomas Aquinas for equating concepts with realities.

Grounded in Plotinus and other Neoplatonic writers yet also in Aristotelian logic and metaphysics, Ibn Gabirol developed a system in which he introduced the conception of a divine will, like the Logos (or divine "word") of Philo. It is an essential unity of creativity of and with God, mutually related like sun and sunlight, which mediates actively between the transcendent deity and the cosmos that God created out of nothingness (to be understood as the potentiality for creation). Matter emanates directly from the deity as a prime matter that supports all substances and even the "intelligent" substances, the sphere-moving powers and angels.

This concept was accepted by the Franciscan school of Scholastics but rejected by the Dominicans, including St. Thomas, for whom form (and only one, not many) and not matter is the creative principle. Since matter, according to Aristotle and Plotinus, "yearns for formation" and, thus, moving toward the nearness of God, causes the rotation of the spheres, the finest matter of the highest spheres is propelled by the strongest "yearning," which issues from God and returns to him and is active in man.

SAINT ANSELM OF CANTERBURY

(b. 1033/34, Aosta, Lombardy—d. April 21, 1109, possibly at Canterbury, Kent, Eng., canonized 1163?; feast day April 21)

St. Anselm was the founder of Scholasticism, a philosophical school of thought that dominated the Middle Ages. He was recognized in modern times as the originator of the ontological argument for the existence of God (based on the idea of an absolutely perfect being, the fact of the idea being in itself a demonstration of existence).

Anselm's mother, Ermenberga, belonged to a noble Burgundian family and possessed considerable property. His father, Gondolfo, was a Lombard nobleman who intended that Anselm would make a career of politics and did not approve of his early decision to enter the monastic life. Anselm received an excellent Classical education and was considered one of the better Latinists of his day. In 1057 Anselm left Aosta to enter the Benedictine monastery at Bec. In 1060 or 1061 he took his monastic vows. He was elected prior of the monastery after Lanfranc became abbot of Caen in 1063. In 1078 he became abbot of Bec.

Saint Anselm, depicted later in life, c. *1090.* Hulton Archive/ Getty Images

Under Anselm, Bec became a centre of monastic learning and some theological questioning. Anselm continued his efforts to satisfactorily answer questions concerning the nature and existence of God. His *Proslogium* ("Address," or "Allocution"), originally titled *Fides quaerens intellectum* ("Faith Seeking Understanding"), established the ontological argument for the existence of God. In it he argued that even a fool has an idea of a being greater than which no other being can be conceived to exist; that such a being must really exist, for the very idea of such a being implies its existence.

Anselm was named archbishop of Canterbury by William II Rufus, the son and successor of William the Conqueror, in March 1093. Anselm accepted the position somewhat reluctantly but with an intention of reforming the English Church. Anselm later became a major figure in the investiture controversy; i.e., over the question as to whether a secular ruler (e.g., emperor or king) or the pope had the primary right to invest an ecclesiastical authority, such as a bishop, with the symbols of his office.

Anselm spent the last two years of his life in peace. In 1163, with new canons requiring approvals for canonization (official recognition of persons as saints), Archbishop Thomas Becket of Canterbury (1118?–1170) referred Anselm's cause to Rome. Anselm was probably canonized at this time, for the Canterbury records for 1170 make frequent mention of the pilgrimages to his new shrine in the cathedral. For several centuries he was venerated locally. Clement XI (pope from 1700 to 1721) declared Anselm a doctor (teacher) of the church in 1720.

AL-GHAZĀLĪ

(b. 1058, Ṭūs, Iran—d. Dec. 18, 1111, Ṭūs)

Al-Ghazālī was a Muslim theologian and mystic whose great work, *Iḥyāʾ ʾulūm ad-dīn* ("The Revival of the Religious Sciences"), made Ṣūfism (Islamic mysticism) an acceptable part of orthodox Islam.

Al-Ghazālī was educated at Ṭūs (near Meshed in eastern Iran), then in Jorjān, and finally at Nishapur (Neyshābūr), where his teacher was al-Juwaynī. After the latter's death in 1085, al-Ghazālī was invited to go to the court of Niẓām al-Mulk, the powerful vizier of the Seljuq sultans. The vizier was so impressed by al-Ghazālī's scholarship that in 1091 he appointed him chief professor in the Niẓāmīyah college in Baghdad.

He passed through a spiritual crisis that rendered him physically incapable of lecturing for a time. In November 1095 he abandoned his career and left Baghdad on the pretext of going on pilgrimage to Mecca. After some time in Damascus and Jerusalem, with a visit to Mecca in November 1096, al-Ghazālī settled in Ṭūs, where Ṣūfī disciples joined him in a virtually monastic communal life. In 1106 he was persuaded to return to teaching at the Niẓāmīyah college at Nishapur. He continued lecturing in Nishapur at least until 1110, when he returned to Ṭūs, where he died the following year.

Al-Ghazālī's greatest work is *Iḥyāʾ ʿulūm ad-dīn*. In 40 "books" he explained the doctrines and practices of Islam and showed how these can be made the basis of a profound devotional life, leading to the higher stages of Ṣūfism, or mysticism. The relation of mystical experience to other forms of cognition is discussed in *Mishkāt al-anwār (The Niche for Lights)*. Al-Ghazālī's abandonment of his career and adoption of a mystical, monastic life is defended in the autobiographical work *al-Munqidh min aḍ-ḍalāl (The Deliverer from Error)*.

His philosophical studies began with treatises on logic and culminated in the *Tahāfut (The Inconsistency—or Incoherence—of the Philosophers)*, in which he defended Islam against such philosophers as Avicenna who sought to demonstrate certain speculative views contrary to accepted Islamic teaching.

Most of his activity was in the field of jurisprudence and theology. Toward the end of his life he completed a work on general legal principles, *al-Mustaṣfā (Choice Part, or Essentials)*. His compendium of standard theological doctrine (translated into Spanish), *al-Iqtiṣād fī al-Iʿtiqād (The Just Mean in Belief)*, was probably written before he became a mystic, but there is nothing in the authentic writings to show that he rejected these doctrines, even though he came to hold that theology—the rational, systematic presentation of religious truths—was inferior to mystical experience. From a similar standpoint he wrote a polemical work against the militant sect of the Assassins (Ismāʿīlīyah), and he also wrote (if it is authentic) a criticism of Christianity, as well as a book of *Counsel for Kings* (*Naṣīḥat al-mulūk*).

PETER ABELARD

(b. 1079, Le Pallet, near Nantes, Brittany [now in France]—d. April 21, 1142, Priory of Saint-Marcel, near Chalon-sur-Saône, Burgundy [now in France])

Peter Abelard, a French theologian and philosopher, is best known for his solution of the problem of universals and for his original use of dialectics. He is also known for his poetry and for his celebrated love affair with Héloïse.

Abelard was born the son of a knight in Brittany south of the Loire River. He sacrificed his inheritance and the prospect of a military career in order to study philosophy, particularly logic, in France. He provoked bitter quarrels with two of his masters, Roscelin of Compiègne and Guillaume de Champeaux, who represented opposite poles of philosophy in regard to the question of the existence of universals. (A universal is a quality or property that each individual member of a class of things must possess if the same general word is to apply to all the things in that class. Redness, for example, is a universal possessed by all red objects.) Roscelin was a nominalist who asserted that universals are nothing more than mere words; Guillaume in Paris upheld a form of Platonic realism according to which universals exist. Abelard in his own logical writings brilliantly elaborated an independent philosophy of language. While showing how words could be used significantly, he stressed that language itself is not able to demonstrate the truth of things (*res*) that lie in the domain of physics.

In 1113 or 1114, Abelard went north to Laon to study theology under Anselm of Laon, the leading biblical scholar of the day. He quickly developed a strong contempt for Anselm's teaching, which he found vacuous, and returned to Paris. There he taught openly but was also given as a private pupil the young Héloïse, niece of one of the clergy of the cathedral of Paris, Canon Fulbert. Abelard and Héloïse fell in love and had a son whom they called Astrolabe. They then married secretly. To escape her uncle's wrath Héloïse withdrew into the convent of Argenteuil outside Paris. Abelard suffered castration at Fulbert's instigation. In shame he embraced the monastic life at the royal abbey of Saint-Denis near Paris and made the unwilling Héloïse become a nun at Argenteuil.

CAREER AS A MONK

At Saint-Denis Abelard extended his reading in theology and tirelessly criticized the way of life followed by his fellow monks. His reading of the Bible and of the Fathers of the Church led him to make a collection of quotations that seemed to represent inconsistencies of teaching by the Christian church. He arranged his findings in a compilation entitled *Sic et non* ("Yes and No"). For it he wrote a preface in which, as a logician and as a keen student of language, he formulated basic rules with which students might reconcile apparent contradictions of meaning and distinguish the various senses in which words had been used over the course of many centuries. He also wrote the first version of his book called *Theologia*, which was formally

Peter Abelard, with Héloïse, miniature portrait by Jean de Meun, 14th century; in the Musee Conde, Chantilly, France. Courtesy of the Musée Condé, Chantilly, Fr.; photograph, Giraudon/Art Resource, New York

condemned as heretical and burned by a council held at Soissons in 1121. Abelard's dialectical analysis of the mystery of God and the Trinity was held to be erroneous, and he himself was placed for a while in the abbey of Saint-Médard under house arrest.

In 1125 he accepted election as abbot of the remote Breton monastery of Saint-Gildas-de-Rhuys. His relations with the community deteriorated, and, after attempts had been made upon his life, he returned to France. Héloïse had meanwhile become the head of a new foundation of nuns called the Paraclete. Abelard became the abbot of the new community and provided it with a rule and with a justification of the nun's way of life. He also provided books of hymns he had composed, and in the early 1130s he and Héloïse composed a collection of their own love letters and religious correspondence.

FINAL YEARS

About 1135 Abelard went to the Mont-Sainte-Geneviève outside Paris to teach, and he wrote in a blaze of energy and of celebrity. He produced further drafts of his *Theologia* in which he analyzed the sources of belief in the Trinity and praised the pagan philosophers of classical antiquity for their virtues and for their discovery by the use of reason of many fundamental aspects of Christian revelation.

At a council held at Sens in 1140, Abelard underwent a resounding condemnation, which was soon confirmed by Pope Innocent II. He withdrew to the great monastery of Cluny in Burgundy and retired from teaching. After his death, his body was first sent to the Paraclete; it now lies alongside that of Héloïse in the cemetery of Père-Lachaise in Paris.

AVERROËS

(b. 1126, Córdoba [Spain] — d. 1198, Marrakech, Almohad empire [now in Morocco])

A verroës was an influential Islamic religious philosopher who integrated Islamic traditions with ancient Greek thought.

Averroës was born into a distinguished family of jurists at Córdoba. Thoroughly versed in the traditional Muslim sciences (especially exegesis of the Qur'ān—Islamic scripture—and Ḥadīth, or Traditions, and *fiqh*, or Law), trained in medicine, and accomplished in philosophy, Averroës rose to be chief *qāḍī* (judge) of Córdoba, an office also held by his grandfather (of the same name) under the Almoravids. After the death of the philosopher Ibn Ṭufayl, Averroës succeeded him as personal physician to the caliphs Abū Ya'qūb Yūsuf in 1182 and his son Abū Yūsuf Ya'qūb in 1184.

At some point between 1153 and 1169, Ibn Ṭufayl had introduced Averroës to Abū Ya'qūb, himself a keen student of philosophy. Soon afterward Averroës received the ruler's request to provide a badly needed correct interpretation of the philosophy of the Greek philosopher Aristotle, a task to which he devoted many years of his busy life as judge, beginning at Sevilla (Seville) and continuing at Córdoba. The exact year of his appointment as chief *qāḍī* of Córdoba, one of the key posts in the government, is not known.

AVERROËS' DEFENSE OF PHILOSOPHY

Averroës' own first work is *General Medicine* (*Kulliyāt*, Latin *Colliget*), written between 1162 and 1169. Only a few of his legal writings and none of his theological writings are preserved. Undoubtedly his most important writings are three closely connected religious-philosophical polemical treatises, composed in the years 1179 and 1180: the *Faṣl al-Makāl*, with its appendix; the *Kashf al-Manāhij*; and the *Tahāfut al-Tahāfut* in defense of philosophy. In the two first named, Averroës stakes a bold claim: Only the metaphysician employing certain proof (syllogism) is capable and competent (as well as obliged) to interpret the doctrines contained in the prophetically revealed law (Shar' or Sharī'ah), and not the Muslim *mutakallimūn* (dialectic theologians), who rely on dialectical arguments. To establish the true, inner meaning of religious beliefs and convictions is the aim of philosophy in its quest for truth. This inner meaning must not be divulged to the masses, who must accept the plain, external meaning of Scripture contained in stories, similes, and metaphors. Averroës applied Aristotle's three arguments (demonstrative, dialectical, and persuasive—i.e., rhetorical and poetical) to the philosophers, the theologians, and the masses. The third work is devoted to a defense of philosophy against his predecessor al-Ghazālī's telling attack directed against Avicenna and al-Qārābī in particular.

Averroës acknowledged the support of Abū Ya'qūb, to whom he dedicated his *Commentary on Plato's Republic*. Yet Averroës pursued his philosophical quest in the face of strong opposition from the *mutakallimūn*, who, together with the jurists, occupied a position of eminence and of great influence over the fanatical masses. This may explain why he suddenly fell from grace when Abū Yūsuf—on the occasion of a *jihad* (holy war) against Christian Spain— dismissed him from high office and banished him to Lucena in 1195. But Averroës' disgrace was only short-lived, since the caliph recalled Averroës to his presence after his return to Marrakech. After his death, Averroës was first buried at Marrakech, and later his body was transferred to the family tomb at Córdoba.

ZHU XI

(b. Oct. 18, 1130, Youxi, Fujian province, China—d. April 23, 1200, China)

Zhu Xi was a Chinese philosopher whose synthesis of neo-Confucian thought long dominated Chinese intellectual life.

Zhu Xi was the son of a local official. He was educated in the Confucian tradition by his father and passed the highest civil service examination at the age of 18, when the average age for such an accomplishment was 35. Zhu Xi's first official position (1151–58) was as a registrar in Tongan, Fujian. There he proceeded to reform the management of taxation and police, improve the library and the standards of the local school, and draw up a code of proper formal conduct and ritual, none being previously available.

Before proceeding to Tongan, Zhu Xi called on Li Tong, a thinker in the tradition of Song Confucianism who decisively influenced his future thinking. He visited Li again in 1158 and spent several months studying with him in 1160. Li was one of the ablest followers of the 11th-century neo-Confucians who had created a new metaphysical system to compete with Buddhist and Daoist philosophy and regain the Confucian intellectual ascendancy lost for nearly a millennium. Under his influence, Zhu's allegiance turned definitely to Confucianism at this time.

After his assignment at Tongan ended, Zhu Xi did not accept another official appointment until 1179. He did, however, continue to express his political views in memorandums addressed to the emperor. Though Zhu Xi also remained involved in public affairs, his persistent refusal to accept a substantive public office reflected his dissatisfaction with the men in power and their policies, his spurning of factional politics, and his preference for the life of a teacher and scholar, which was made possible by his receipt of a series of government sinecures.

These years were productive in thought and scholarship as indicated both by his formal writings and by his correspondence with friends and scholars of diverse views. In 1175, for instance, Zhu Xi held a famous philosophical debate with the philosopher Lu Jiuyuan (Lu Xiangshan) at which neither man was able to prevail. In contrast to Lu's insistence on the exclusive value of inwardness, Zhu Xi emphasized the value of inquiry and study, including book learning. Consistent with this view was Zhu Xi's own prolific literary output. In a number of works, including a compilation of the works of the Cheng brothers and studies of Zhou Dunyi (1017–73) and Zhang Zai (1020–77), he expressed his esteem for these four philosophers, whose ideas he incorporated and synthesized into his own thought. According to Zhu Xi, these thinkers had restored the transmission of the Confucian Way (dao), a process that had been lost after the death of Mencius. In 1175 Zhu Xi and his friend Lu Ziqian (1137–81) compiled passages from the works of the four to form their famous anthology, *Jinsi Lu* ("Reflections on Things at Hand"). Zhu Xi's philosophical ideas also found expression during this period in his enormously influential commentaries on the *Lunyu* (known in English as the *Analects* of Confucius) and on the *Mencius*, both completed in 1177.

Zhu Xi also took a keen interest in history and directed a reworking and condensation of Sima Guang's history, the *Zizhi tongjian* ("Comprehensive Mirror for Aid in Government"), so that it would illustrate moral principles in government. The resulting work, known as the *Tongjian gangmu* ("Outline and Digest of the General Mirror"), basically completed in 1172, was not only widely read throughout eastern Asia but also served as the basis for the first comprehensive history of China published in Europe, J.-A.-M. Moyriac de Mailla's *Histoire générale de la Chine* (1777–85).

On several occasions during his later career Zhu was invited to the imperial court and seemed destined for more influential positions, but his invariably frank and forceful opinions and his uncompromising attacks on corruption and political expediency each time brought his dismissal or his transfer to a new post conveniently distant from the capital. On the last of these occasions, near the end of his life, his enemies retaliated with virulent accusations concerning his views and conduct, and he was barred from political activity. He was still in political disgrace when he died in 1200. Zhu Xi's reputation was rehabilitated soon after his death, however, and post-humous honours for him followed in 1209 and 1230, culminating in the placement of his tablet in the Confucian Temple in 1241. In later centuries, rulers more authoritarian than those he had criticized, discreetly forgetting his political and intellectual nonconformity, made his philo-sophic system the sole orthodox creed, which it remained until the end of the 19th century.

MOSES MAIMONIDES

(b. March 30, 1135, Córdoba [Spain]—d. Dec. 13, 1204, Egypt)

Moses Maimonides was a Jewish philosopher, jurist, and physician and the foremost intellectual figure of medieval Judaism. His first major work, begun at age 23 and completed 10 years later, was a commentary on the Mishna, the collected Jewish oral laws. A monumental code of Jewish law followed in Hebrew, *The Guide for the Perplexed* in Arabic, and numerous other works, many of major importance. His contributions in religion, philosophy, and medicine have influenced Jewish and non-Jewish scholars alike.

LIFE

Maimonides was born into a distinguished family in Córdoba (Cordova), Spain. The young Moses studied with his learned father, Maimon, and other masters and at an early age astonished his teachers by his remarkable depth and versatility. Before Moses reached his 13th birthday, his peaceful world was suddenly disturbed by the ravages of war and persecution.

As part of Islamic Spain, Córdoba had accorded its citizens full religious freedom. But now the Islamic Mediterranean world was shaken by a revolutionary and fanatical Islamic sect, the Almohads (Arabic: *al-Muwaḥḥidūn*, "the Unitarians"), who captured Córdoba in 1148, leaving the Jewish community faced with the grim alternative of submitting to Islam or leaving the city. The Maimons temporized by practicing their Judaism in the privacy of their homes, while disguising their ways in public as far as possible to appear like Muslims. They remained in Córdoba for some 11 years, and Maimonides continued his education in Judaic studies as well as in the scientific disciplines in vogue at the time.

When the double life proved too irksome to maintain in Córdoba, the Maimon family finally left the city about 1159 to settle in Fez, Morocco. Although it was also under Almohad rule, Fez was presumably more promising than Córdoba because there the Maimons would be strangers, and their disguise would be more likely to go undetected. Moses continued his studies in his favourite subjects, rabbinics and Greek philosophy, and added medicine to them. Fez proved to be no more than a short respite, however. In 1165 Rabbi Judah ibn Shoshan, with whom Moses had studied, was arrested as a practicing Jew and was found guilty and then executed. This was a sign to the Maimon family to move again, this time to Palestine, which was in a depressed economic state and could not offer them the basis of a livelihood. After a few months they moved again, now to Egypt, settling in Fostat, near Cairo. There Jews were free to practice their faith openly, though any Jew who had once submitted to Islam courted death if he relapsed to Judaism. Moses himself was once accused of being a renegade Muslim, but he was able to prove that he had never really adopted the faith of Islam and so was exonerated.

Though Egypt was a haven from harassment and persecution, Moses was soon assailed by personal problems. His father died shortly after the family's arrival in Egypt. His younger brother, David, a prosperous jewelry merchant on whom Moses leaned for support, died in a shipwreck, taking the entire family fortune with him, and Moses was left as the sole support of his family. He could not turn to the rabbinate because in those days the rabbinate was conceived of as a public service that did not offer its practitioners any remuneration. Pressed by economic necessity, Moses took advantage of his medical studies and became a practicing physician. His fame as a physician spread rapidly, and he soon became the court physician to the sultan Saladin, the famous Muslim military leader, and to his son al-Afḍal. He also continued a private practice and lectured before his fellow physicians at the state hospital. At the same time he became the leading member of the Jewish community, teaching in public and helping his people with various personal and communal problems.

Maimonides married late in life and was the

Moses Maimonides, shown in a drawing dated to 1175. Hulton Archive/ Getty Images

father of a son, Abraham, who was to make his mark in his own right in the world of Jewish scholarship.

Works

The writings of Maimonides were numerous and varied. His earliest work, composed in Arabic at the age of 16, was the *Millot ha-Higgayon* ("Treatise on Logical Terminology"), a study of various technical terms that were employed in logic and metaphysics. Another of his early works, also in Arabic, was the *Essay on the Calendar* (Hebrew title: *Ma'amar ha'ibur*).

The first of Maimonides' major works, begun at the age of 23, was his commentary on the *Mishna*, *Kitāb al-Sirāj*, also written in Arabic. The *Mishna* is a compendium of decisions in Jewish law that dates from earliest times to the 3rd century. Maimonides' commentary clarified individual words and phrases, frequently citing relevant information in archaeology, theology, or science. Possibly the work's most striking feature is a series of introductory essays dealing with general philosophic issues touched on in the *Mishna*. One of these essays summarizes the teachings of Judaism in a creed of *Thirteen Articles of Faith*.

He completed the commentary on the *Mishna* at the age of 33, after which he began his magnum opus, the code of Jewish law, on which he also laboured for 10 years. Bearing the name of *Mishne Torah* ("The Torah Reviewed") and written in a lucid Hebrew style, the code offers a brilliant systematization of all Jewish law and doctrine. He wrote two other works in Jewish law of lesser scope: the *Sefer ha-mitzwot* (*Book of Precepts*), a digest of law for the less sophisticated reader, written in Arabic; and the *Hilkhot ha-Yerushalmi* ("Laws of Jerusalem"), a digest of the laws in the Palestinian Talmud, written in Hebrew.

His next major work, which he began in 1176 and on which he laboured for 15 years, was his classic in religious philosophy, the *Dalālat al-ḥāḥirīn* (*The Guide for the Perplexed*), later known under its Hebrew title as the *Moreh nevukhim*. A plea for what he called a more rational philosophy of Judaism, it constituted a major contribution to the accommodation between science, philosophy, and religion. It was written in Arabic and sent as a private communication to his favourite disciple, Joseph ibn Aknin. The work was translated into Hebrew in Maimonides' lifetime and later into Latin and most European languages. It has exerted a marked influence on the history of religious thought.

Maimonides complained often that the pressures of his many duties robbed him of peace and undermined his health. He died in 1204 and was buried in Tiberias, in the Holy Land, where his grave continues to be a shrine drawing a constant stream of pious pilgrims.

IBN AL-ʿARABĪ

(b. July 28, 1165, Murcia, Valencia [Spain] — d. Nov. 16, 1240, Damascus [Syria])

Ibn al-ʿArabī was a celebrated Muslim mystic-philosopher who gave the esoteric, mystical dimension of Islamic thought its first full-fledged philosophic expression. His major works are the monumental *Al-Futūḥāt al-Makkiyyah* ("The Meccan Revelations") and *Fuṣūṣ al-ḥikam* (1229; "The Bezels of Wisdom").

Ibn al-Arabī was born in the southeast of Spain, a man of pure Arab blood whose ancestry went back to the prominent Arabian tribe of Ṭāʾī. It was in Sevilla (Seville), then an outstanding centre of Islamic culture and learning, that he received his early education. He stayed there for 30 years, studying traditional Islamic sciences; he studied with a number of mystic masters who found in him a young man of marked spiritual inclination and unusually keen intelligence. During those years he travelled a great deal and visited various cities of Spain and North Africa in search of masters of the Sufi (mystical) Path who had achieved great spiritual progress and thus renown.

It was during one of these trips that Ibn al-Arabī had a dramatic encounter with the great Aristotelian philosopher Ibn Rushd (Averroës; 1126–98) in the city of Córdoba. Averroës, a close friend of the boy's father, had asked that the interview be arranged because he had heard of the extraordinary nature of the young, still beardless lad. After the early exchange of only a few words, it is said, the mystical depth of the boy so overwhelmed the old philosopher that he became pale and, dumbfounded, began trembling.

In 1198, while in Murcia, Ibn al-Arabī had a vision in which he felt he had been ordered to leave Spain and set out for the East. Thus began his pilgrimage to the Orient, from which he never was to return to his homeland.

The first notable place he visited on this journey was Mecca (1201), where he "received a divine commandment" to begin his major work *Al-Futūḥāt al-Makkiyyah*, which was to be completed much later in Damascus. In 560 chapters, it is a work of tremendous size, a personal encyclopaedia extending over all the esoteric sciences in Islam as Ibn al-Arabī understood and had experienced them, together with valuable information about his own inner life.

It was also in Mecca that Ibn al-Arabī became acquainted with a young girl of great beauty who, as a living embodiment of the eternal *sophia* (wisdom), was to play in his life a role much like that which Beatrice played for Dante. Her memories were eternalized by Ibn al-Arabī in a collection of love poems (*Tarjumān al-ashwāq*; "The Interpreter of Desires"), upon which he himself composed a mystical commentary. His daring "pantheistic" expressions drew down on him the wrath of Muslim orthodoxy, some of whom prohibited the reading of his works at the same time that others were elevating him to the rank of the prophets and saints.

After Mecca, Ibn al-Arabī visited Egypt (also in 1201) and then Anatolia, where, in Qonya, he met Ṣadr al-Dīn al-Qūnawī, who was to become his most important follower and successor in the East. From Qonya he went on to Baghdad and Aleppo (modern Ḥalab, Syria). By the time his long pilgrimage had come to an end at Damascus (1223), his fame had spread all over the Islamic world. Venerated as the greatest spiritual master, he spent the rest of his life in Damascus in peaceful contemplation, teaching, and writing. It was during his Damascus days that one of the most important works in mystical philosophy in Islam, *Fuṣūṣ al-ḥikam*, was composed in 1229, about 10 years before his death. Consisting only of 27 chapters, the book is incomparably smaller than *Al-Futūḥāt al-Makkiyyah*, but its importance as an expression of Ibn al-Arabī's mystical thought in its most mature form cannot be overemphasized.

SHINRAN

(b. 1173, near Kyōto, Japan—d. Jan. 9, 1263, Kyōto)

Shinran was a Buddhist teacher recognized as the founder of the Jōdo Shinshū (True Pure Land School), which advocates that faith, recitation of the name of the buddha Amida (Amitabha), and birth in the paradise of the Pure Land. For centuries Jōdo Shinshū has been one of the largest schools of Buddhism in Japan. During his lifetime Shinran was an insignificant figure, but in modern times he has been recognized as an eminent and sophisticated religious thinker.

The details of Shinran's life are sketchy because few historical sources about him have survived. The most important of these, a hagiography (saint's life) known pop-ularly as the *Godenshō* ("The Biography"), was written in 1295 by his great-grandson Kakunyo (1270–1351). Other works that offer insights into his life are Shinran's own religious writings and the letters of his wife, Eshin Ni (1182–1268?), which were discovered in 1921.

According to the *Godenshō*, Shinran was inducted into the Buddhist priesthood at age nine by Jien (1155–1225), an abbot of the Tendai school of Buddhist thought. Shinran's entry into the order may have been the result of the declining fortunes of his extended family, who belonged to the low-level aristocratic Hino clan, or of the death of his parents. He served for 20 years at the Tendai monastery on Mt. Hiei, northeast of Kyōto, as a *dōsō* ("hall priest"), performing Pure Land Buddhist rituals and practices. In 1201 he left Mt. Hiei and secluded himself for 100 days in the Rokkaku Temple in Kyōto. During this retreat he had a dream in which Prince Shōtoku (574–622), the semilegendary promulgator of Buddhism in Japan, revealed that the bodhisattva Kannon would become Shinran's conjugal partner for life and would lead him to the Pure Land paradise at death. Inspired by this vision, Shinran abandoned monastic life at Mt. Hiei and became a disciple of Hōnen (1133–1212), the renowned master of Pure Land Buddhism. Subsequently, Shinran married and had children, thereby departing from Buddhism's ancient tradition of clerical celibacy.

As a fervent follower of Hōnen, Shinran adopted his teaching of the "exclusive *nembutsu*" (*senju nembutsu*): invoking the name of Amida Buddha is the sole practice assuring enlightenment in the Pure Land. Hōnen's religious move-ment provoked controversy and was censured by several powerful temples, including the Tendai monastery on Mt. Hiei and the Kōfuku Temple in Nara. In 1207 the ruling authorities suppressed the movement, resulting in Shinran's banishment to the remote province of Echigo. It was about this time that he married Eshin Ni and began a family. During his banishment and subsequent 20-year residency in the Kantō region (the vicinity of present-day Tokyo), Shinran deepened his religious ideas and actively propagated Pure Land teachings. He attracted an enthusiastic following of his own as a peripatetic preacher, emulating perhaps the itinerant priests of the Zenkō Temple, whose sacred Amida icon Shinran revered. During this period he also compiled an early draft of his magnum opus, *Kyōgyōshinshō* ("Teaching, Practice, Faith, and Attainment"), a collection of scriptural quotations on Pure Land teachings interspersed with Shinran's interpretations or comments.

In the early 1230s Shinran left the Kantō region and returned to Kyōto, where he spent the last three decades of his long life. His many followers remained in contact with him through letters and visits and offered monetary gifts to sustain him in old age. Shinran dedicated considerable time in this period to writing. In addition to completing the *Kyōgyōshinshō*, he composed doctrinal treatises, commentaries, religious tracts, hymns of praise (*wasan*), and other works, both to confirm his own understanding of Pure Land Buddhism and to convey his views to others.

In the last decade of his life, Shinran endured a particularly agonizing estrangement from his son Zenran (died 1292). Zenran had become embroiled in a dispute with Shinran's followers in the Kantō region over provocative beliefs and behaviour, such as the assertion by some of license to commit wrongdoings. To counter them, Zenran made extravagant claims that Shinran had secretly imparted authority to him. Only by disowning him was Shinran able to quell the confusion among his followers and to reassure them of his true teachings.

According to the *Godenshō*, Shinran died in Kyōto at the age of 90. On his deathbed he chanted the *nembutsu* steadfastly, and at his side were his youngest daughter, Kakushin Ni (1224–83), and several other followers. After his cremation, Shinran's ashes were interred in eastern Kyōto. In 1272 they were moved to a nearby site where a memorial chapel was constructed, which would be the precursor of the Hongan Temple, the headquarters of the Shinshū school.

In premodern times the Jodo Shinshū regarded Shinran as an earthly incarnation of the buddha Amida, appearing in the world to spread the Pure Land teachings. Such a characterization was common in medieval Buddhism and congruent with Shinran's own veneration of Hōnen as an incarnation of Amida. The Hongan Temple preserved and promoted this image, especially during the Shinshū's emergence as Japan's largest and most powerful religious movement under the leadership of Shinran's descendant Rennyo (1415–99). In modern times, however, Shinran has been depicted in a more humanistic fashion, as a visionary thinker and as the archetypal religious seeker.

SAINT THOMAS AQUINAS

(b. 1224/25, Roccasecca, near Aquino, Terra di Lavoro, Kingdom of Sicily—d. March 7, 1274, Fossanova, near Terracina, Latium, Papal States; canonized July 18, 1323; feast day January 28, formerly March 7)

S t. Thomas Aquinas was an Italian Dominican theologian and the foremost medieval Scholasticist. His doctrinal system and the explanations and developments made by his followers are known as Thomism. He is nevertheless recognized by the Roman Catholic Church as its foremost Western philosopher and theologian.

EARLY YEARS

Thomas was born to parents who were in possession of a modest feudal domain on a boundary constantly disputed by the emperor and the pope. Thomas was placed in the monastery of Monte Cassino near his home as an oblate (i.e., offered as a prospective monk) when he was still a young boy; his family doubtless hoped that he would someday become abbot to their advantage. In 1239, after nine years in this sanctuary of spiritual and cultural life, young Thomas was forced to return to his family when the emperor expelled the monks because they were too obedient to the pope. He was then sent to the University of Naples, recently founded by the emperor, where he first encountered the scientific and philosophical works that were being translated from the Greek and the Arabic.

In this setting Thomas decided to join the Friars Preachers, or Dominicans, a new religious order founded 30 years earlier, which departed from the traditional paternalistic form of government for monks to the more democratic form of the mendicant friars (i.e., religious orders whose corporate as well as personal poverty made it necessary for them to beg alms) and from the monastic life of prayer and manual labour to a more active life of preaching and teaching. A dramatic episode marked the full significance of his decision. His parents had him abducted on the road to Paris, where his

Portrait of Thomas Aquinas, created c. 1270. Hulton Archive/Getty Images

shrewd superiors had immediately assigned him so that he would be out of the reach of his family but also so that he could pursue his studies in the most prestigious and turbulent university of the time.

STUDIES IN PARIS

Thomas held out stubbornly against his family despite a year of captivity. He was finally liberated and in the autumn of 1245 went to Paris to the convent of Saint-Jacques, the great university centre of the Dominicans; there he studied under Albertus Magnus, a tremendous scholar with a wide range of intellectual interests.

When Thomas Aquinas arrived at the University of Paris, the influx of Arabian-Aristotelian science was arousing a sharp reaction among believers; and several times the church authorities tried to block the naturalism and rationalism that were emanating from this philosophy and, according to many ecclesiastics, seducing the younger generations. Thomas did not fear these new ideas, but, like Albertus Magnus (and Roger Bacon, also lecturing at Paris), he studied the works of Aristotle and eventually lectured publicly on them.

During the summer of 1248, Aquinas left Paris with Albertus, who was to assume direction of the new faculty established by the Dominicans at the convent in Cologne. He remained there until 1252, when he returned to Paris to prepare for the degree of master of theology. After taking his bachelor's degree, he received the *licentia docendi* ("license to teach") at the beginning of 1256 and shortly afterward finished the training necessary for the title and privileges of master. Thus, in the year 1256 he began teaching theology in one of the two Dominican schools incorporated in the University of Paris.

LATER YEARS

In 1259 Thomas was appointed theological adviser and lecturer to the papal Curia, then the centre of Western humanism. He returned to Italy, where he spent two years at Anagni at the end of the reign of Alexander IV and four years at Orvieto with Urban IV. From 1265 to 1267 he taught at the convent of Santa Sabina in Rome and then, at the request of Clement IV, went to the papal Curia in Viterbo. Suddenly, in November 1268, he was sent to Paris, where he became involved in a sharp doctrinal polemic that had just been triggered off.

The works of Averroës, the outstanding representative of Arabic philosophy in Spain, who was known as the great commentator and interpreter of Aristotle, were just becoming known to the Parisian masters. Averroës asserted that the structure of religious knowledge was entirely heterogeneous to rational knowledge: two truths—one of faith, the other of reason—can, in the final analysis, be contradictory. This dualism was denied by Muslim orthodoxy and was still less acceptable to Christians. With the appearance of Siger of Brabant, however, and from 1266 on, the quality of Averroës's exegesis and the wholly rational bent of his thought began to attract disciples in the faculty of arts at the University of Paris. Thomas Aquinas rose in protest against his colleagues; nevertheless, the parties retained a mutual esteem.

In the course of this dispute, the very method of theology was called into question. According to Aquinas, reason is able to operate within faith and yet according to its own laws. The mystery of God is expressed and incarnate in human language; it is thus able to become the object of an active, conscious, and organized elaboration in which the rules and structures of rational activity are integrated in the light of faith. In the Aristotelian sense of the word, then (although not in the modern sense), theology is a "science"; it is knowledge that is rationally derived from propositions that are accepted as certain because they are revealed by God. The theologian accepts authority and faith as his starting point and then proceeds to conclusions using reason; the philosopher, on the other hand, relies solely on the natural light of reason. Thomas was the first to view theology expressly in this way or at least to present it systematically, and in doing so he raised a storm of opposition in various quarters.

The logic of Aquinas's position regarding faith and reason required that the fundamental consistency of the realities of nature be recognized. A *physis* ("nature") has necessary laws; recognition of this fact permits the construction of a science according to a *logos* ("rational structure"). Thomas thus avoided the temptation to sacralize the forces of nature through a naïve recourse to the miraculous or the Providence of God. For him, a whole "supernatural" world that cast its shadow over things and men, in Romanesque art as in social customs, had blurred men's imaginations. Nature, discovered in its profane reality, should assume its proper religious value and lead to God by more rational ways, yet not simply as a shadow of the supernatural. This understanding is exemplified in the way that Francis of Assisi admired the birds, the plants, and the Sun.

Although he was an Aristotelian, Thomas was certain that he could defend himself against a heterodox interpretation of "the Philosopher," as Aristotle was known. Thomas held that human liberty could be defended as a rational thesis while admitting that determinations are found in nature. In his theology of Providence, he taught a continuous creation, in which the dependence of the created on the creative wisdom guarantees the reality of the order of nature. God moves sovereignly all that he creates, but the supreme government that he exercises over the universe is conformed to the laws of a creative Providence that wills each being to act according to its proper nature. This autonomy finds its highest realization in the rational creature: humans are literally self-moving in their intellectual, volitional, and physical existence. Their freedom, far from being destroyed by their relationship to God, finds its foundation in this very relationship.

In January 1274 Thomas was personally summoned by Gregory X to the second Council of Lyons, which was an attempt to repair the schism between the Latin and Greek churches. On his way he was stricken by illness; he stopped at the Cistercian abbey of Fossanova, where he died on March 7.

JOHN DUNS SCOTUS

(b. c. 1266, Duns, Lothian [now in Scottish Borders], Scotland—d. Nov. 8, 1308, Cologne [Germany])

John Duns Scotus was an influential Franciscan realist philosopher and scholastic theologian.

There is perhaps no other great medieval thinker whose life is as little known as that of Duns Scotus. He apparently spent 13 years (1288–1301) at the University of Oxford preparing for inception as master of theology. There is no record of where he took the eight years of preliminary philosophical training (four for a bachelor's and four for the master's degrees) required to enter such a program.

After studying theology for almost four years, John Duns was ordained priest at St. Andrew's Church in Northampton on March 17, 1291. In view of the minimum age requirements for the priesthood, this suggests that Duns Scotus must have been born no later than March 1266.

YEARS AT THE UNIVERSITY OF PARIS

When the turn came for the English province to provide a talented candidate for the Franciscan chair of theology at the more prestigious University of Paris, Duns Scotus was appointed. One *reportatio* of his Paris lectures indicates that he began commenting on the *Sentences* there in the autumn of 1302 and continued to June 1303. Before the term ended, however, the university was affected by the long-smouldering feud between King Philip IV and Pope Boniface VIII. The issue was taxation of church property to support the king's wars with England. When Boniface excommunicated him, the monarch retaliated by calling for a general church council to depose the pope. He won over the French clergy and the university. On June 24, 1303, a great antipapal demonstration took place. Friars paraded in the Paris streets.

On the following day royal commissioners examined each member of the Franciscan house to determine whether he was with or against the king. Some 70 friars, mostly French, sided with Philip, while the rest (some 80 odd) remained loyal to the pope, among them Duns Scotus and Master Gonsalvus Hispanus. As a result of his harassment and imprisonment by the king's minister, however, Boniface died in October and was succeeded by Pope Benedict XI. In the interests of peace, Benedict lifted the ban against the university in April 1304, and shortly afterward the king facilitated the return of students.

Where Duns Scotus spent the exile is unclear. Possibly his Cambridge lectures stem from this period, although they may have been given during the academic year of 1301–02 before coming to Paris. At any rate, Duns Scotus was back before the summer of 1304, for he was the bachelor respondent in the *disputatio in aula* ("public disputation") when his predecessor, Giles of Ligny, was promoted to master. On November 18 of that same year, Gonsalvus, who had been elected minister general of the Franciscan order at the Pentecost chapter, or meeting, assigned Duns Scotus as Giles's successor.

The period following Duns Scotus's inception as master in 1305 was one of great literary activity. Aided by a staff of associates and secretaries, he set to work to complete his *Ordinatio* begun at Oxford, using not only the Oxford and Cambridge lectures but also those of Paris. A search of manuscripts reveals a magisterial dispute Duns Scotus conducted with the Dominican master, Guillaume Pierre Godin, against the thesis that matter is the principle of individuation (the metaphysical principle that makes an individual thing different from other things of the same species). Duns Scotus did conduct one solemn quodlibetal disputation, so called because the master accepted questions on any topic (*de quodlibet*) and from any bachelor or master present (*a quodlibet*). The 21 questions Duns Scotus treated were later revised, enlarged, and organized under two main topics, God and creatures.

The short but important *Tractatus de primo principio*, a compendium of what reason can prove about God, draws heavily upon the *Ordinatio*. The remaining authentic works seem to represent questions discussed privately for the benefit of the Franciscan student philosophers or theologians. They include, in addition to the *Collationes* (from both Oxford and Paris), the *Quaestiones in Metaphysicam Aristotelis* and a series of logical questions occasioned by the Neoplatonist Porphyry's *Isagoge* and Aristotle's *De praedicamentis*, *De interpretatione*, and *De sophisticis elenchis*.

FINAL PERIOD AT COLOGNE

In 1307 Duns Scotus was appointed professor at Cologne. Some have suggested that Gonsalvus sent him to Cologne for his own safety. Although Duns Scotus's brilliant defense of the Immaculate Conception marked the turning point in the history of the doctrine, it was immediately challenged by secular and Dominican colleagues. When the question arose in a solemn quodlibetal disputation, the secular master Jean de Pouilly, for example, declared the Scotist thesis not only improbable but even heretical. At a time when Philip IV had initiated heresy trials against the wealthy Knights Templars, Pouilly's words have an ominous ring. There seems to have been something hasty about Duns Scotus's departure in any case. Duns Scotus lectured at Cologne until his death. His body at present lies in the nave of the Franciscan church near the Cologne cathedral, and in many places he is venerated as blessed.

Despite their imperfect form, Duns Scotus's works were widely circulated. His claim that universal concepts are based on a "common nature" in individuals was one of the central issues in the 14th-century controversy between Realists and Nominalists concerning the question of whether general types are figments of the mind or are real.

WILLIAM OF OCKHAM

(b. c. 1285, Ockham, Surrey?, Eng.—d. 1347/49, Munich, Bavaria [now in Germany])

William of Ockham was a Franciscan philosopher, theologian, and political writer. He is regarded as the founder of a form of nominalism—the school of thought that denies that universal concepts such as "father" have any reality apart from the individual things signified by the universal or general term.

EARLY LIFE

Little is known of Ockham's childhood. It seems that he was still a youngster when he entered the Franciscan order. Ockham's early schooling in a Franciscan convent concentrated on the study of logic; throughout his career, his interest in logic never waned, because he regarded the science of terms as fundamental and indispensable for practicing all the sciences of things, including God, the world, and ecclesiastical or civil institutions.

After his early training, Ockham took the traditional course of theological studies at the University of Oxford and apparently between 1317 and 1319 lectured on the *Sentences* of Peter Lombard. His opinions aroused strong opposition from members of the theological faculty of Oxford, however, and he left the university without obtaining his master's degree in theology. Ockham thus remained, academically speaking, an undergraduate.

When he left his country for Avignon, Fr., in the autumn of 1324 at the pope's request, he was acquainted with a university environment shaken not only by disputes but also by the challenging of authority: that of the bishops in doctrinal matters and that of the chancellor of the university, John Lutterell, who was dismissed from his post in 1322 at the demand of the teaching staff.

However abstract and impersonal the style of Ockham's writings may be, they reveal at least two aspects of Ockham's intellectual and spiritual attitude. On the one hand, with his passion for logic he insisted on evaluations that are severely rational, on distinctions between the necessary and the incidental and differentiation between evidence and degrees of probability. On the other hand, as a theologian he referred to the primary importance of the God of the creed whose omnipotence determines the gratuitous salvation of humans. The medieval rule of economy, that "plurality should not be assumed without necessity," has come to be known as "Ockham's razor"; the principle was used by Ockham to eliminate many entities that had been devised, especially by the scholastic philosophers, to explain reality.

TREATISE TO JOHN XXII

Ockham met John Lutterell again at Avignon; in a treatise addressed to Pope John XXII, the former chancellor of Oxford denounced Ockham's teaching on the *Sentences*, extracting from it 56 propositions that he showed to be in serious error. Ockham, however, presented to the pope another copy of the *Ordinatio* in which he had made some corrections. It appeared that he would be condemned for his teaching, but the condemnation never came.

At the convent where he resided in Avignon, Ockham met Bonagratia of Bergamo, a doctor of civil and canon law who was being persecuted for his opposition to John XXII on the problem of Franciscan poverty. On Dec. 1, 1327, the Franciscan general Michael of Cesena arrived in Avignon and stayed at the same convent; he, too, had been summoned by the pope in connection with the dispute over the holding of property. They were at odds over the theoretical problem of whether Christ and his Apostles had owned the goods they used. Michael maintained that because Christ and his Apostles had renounced all ownership and all rights to property, the Franciscans were justified in attempting to do the same thing.

The relations between John and Michael grew steadily worse, to such an extent that, on May 26, 1328, Michael fled from Avignon accompanied by Bonagratia and William. They stayed in Pisa under the protection of Emperor Louis IV the Bavarian, who had been excommunicated in 1324 and proclaimed by John XXII to have forfeited all rights to the empire. They followed him to Munich in 1330, and thereafter Ockham wrote fervently against the papacy in defense of both the strict Franciscan notion of poverty and the empire.

Instructed by his superior general in 1328 to study three papal bulls on poverty, Ockham found that they contained many errors that showed John XXII to be a heretic who had forfeited his mandate by reason of his heresy. His status of pseudo-pope was confirmed in Ockham's view in 1330–31 by his sermons proposing that the souls of the saved did not enjoy the vision of God immediately after death but only after they were rejoined with the body at the Last Judgment, an opinion that contradicted tradition and was ultimately rejected.

Excommunicated after his flight from Avignon, Ockham maintained the same basic position on poverty after the death of John XXII in 1334, during the reign of Benedict XII (1334–42), and after the election of Clement VI. In these final years he found time to write two treatises on logic, which bear witness to the leading role that he consistently assigned to that discipline. Ockham was long thought to have died at a convent in Munich in 1349 during the Black Death, but he may actually have died there in 1347.

NICCOLÒ MACHIAVELLI

(b. May 3, 1469, Florence, Italy—d. June 21, 1527, Florence)

Niccolò Machiavelli was an Italian Renaissance political philosopher and a statesman who is best known as the author of *The Prince* (*Il Principe*), a work that brought him a reputation as an atheist and an immoral cynic.

From the 13th century onward, Machiavelli's family was wealthy and prominent, holding on occasion Florence's most important offices. His father, Bernardo, a doctor of laws, was nevertheless among the family's poorest members.

Bernardo kept a library in which Niccolò must have read, but little is known of Niccolò's education and early life in Florence, at that time a thriving centre of philosophy and a brilliant showcase of the arts. In a letter to a friend in 1498, Machiavelli writes of listening to the sermons of Girolamo Savonarola (1452–98), a Dominican friar who moved to Florence in 1482 and in the 1490s attracted a party of popular supporters with his thinly veiled accusations against the government, the clergy, and the pope. Savonarola, who effectively ruled Florence for several years after 1494, was featured in *The Prince* (1513) as an example of an "unarmed prophet" who must fail.

On May 24, 1498, Savonarola was hanged as a heretic and his body burned in the public square. Several days later, emerging from obscurity at the age of 29, Niccolò Machiavelli became head of the second chancery (*cancelleria*), a post that placed him in charge of the republic's foreign affairs in subject territories. He held the post until 1512, having gained the confidence of Piero Soderini (1452–1522), the gonfalonier (chief magistrate) for life in Florence from 1502.

In 1512 the Florentine republic was overthrown and the gonfalonier deposed by a Spanish army that Julius II had enlisted into his Holy League. The Medici family returned to rule Florence, and Machiavelli, suspected of conspiracy, was imprisoned, tortured, and sent into exile in 1513 to his father's small property in San Casciano, just south of Florence. There he wrote his two major works, *The Prince* and *Discourses on Livy*, both of which were published after his death.

Machiavelli was first employed in 1520 by Cardinal Giulio de' Medici to resolve a case of bankruptcy in Lucca, where he took the occasion to write a sketch of its government and to compose his *The Life of Castruccio Castracani of*

Lucca (1520; *La vita di Castruccio Castracani da Lucca*). Later that year the cardinal agreed to have Machiavelli elected official historian of the republic, a post to which he was appointed in November 1520.

In April 1526 Machiavelli was made chancellor of the Procuratori delle Mura to superintend Florence's fortifications. By this time Cardinal Giulio had become Pope Clement VII. The pope formed a Holy League at Cognac against Holy Roman Emperor Charles V (reigned 1519–56), and Machiavelli went with the army to join his friend Francesco Guicciardini (1482–1540), the pope's lieutenant, with whom he remained until the sack of Rome by the emperor's forces brought the war to an end in May 1527. Now that Florence had cast off the Medici, Machiavelli hoped to be restored to his old post at the chancery. But the few favours that the Medici had doled out to him caused the supporters of the free republic to look upon him with suspicion. Denied the post, he fell ill and died within a month.

THE PRINCE

The first and most persistent view of Machiavelli is that of a teacher of evil. *The Prince* is in the tradition of the "Mirror for Princes"—i.e., books of advice that enabled princes to see themselves as though reflected in a mirror—which began with the *Cyropaedia* by the Greek historian Xenophon (431–350 BCE) and continued into the Middle Ages. Prior to Machiavelli, works in this genre advised princes to adopt the best prince as their model, but Machiavelli's version recommends that a prince go to the "effectual truth" of things and forgo the standard of "what should be done" lest he bring about his ruin. To maintain himself a prince must learn how not to be good and use or

Niccolò Machiavelli, in an engraving of a portrait by Raphael Morghen.
Hulton Archive/Getty Images

not use this knowledge "according to necessity." A second "amoral" interpretation fastens on Machiavelli's frequent resort to "necessity" in order to excuse actions that might otherwise be condemned as immoral.

Machiavelli divides principalities into those that are acquired and those that are inherited. In general, he argues that the more difficult it is to acquire control over a state, the easier it is to hold on to it. The reason for this is that the fear of a new prince is stronger than the love for a hereditary prince; hence, the new prince, who relies on "a dread of punishment that never forsakes you," will succeed, but a prince who expects his subjects to keep their promises of support will be disappointed.

The new prince relies on his own virtue, but, if virtue is to enable him to acquire a state, it must have a new meaning distinct from the New Testament virtue of seeking peace. Machiavelli's notion of *virtù* requires the prince to be concerned foremost with the art of war and to seek not merely security but also glory, for glory is included in necessity. *Virtù* for Machiavelli is virtue not for its own sake but rather for the sake of the reputation it enables princes to acquire. Virtue, according to Machiavelli, aims to reduce the power of fortune over human affairs because fortune keeps men from relying on themselves. At first Machiavelli admits that fortune rules half of men's lives, but then, in an infamous metaphor, he compares fortune to a woman who lets herself be won more by the impetuous and the young. A prince who possesses the virtue of mastery can command fortune and manage people to a degree never before thought possible.

In the last chapter of *The Prince*, Machiavelli writes a passionate "exhortation to seize Italy and to free her from the barbarians"—apparently France and Spain, which had been overrunning the disunited peninsula. He calls for a redeemer, mentioning the miracles that occurred as Moses led the Israelites to the promised land, and closes with a quotation from a patriotic poem by Petrarch (1304–74). The final chapter has led many to a third interpretation of Machiavelli as a patriot rather than as a disinterested scientist.

WANG YANGMING

(b. 1472, Yuyao, Zhejiang province, China—d. 1529, Nan'an, Jiangxi)

Wang Yangming was a Chinese scholar-official whose idealistic interpretation of neo-Confucianism influenced philosophical thinking in East Asia for centuries.

Wang was the son of a high government official. In 1492 he obtained the civil service degree "a recommended person." Having failed in the metropolitan civil service examinations in 1493 and 1495, he shifted his interest to military arts and Daoist techniques for longevity. In 1499, however, Wang passed the "advanced scholar" (*jinshi*) examination and was appointed a Ministry of Works official. He recommended to the emperor eight measures for frontier defense, strategy, and administration, which earned him early recognition. In 1500 he was appointed a Ministry of Justice secretary and in 1501 was ordered to check prisoners' records near Nanjing. He corrected injustices in many cases.

A critical event occurred in 1506, when Wang defended a supervising censor who had been imprisoned for attacking a powerful, corrupt eunuch. For his actions Wang was beaten with 40 strokes, imprisoned for several months, and banished to remote Guizhou as head of a dispatch station, where he lived among aborigines and often fell sick. The hardship and solitude led him to realize, suddenly one night at the age of 36, that to investigate the principles (*li*) of things is not to seek for them in actual objects, as the rationalistic Zhu Xi had taught, but in one's own mind.

Thus he brought Idealist (*xinxue*) neo-Confucianism—as first taught by a 12th-century philosopher, Lu Xiangshan—to its highest expression.

A year later he pronounced another epoch-making theory: that knowledge and action are one (*zhixing heyi*). One knows filial piety (*xiao*), he argued, only when one acts upon it, and correct action requires correct knowledge. As a magistrate in Jiangxi in 1510, he carried out many reforms, including a novel "joint registration system" whereby 10 families shared responsibility for security. An imperial audience followed and then appointments as Ministry of Justice secretary, Ministry of Personnel director (1511), Imperial Studs vice minister (1512), State Ceremonials minister (1514), and assistant censor in chief and governor of southern Jiangxi and adjacent areas (1516).

In 1521 the new emperor appointed him war minister and awarded him the title of earl of Xinjian. His father died in 1522, and he remained home to mourn his loss. For more than five years he stayed home and discussed doctrines with his followers, who came from various parts of China and numbered in the hundreds. These conversations and those earlier constitute his main work, *Chuanxilu* ("Instructions for Practical Living"). In 1521 he had enunciated his doctrine of complete realization of the innate knowledge of the good.

FRANCIS BACON, VISCOUNT SAINT ALBAN (OR ALBANS), BARON OF VERULAM

(b. Jan. 22, 1561, York House, London, Eng.—d. April 9, 1626, London)

Francis Bacon was a philosopher, lawyer, and statesman who served as lord chancellor of England from 1618 to 1621.

Bacon attended Trinity College, Cambridge, and then went to Paris (1576). Recalled abruptly after the death of his father (1579), he took up residence at Gray's Inn, an institution for legal education, and became a barrister in 1582. He progressed through several legal positions, becoming a member of Parliament in 1584, but had little success in gaining political power. About 1591 Robert Devereux, 2nd earl of Essex and a favourite of Queen Elizabeth, became his patron. By 1600, however, Bacon was the queen's learned counsel in the trial of Essex, and in 1601 he drew up a report denouncing Essex as a traitor.

With the accession of James I in 1603, Bacon sought anew to gain influence by means of unsparing service in Parliament, persistent letters of self-recommendation, and the help of important associates. He was engaged in a series of conflicts with Sir Edward Coke, the great jurist, in an effort to safeguard the royal prerogative. After a succession of legal posts, he was appointed lord chancellor and Baron Verulam in 1618; in 1620/21 he was created Viscount St. Albans. Between 1608 and 1620 he prepared at least 12 draftings of his most celebrated work, the *Novum Organum*, in which he presented his scientific method; he developed his Instauratio Magna, a plan to reorganize the sciences; and he wrote several minor philosophical works.

Bacon fell from power in 1621, following his being charged with bribery. He spent his final years writing what are considered some of his most valuable works.

THE IDOLS OF THE MIND

In the first book of *Novum Organum* Bacon discusses the causes of human error in the pursuit of knowledge. Aristotle had discussed logical fallacies, commonly found in human reasoning, but Bacon was original in looking behind the forms of reasoning to underlying psychological causes. He invented the metaphor of "idol" to refer to such causes of human error.

Bacon distinguishes four idols, or main varieties of proneness to error. The idols of the tribe are certain intellectual faults that are universal to mankind, or, at any rate, very common. One, for example, is a tendency toward oversimplification, that is, toward supposing, for the sake of tidiness, that there exists more order in a field of inquiry than there actually is. Another is a propensity to be overly influenced by particularly sudden or exciting occurrences that are in fact unrepresentative.

The idols of the cave are the intellectual peculiarities of individuals. One person may concentrate on the likenesses, another on the differences, between things. One may fasten on detail, another on the totality.

The idols of the marketplace are the kinds of error for which language is responsible. It has always been a distinguishing feature of English philosophy to emphasize the unreliable nature of language, which is seen, nominalistically, as a human improvisation. Nominalists argue that even if the power of speech is given by God, it was Adam who named the beasts and thereby gave that power its concrete realization. But language, like other human achievements, partakes of human imperfections. Bacon was particularly concerned with the superficiality of distinctions drawn in everyday language, by which things fundamentally different are classed together (whales and fishes as fish, for example) and things fundamentally similar are distinguished (ice, water, and steam). But he was also concerned, like later critics of language, with the capacity of words to embroil men in the discussion of the meaningless (as, for example, in discussions of the deity Fortune).

The fourth and final group of idols is that of the idols of the theatre, that is to say mistaken systems of

Artist Paul Van Somer's portrait of Francis Bacon. Hulton Archive/ Getty Images

philosophy in the broadest, Baconian sense of the term, in which it embraces all beliefs of any degree of generality. Bacon's critical polemic in discussing the idols of the theatre is lively but not very penetrating philosophically. He speaks, for example, of the vain affectations of the humanists, but they were not a very apt subject for his criticism. Humanists were really anti-philosophers who not unreasonably turned their attention to nonphilosophical matters because of the apparent inability of philosophers to arrive at conclusions that were either generally agreed upon or useful. Bacon does have something to say about the skeptical philosophy to which humanists appealed when they felt the need for it. Insofar as skepticism involves doubts about deductive reasoning, he has no quarrel with it. Insofar as it is applied not to reason but to the ability of the senses to supply the reason with reliable premises to work from, he brushes it aside too easily.

THE NEW METHOD

The core of Bacon's philosophy of science is the account of inductive reasoning given in Book II of *Novum Organum*. The defect of all previous systems of beliefs about nature, he argued, lay in the inadequate treatment of the general propositions from which the deductions were made. Either they were the result of precipitate generalization from one or two cases, or they were uncritically assumed to be self-evident on the basis of their familiarity and general acceptance.

In order to avoid hasty generalization Bacon urges a technique of "gradual ascent," that is, the patient accumulation of well-founded generalizations of steadily increasing degrees of generality. This method would have the beneficial effect of loosening the hold on men's minds of ill-constructed everyday concepts that obliterate important differences and fail to register important similarities.

The crucial point, Bacon realized, is that induction must work by elimination not, as it does in common life and the defective scientific tradition, by simple enumeration. Thus he stressed "the greater force of the negative instance"—the fact that while "all A are B" is only very weakly confirmed by "this A is B," it is shown conclusively to be false by "this A is not B." He devised tables, or formal devices for the presentation of singular pieces of evidence, in order to facilitate the rapid discovery of false generalizations. What survives this eliminative screening, Bacon assumes, may be taken to be true.

The conception of a scientific research establishment, which Bacon developed in his utopia, *The New Atlantis*, may be a more important contribution to science than his theory of induction. Here the idea of science as a collaborative undertaking, conducted in an impersonally methodical fashion and animated by the intention to give material benefits to mankind, is set out with literary force.

THOMAS HOBBES

(b. April 5, 1588, Westport, Wiltshire, Eng.—d. Dec. 4, 1679, Hardwick Hall, Derbyshire)

Thomas Hobbes was an English philosopher who is best known for his political philosophy, especially as articulated in his masterpiece *Leviathan* (1651).

Hobbes's father was a quick-tempered vicar of a small Wiltshire parish church. Disgraced after engaging in a brawl at his own church door, he disappeared and abandoned his three children to the care of his brother, a well-to-do glover in Malmesbury. For nearly the whole of his adult life, Hobbes worked for different branches of the wealthy and aristocratic Cavendish family. Upon taking his degree at Oxford in 1608, he was employed as page and tutor to the young William Cavendish, afterward the second earl of Devonshire. Over the course of many decades Hobbes served the family and their associates as translator, travelling companion, keeper of accounts, business representative, political adviser, and scientific collaborator. Hobbes also worked for the marquess of Newcastle-upon-Tyne, a cousin of William Cavendish, and Newcastle's brother, Sir Charles Cavendish.

INTELLECTUAL DEVELOPMENT

The two branches of the Cavendish family nourished Hobbes's enduring intellectual interests in politics and natural science, respectively. Through them, Hobbes became a member of several networks of intellectuals in England. Farther afield, in Paris, he became acquainted with the circle of scientists, theologians, and philosophers presided over by the theologian Marin Mersenne. This circle included René Descartes.

Hobbes was exposed to practical politics before he became a student of political philosophy. Hobbes attended many meetings of the governing body of the Virginia Company, a trading company established by James I to colonize parts of the eastern coast of North America, and came into contact with powerful men there. (Hobbes himself was given a small share in the company by his employer.)

In the late 1630s Parliament and the king were in conflict over how far normal kingly powers could be exceeded in exceptional circumstances, especially in regard to raising money for armies. In 1640 Hobbes wrote a treatise defending King Charles I's own wide interpretation of his prerogatives. Royalist members of Parliament used arguments from Hobbes's treatise in debates, and the treatise itself circulated in manuscript form. *The Elements of Law, Natural and Politic* (written in 1640, published in a misedited unauthorized version in 1650) was Hobbes's first work of political philosophy, though he did not intend it for publication as a book.

When strife became acute in 1640, Hobbes feared for his safety. Shortly after completing *The Elements of Law*, he fled to Paris, where he rejoined Mersenne's circle and made contact with other exiles from England. He would remain in Paris for more than a decade, working on optics and on *De Cive, De Corpore*, and *Leviathan*.

Political Philosophy

Hobbes presented his political philosophy in different forms for different audiences. *De Cive* states his theory in what he regarded as its most scientific form. Its break from the ancient authority par excellence—Aristotle—could not have been more loudly advertised. After only a few paragraphs, Hobbes rejects one of the most famous theses of Aristotle's politics, namely that human beings are naturally suited to life in a polis and do not fully realize their natures until they exercise the role of citizen. Hobbes turns Aristotle's claim on its head: human beings, he insists, are by nature unsuited to political life. They naturally denigrate and compete with each other, are very easily swayed by the rhetoric of ambitious men, and think much more highly of themselves than of other people. There is no natural self-restraint, even when human beings are moderate in their appetites, for a ruthless and bloodthirsty few can make even the moderate feel forced to take violent preemptive action in order to avoid losing everything.

War comes more naturally to human beings than political order. Indeed, political order is possible only when human beings abandon their natural condition of judging and pursuing what seems best to each and delegate this judgment to someone else. This delegation is effected when the many contract together to submit to a sovereign in return for physical safety and a modicum of well-being. Although Hobbes did not assume that there was ever a real historical event in which a mutual promise was made to delegate self-government to a sovereign, he claimed that the best way to understand the state was to conceive of it as having resulted from such an agreement.

The sovereign is not a party to the social contract; he receives the obedience of the many as a free gift in their hope that he will see to their safety. The sovereign makes no promises to the many in order to win their submission. Indeed, because he does not transfer his right of self-government to anyone, he retains the total liberty that his subjects trade for safety. He is not bound by law, including his own laws. Nor does he do anything unjustly if he makes decisions about his subjects' safety and well-being that they do not like.

Hobbes's masterpiece, *Leviathan* (1651), does not significantly depart from the view of *De Cive* concerning the relation between protection and obedience, but it devotes much more attention to the civil obligations of Christian believers and the proper and improper roles of a church within a state. Hobbes argues that believers do not endanger their prospects of salvation by obeying a sovereign's decrees to the letter, and he maintains that churches do not have any authority that is not granted by the civil sovereign.

RETURN TO ENGLAND

There are signs that Hobbes intended *Leviathan* to be read by a monarch, who would be able to take the rules of statecraft from it. A specially bound copy was given to Prince Charles while he was in exile in Paris. Unfortunately, Hobbes's suggestion in *Leviathan* that a subject had the right to abandon a ruler who could no longer protect him gave serious offense to the prince's advisers. Barred from the exiled court and under suspicion by the French authorities for his attack on the papacy, Hobbes found his position in Paris becoming daily more intolerable. At the end of 1651, at about the time that *Leviathan* was published, he returned to England and made his peace with the new regime of Oliver Cromwell. Hobbes submitted to that authority for a long time before the monarchy was restored in 1660.

From the time of the Restoration in 1660, Hobbes enjoyed a new prominence. Charles II received Hobbes again into favour. It was not until 1666, when the House of Commons prepared a bill against atheism and profaneness, that Hobbes felt seriously endangered. Hobbes, then verging upon 80, burned such of his papers as he thought might compromise him.

Although he was impugned by enemies at home, no Englishman of the day stood in such high repute abroad as Hobbes, and distinguished foreigners who visited England were always eager to pay their respects to the old man, whose vigour and freshness of intellect remained unquenched. In his last years Hobbes amused himself by returning to the Classical studies of his youth. In 1675 he produced a translation of the *Odyssey* in rugged English rhymes, with a lively preface, "Concerning the Virtues of an Heroic Poem." A translation of the *Iliad* appeared in the following year. As late as four months before his death, he was promising his publisher "somewhat to print in English."

RENÉ DESCARTES

(b. March 31, 1596, La Haye, Touraine, France—d. Feb. 11, 1650, Stockholm, Swed.)

René Descartes was a French philosopher, mathematician, and scientist who is generally regarded as the founder of modern Western philosophy. One of the first philosophers to abandon scholastic Aristotelianism, he formulated the first modern version of mind-body dualism, from which stems the mind-body problem, and promoted the development of a new science grounded in observation and experiment. Applying an original system of methodical doubt, he dismissed apparent knowledge derived from authority, the senses, and reason and erected new epistemic foundations on the basis of the intuition that, when he is thinking, he exists; this he expressed in the dictum "I think, therefore I am."

EARLY LIFE AND EDUCATION

Although Descartes's birthplace, La Haye (now Descartes), France, is in Touraine, his family connections lie south, across the Creuse River in Poitou, where his father, Joachim, owned farms and houses in Châtellerault and Poitiers. Because Joachim was a councillor in the Parlement of Brittany in Rennes, Descartes inherited a modest rank of nobility. Descartes's mother died when he was one year old. His father remarried in Rennes, leaving him in La Haye to be raised first by his maternal grandmother and then by his great-uncle in Châtellerault. Although the Descartes family was Roman Catholic, the Poitou region was controlled by the Protestant Huguenots, and Châtellerault, a Protestant stronghold, was the site of negotiations over the Edict of Nantes (1598), which gave Protestants freedom of worship in France following the intermittent Wars of Religion between Protestant and Catholic forces in France. Descartes returned to Poitou regularly until 1628.

In 1606 Descartes was sent to the Jesuit college at La Flèche, established in 1604 by Henry IV. In 1614 Descartes went to Poitiers, where he took a law degree in 1616. At this time, Huguenot Poitiers was in virtual revolt against the young King Louis XIII (reigned 1610–43). Descartes's father probably expected him to enter Parlement, but the minimum age for doing so was 27, and Descartes was only 20. In 1618 he went to Breda in the Netherlands, where he spent 15 months as an informal student of mathematics and military architecture in the peacetime army of the Protestant stadtholder, Prince Maurice (ruled 1585–1625).

Descartes spent the period 1619 to 1628 travelling in northern and southern Europe, where, as he later explained, he studied "the book of the world." While in Bohemia in 1619, he invented analytic geometry, a method of solving geometric problems algebraically and algebraic problems geometrically. He also devised a universal method of deductive reasoning, based on mathematics, that is applicable to all the sciences.

In 1622 Descartes moved to Paris. There he gambled, rode, fenced, and went to the court, concerts, and the theatre. He befriended the mathematician Claude Mydorge (1585–1647) and Father Marin Mersenne (1588–1648), a man of universal learning who corresponded with hundreds of scholars, writers, mathematicians, and scientists and who became Descartes's main contact with the larger intellectual world.

In 1628 Descartes left for the Netherlands, which was Protestant, and—taking great precautions to conceal his address—did not return to France for 16 years.

RESIDENCE IN THE NETHERLANDS

Descartes said that he went to the Netherlands to enjoy a greater liberty than was available anywhere else and to avoid the distractions of Paris and friends so that he could have the leisure and solitude to think. (He had inherited enough money and property to live independently.) The Netherlands was a haven of tolerance, where Descartes could be an original, independent thinker without fear of being burned at the stake—as was the Italian philosopher Lucilio Vanini (1585–1619) for proposing natural explanations of miracles—or being drafted into the armies then prosecuting the Catholic Counter-Reformation.

In 1629 Descartes went to the university at Franeker, where he stayed with a Catholic family and wrote the first draft of his *Meditations*. He matriculated at the University of Leiden in 1630.

In 1635 Descartes's daughter Francine was born to Helena Jans and was baptized in the Reformed Church in Deventer. Although Francine is typically referred to by commentators as Descartes's "illegitimate" daughter, her baptism is recorded in a register for legitimate births. Her death of scarlet fever at the age of five was the greatest sorrow of Descartes's life. Referring to her death, Descartes said that he did not believe that one must refrain from tears to prove oneself a man.

MEDITATIONS

In 1641 Descartes published the *Meditations on First Philosophy, in Which Is Proved the Existence of God and the Immortality of the Soul.* Written in Latin and dedicated to the Jesuit professors at the Sorbonne in Paris, the work included critical responses by several eminent thinkers—collected by Mersenne from the Jansenist philosopher and theologian Antoine Arnauld (1612–94), the English philosopher Thomas Hobbes (1588–1679), and the Epicurean atomist Pierre Gassendi (1592–1655)—as well as Descartes's replies.

The *Meditations* is characterized by Descartes's use of methodic doubt, a systematic procedure of rejecting as

A 1630 portrait of noted French philosopher René Descartes. Hulton Archive/ Getty Images

though false all types of belief in which one has ever been, or could ever be, deceived. Thus, Descartes's apparent knowledge based on authority is set aside, because even experts are sometimes wrong. His beliefs from sensory experience are declared untrustworthy, because such experience is sometimes misleading, as when a square tower appears round from a distance. Even his beliefs about the objects in his immediate vicinity may be mistaken, because, as he notes, he often has dreams about objects that do not exist, and he has no way of knowing with certainty whether he is dreaming or awake. Finally, his apparent knowledge of simple and general truths of reasoning that do not depend on sense experience—such as "$2 + 3 = 5$" or "a square has four sides"—is also unreliable, because God could have made him in such a way that, for example, he goes wrong every time he counts. As a way of summarizing the universal doubt into which he has fallen, Descartes supposes that an "evil genius of the utmost power and cunning has employed all his energies in order to deceive me."

Although at this stage there is seemingly no belief about which he cannot entertain doubt, Descartes finds certainty in the intuition that, when he is thinking—even if he is being deceived—he must exist. In the *Discourse*, Descartes expresses this intuition in the dictum "I think, therefore I am"; but because "therefore" suggests that the intuition is an argument—though it is not—in the *Meditations* he says merely, "I think, I am" ("Cogito, sum"). The cogito is a logically self-evident truth that also gives intuitively certain knowledge of a particular thing's existence—that is, one's self. Nevertheless, it justifies accepting as certain only the existence of the person who thinks it. If all one ever knew for certain was that one exists, and if one adhered to Descartes's method of doubting all that is uncertain, then one would be reduced to solipsism, the view that nothing exists but one's self and thoughts. To escape solipsism, Descartes argues that all ideas that are as "clear and distinct" as the cogito must be true, for, if they were not, the cogito also, as a member of the class of clear and distinct ideas, could be doubted. Since "I think, I am" cannot be doubted, all clear and distinct ideas must be true.

On the basis of clear and distinct innate ideas, Descartes then establishes that each mind is a mental substance and each body a part of one material substance. The mind or soul is immortal, because it is unextended and cannot be broken into parts, as can extended bodies. Descartes also advances a proof for the existence of God. He begins with the proposition that he has an innate idea of God as a perfect being and then concludes that God necessarily exists, because, if he did not, he would not be perfect. This ontological argument for God's existence, originally due to the English logician St. Anselm of Canterbury (1033/34–1109), is at the heart of Descartes's rationalism, for it establishes certain knowledge about an existing thing solely on the basis of reasoning from innate ideas, with no help from sensory experience. Descartes then argues that, because God is perfect, he does not deceive human beings; and therefore, because God leads us to believe that the material world exists, it does exist. In this way Descartes claims to establish metaphysical foundations for the existence of his own mind, of God, and of the material world.

The inherent circularity of Descartes's reasoning was exposed by Arnauld, whose objection has come to be known as the Cartesian Circle. According to Descartes, God's existence is established by the fact that Descartes has a clear and distinct idea of God; but the truth of Descartes's clear and distinct ideas are guaranteed by the fact that God exists and is not a deceiver. Thus, in order to show that God exists, Descartes must assume that God exists.

FINAL YEARS

In 1644, 1647, and 1648, after 16 years in the Netherlands, Descartes returned to France for brief visits on financial business and to oversee the translation into French of the *Principles of Philosophy* (1644), a compilation of his physics and metaphysics, the *Meditations*, and the *Objections and Replies*. During Descartes's final stay in Paris in 1648, the French nobility revolted against the crown in a series of wars known as the Fronde. Descartes left precipitously on Aug. 17, 1648, only days before the death of his old friend Mersenne.

Hector Pierre Chanut, the brother-in-law of Claude Clerselier (one of Descartes' translators), engineered an invitation for Descartes to the court of Queen Christina, who by the close of the Thirty Years' War (1618–48) had become one of the most important and powerful monarchs in Europe. Descartes went reluctantly, arriving early in October 1649.

In Sweden—where, Descartes said, in winter men's thoughts freeze like the water—the 22-year-old Christina perversely made the 53-year-old Descartes rise before 5:00 AM to give her philosophy lessons, even though she knew of his habit of lying in bed until 11 o'clock in the morning. While delivering these statutes to the queen in the morning hours on Feb. 1, 1650, he caught a chill and soon developed pneumonia. He died in Stockholm on February 11.

JOHN LOCKE

(b. Aug. 29, 1632, Wrington, Somerset, Eng.—d. Oct. 28, 1704, High Laver, Essex)

John Locke was an English philosopher who laid the foundation of modern philosophical empiricism and political liberalism. He was an inspirer of both the

European Enlightenment and the Constitution of the United States. Much of what he advocated in the realm of politics was accepted in England after the Glorious Revolution of 1688–89 and in the United States after the country's declaration of independence in 1776.

Locke's family was sympathetic to Puritanism but remained within the Church of England, a situation that coloured his later life and thinking. Raised in Pensford, near Bristol, Locke was 10 years old at the start of the English Civil Wars between the monarchy of Charles I and parliamentary forces under the eventual leadership of Oliver Cromwell.

After the first Civil War ended in 1646, Locke's father was able to obtain for his son, who had evidently shown academic ability, a place at Westminster School in distant London. It was to this already famous institution that Locke went in 1647, at age 14. The curriculum of Westminster centred on Latin, Greek, Hebrew, Arabic, mathematics, and geography. In 1650 Locke was elected a King's Scholar, an academic honour and financial benefit that enabled him to buy several books, primarily classic texts in Greek and Latin. Although Locke was evidently a good student, he did not enjoy his schooling; in later life he attacked boarding schools for their overemphasis on corporal punishment and for the uncivil behaviour of pupils.

OXFORD

In the autumn of 1652 Locke, at the comparatively late age of 20, entered Christ Church, the largest of the colleges of the University of Oxford and the seat of the court of Charles I during the Civil Wars.

He later reported that he found the undergraduate curriculum at Oxford dull and unstimulating. It was still largely that of the medieval university, focusing on Aristotle (especially his logic) and largely ignoring important new ideas about the nature and origins of knowledge that had been developed in writings by Francis Bacon (1561–1626), René Descartes (1596–1650), and other natural philosophers. Although their works were not on the official syllabus, Locke was soon reading them. He graduated with a bachelor's degree in 1656 and a master's two years later, about which time he was elected a student (the equivalent of fellow) of Christ Church.

The restoration of the English monarchy in 1660 was a mixed blessing for Locke. It led many of his scientific collaborators to return to London, where they soon founded the Royal Society, which provided the stimulus for much scientific research. But in Oxford the new freedom from Puritan control encouraged unruly behaviour and religious enthusiasms among the undergraduates. These excesses led Locke to be wary of rapid social change, an attitude that no doubt partly reflected his own childhood during the Civil Wars.

In 1666 Locke was introduced to Lord Anthony Ashley Cooper by a mutual acquaintance. As a member and eventually the leader of a group of opposition politicians known as the Whigs, Ashley was one of the most powerful figures in England in the first two decades after the Restoration. Ashley was so impressed with Locke at their first meeting that in the following year he asked him to join his London household in Exeter House in the Strand as his aide and personal physician, though Locke did not then have a degree in medicine.

By 1668 Locke had become a fellow of the Royal Society and was conducting medical research with his friend Thomas Sydenham, the most distinguished physician of the period. Although Locke was undoubtedly the junior partner in their collaboration, they worked together to produce important research based on careful observation and a minimum of speculation. The method that Locke acquired and helped to develop in this work reinforced his commitment to philosophical empiricism.

Throughout his time in Exeter House, Locke kept in close contact with his friends. Indeed, the long gestation of his most important philosophical work, *An Essay Concerning Human Understanding* (1689), began at a meeting with friends in his rooms, probably in February 1671.

In 1672 Ashley was raised to the peerage as the first earl of Shaftesbury, and at the end of that year he was appointed lord chancellor of England. He was soon dismissed, however, having lost favour with Charles II. For a time Shaftesbury and Locke were in real danger, and it was partly for this reason that Locke travelled to France in 1675.

EXILE IN FRANCE

Locke remained in France for nearly four years (1675–79), spending much time in Paris and Montpelier; the latter possessed a large Protestant minority and the most important medical school in Europe, both of which were strong attractions for Locke. He made many friends in the Protestant community, including some leading intellectuals.

Back in England, Shaftesbury had been imprisoned for a year in the Tower of London but was released in February 1678. By the time Locke returned to England in 1679, Shaftesbury had been restored to favour as lord president of the Privy Council. The country, however, was torn by dissension over the exclusion controversy—the debate over whether a law could be passed to forbid (exclude) the succession of Charles II's brother James, a Roman Catholic, to the English throne. Shaftesbury and Locke strongly supported exclusion. The controversy reached its apex in the hysteria of the so-called Popish Plot, a supposed Catholic conspiracy to assassinate Charles and replace him with James.

Two Treatises of Government

When Shaftesbury failed to reconcile the interests of the king and Parliament, he was dismissed; in 1681 he was arrested, tried, and finally acquitted of treason by a London jury. A year later he fled to Holland, where in 1683 he died. None of Shaftesbury's known friends were now safe in England. Locke himself, who was being closely watched, crossed to Holland in September 1683.

Out of this context emerged Locke's major work in political philosophy, *Two Treatises of Government* (1690). In the preface to the work, composed at a later date, Locke makes clear that the arguments of the two treatises are continuous and that the whole constitutes a justification of the Glorious Revolution, which brought the Protestant William III and Mary II to the throne following the flight of James II to France.

The first treatise was aimed squarely at the work of another 17th-century political theorist, Sir Robert Filmer, whose *Patriarcha* (1680, though probably written in the 1630s) defended the theory of divine right of kings: the authority of every king is divinely sanctioned by his descent from Adam—according to the Bible, the first king and the father of humanity. Locke claims that Filmer's doctrine defies "common sense." His refutation was widely accepted as decisive, and in any event the theory of the divine right of kings ceased to be taken seriously in England after 1688.

Locke's importance as a political philosopher lies in the argument of the second treatise.

Locke defined political power as a "right" of making laws and enforcing them for "the public good." Power for

Locke never simply means "capacity" but always "morally sanctioned capacity." Morality pervades the whole arrangement of society, and it is this fact, tautologically, that makes society legitimate.

Locke's account of political society is based on a hypothetical consideration of the human condition before the beginning of communal life. In this "state of nature," humans are entirely free. But this freedom is not a state of complete license, because it is set within the bounds of the law of nature. It is a state of equality, which is itself a central element of Locke's account. Each person is naturally free and equal under the law of nature, subject only to the will of "the infinitely wise Maker." Each person, moreover, is required to enforce as well as to obey this law. It is this duty that gives to humans the right to punish offenders. But in such a state of nature, it is obvious that placing the right to punish in each person's hands may lead to injustice and violence. This can be remedied if humans enter into a contract with each other to recognize by common consent a civil government with the power to enforce the law of nature among the citizens of that state. Although any contract is legitimate as long as it does not infringe upon the law of nature, it often happens that a contract can be enforced only if there is some higher human authority to require compliance with it. It is a primary function of society to set up the framework in which legitimate contracts, freely entered into, may be enforced, a state of affairs much more difficult to guarantee in the state of nature and outside civil society.

Before discussing the creation of political society in greater detail, Locke provides a lengthy account of his notion of property, which is of central importance to his political theory. Each person, according to Locke, has property in his own person—that is, each person literally owns his own body. Other people may not use a person's body for any purpose without his permission. But one can acquire property beyond one's own body through labour. By mixing one's labour with objects in the world, one acquires a right to the fruits of that work.

ORGANIZATION OF GOVERNMENT

Locke returns to political society in Chapter VIII of the second treatise. In the community created by the social contract, the will of the majority should prevail, subject to the law of nature. The legislative body is central, but it cannot create laws that violate the law of nature, because the enforcement of the natural law regarding life, liberty, and property is the rationale of the whole system. Laws must apply equitably to all citizens and not favour particular sectional interests, and there should be a division of legislative, executive, and judicial powers.

The significance of Locke's vision of political society can scarcely be exaggerated. His integration of individualism within the framework of the law of nature and his account of the origins and limits of legitimate government authority inspired the U.S. Declaration of Independence (1776) and the broad outlines of the system of government adopted in the U.S. Constitution. In France too, Lockean principles found clear

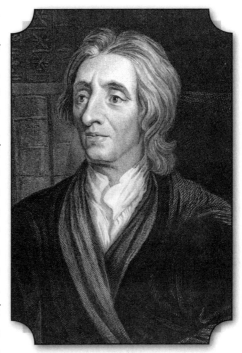

Engraving of John Locke. Hulton Archive/Getty Images

expression in the Declaration of the Rights of Man and of the Citizen and other justifications of the French Revolution of 1789.

AN ESSAY CONCERNING HUMAN UNDERSTANDING

Locke remained in Holland for more than five years (1683–89). While there he completed *An Essay Concerning Human Understanding*.

Locke begins the *Essay* by repudiating the view that certain kinds of knowledge—knowledge of the existence of God, of certain moral truths, or of the laws of logic or mathematics—are innate, imprinted on the human mind at its creation. Locke argues to the contrary that an idea cannot be said to be "in the mind" until one is conscious of it. But human infants have no conception of God or of moral, logical, or mathematical truths, and to suppose that they do, despite obvious evidence to the contrary, is merely an unwarranted assumption to save a position.

In Book II he turns to a positive account. He begins by claiming that the sources of all knowledge are, first, sense experience (the red colour of a rose, the ringing sound of a bell, the taste of salt, and so on) and, second, "reflection" (one's awareness that one is thinking, that one is happy or sad, that one is having a certain sensation, and so on). These are not themselves, however, instances of knowledge in the strict sense, but they provide the mind with the materials of knowledge. Locke calls the materials so provided "ideas." Ideas are objects "before the mind," not in the sense that they are physical objects but in the sense that they represent physical objects to consciousness.

All ideas are either simple or complex. All simple ideas are derived from sense experience, and all complex ideas are derived from the combination ("compounding") of simple and complex ideas by the mind. Whereas complex ideas can be analyzed, or broken down, into the simple or complex ideas of which they are composed, simple ideas cannot be. The complex idea of a snowball, for example, can be analyzed into the simple ideas of whiteness, roundness, and solidity (among possibly others), but none of the latter ideas can be analyzed into anything simpler. In Locke's view, therefore, a major function of philosophical inquiry is the analysis of the meanings of terms through the identification of the ideas that give rise to them. The project of analyzing supposedly complex ideas (or concepts) subsequently became an important theme in philosophy, especially within the analytic tradition, which began at the turn of the 20th century and became dominant at Cambridge, Oxford, and many other universities, especially in the English-speaking world.

KNOWLEDGE

In Book IV of the *Essay*, Locke reaches the putative heart of his inquiry, the nature and extent of human knowledge. His precise definition of knowledge entails that very few things actually count as such for him. In general, he excludes knowledge claims in which there is no evident connection or exclusion between the ideas of which the claim is composed. Thus, it is possible to know that the three angles of a triangle equal two right angles if one knows the relevant Euclidean proof. But it is not possible to know that the next stone one drops will fall downward or that the next glass of water one drinks will quench one's thirst, even though psychologically one has every expectation, through the association of ideas, that it will. These are cases only of probability, not knowledge—as indeed is virtually the whole of scientific knowledge, excluding mathematics.

There are, however, some very important things that can be known. For example, Locke agreed with Descartes that each person can know immediately and without appeal to any further evidence that he exists at the time that he considers it. It can also be proved from self-evident truths by valid argument (by an argument whose conclusion cannot be false if its premises are true) that a first cause, or God, must exist. Various moral claims also can be demonstrated—e.g., that parents have a duty to care for their children and that one should honour one's contracts.

The *Essay*'s influence was enormous, perhaps as great as that of any other philosophical work apart from those of Plato and Aristotle. Its importance in the English-speaking world of the 18th century can scarcely be overstated. Along with the works of Descartes, it constitutes the foundation of modern Western philosophy.

Last Years

Locke remained in Holland until James II was overthrown in the Glorious Revolution. Indeed, Locke himself in February 1689 crossed the English Channel in the party that accompanied the princess of Orange, who was soon crowned Queen Mary II of England. Upon his return he became actively involved in various political projects, including helping to draft the English Bill of Rights, though the version eventually adopted by Parliament did not go as far as he wanted in matters of religious toleration. He was offered a senior diplomatic post by William but declined. His health was rarely good, and he suffered especially in the smoky atmosphere of London. He was therefore very happy to accept the offer of his close friend Damaris Masham, herself a philosopher and the daughter of Ralph Cudworth, to make his home with her family at Oates in High Laver, Essex. There he spent his last years revising the *Essay* and other works, entertaining friends, including Newton, and responding at length to his critics.

After a lengthy period of poor health, he died while Damaris read him the Bible. He was buried in High Laver church.

BENEDICT DE SPINOZA

(b. Nov. 24, 1632, Amsterdam, Neth.—d. Feb. 21, 1677, The Hague)

Benedict de Spinoza, a Dutch-Jewish philosopher, was one of the foremost exponents of 17th-century Rationalism and one of the early and seminal figures of the Enlightenment.

Spinoza's Portuguese parents were among the many Jews who were forcibly converted to Christianity but continued to practice Judaism in secret. After being arrested, tortured, and condemned by the inquisition in Portugal, they escaped to Amsterdam, where the Jewish community was granted toleration by the Dutch authorities on the condition that it not cause scandal or allow any of its members to become public charges.

There is some evidence that Spinoza began to attract attention as a potential heretic when he was in his early 20s. After he and two other young men began teaching classes in Sabbath school, all three were charged with improprieties, though in Spinoza's case the record of the investigation does not survive. The two other men were accused of raising doubts in their students' minds about the historical accuracy of the Bible and about whether there might be other accounts of human history with an equal or even better claim to the truth.

In 1655 a book titled *Prae-Adamitae* (Latin: "Men Before Adam"), by the French courtier Isaac La Peyrère, appeared in Amsterdam. It challenged the accuracy of the Bible and insisted that the spread of human beings to all parts of the globe implies that there must have been humans before Adam and Eve. La Peyrère concluded that the Bible is the history of the Jews, not the history of humanity. Spinoza owned a copy of the work, and many of La Peyrère's ideas about the Bible later appeared in Spinoza's writings.

La Peyrère's heresies may well have been the starting point of Spinoza's falling out with the synagogue in Amsterdam. In the summer of 1656 he was formally excommunicated. A series of horrendous curses were cast upon him, and members of the synagogue were forbidden to have any relationship with him, to read anything he had written, or to listen to anything he had to say.

There is still much debate about why Spinoza was excommunicated.

Ultimately, however, his excommunication may have had more to do with the presentation rather than the content of his beliefs. As suggested by some strongly worded sections of the *Tractatus Theologico-Politicus* (published anonymously in 1670), Spinoza may have been aggressively obnoxious in his criticism of established religion and insensitive to the suffering that older Marranos in the community had undergone.

RIJNSBURG AND THE HAGUE

In 1661 Spinoza moved from Amsterdam to the coastal town of Rijnsburg. In Rijnsburg Spinoza lived alone in a modest but comfortable cottage, where he worked on his philosophy and supported himself by grinding lenses.

In 1661 Spinoza began writing the *Tractatus de Intellectus Emendatione* (*Treatise on the Emendation of the Intellect*), a presentation of his theory of knowledge, which he left unfinished. In about 1662 he completed his only work in Dutch, *Korte verhandeling van God, de mensch en deszelfs welstand* (*Short Treatise on God, Man and His Well-Being*), a brief survey of his overall philosophy. During this period he was also working on the *Ethics*, as his correspondence shows.

In 1663 Spinoza published *Renati des Cartes Principiorum Philosophiae* (1663; *René Descartes's Principles of Philosophy*), the only one of his works to be published under his own name in his lifetime. An exposition of Descartes's *Principia Philosophiae* (1644; *Principles of Philosophy*), it showed a profound understanding of Descartes's system.

In the mid-1660s Spinoza moved again, to the outskirts of The Hague, where he spent the rest of his life. Recognized as a significant intellectual figure, especially after the publication of the *Tractatus* in 1670, Spinoza found himself in the company of professors, diplomats, and writers of great renown.

TRACTATUS THEOLOGICO-POLITICUS

The publication of the *Tractatus Theologico-Politicus* in 1670 made Spinoza notorious. Although his name did not appear on the work, he was quickly known as its author. The *Tractatus* was one of the few books to be officially banned in the Netherlands during this period, though it could be bought easily. It was soon the topic of heated discussion throughout Europe.

Spinoza denies that the Jewish prophets possessed any knowledge beyond that of ordinary mortals, and he denies that the history of the Jews is any more extraordinary than that of other peoples. He contended that much of the content of the Bible was determined by the peculiarities of Hebrew history from the time of the Exodus onward. The particular rituals it describes were relevant to the circumstances in which the ancient Hebrews found themselves but no longer made sense in a modern age; hence, the ceremonial law of the ancient Hebrews could be disregarded.

Spinoza derides those who reinterpret scripture in order to see a rational message in it—as Moses Maimonides did—as well as those who accept its unreasonableness on faith. Instead, one should dispense with the view that the scriptures are a divine document and simply accept them as a historical one.

This line of thought leads Spinoza to assert that the message of the scriptures is to be found not in any collection of ancient parchments but rather in the spirit that pervades them. He reduces this message to a simple set of propositions that any rational person could determine for himself: that God exists, that God causes everything, and that a person should treat others as he would wish others to treat him.

THE PERIOD OF THE ETHICS

Shortly after publication of the *Tractatus*, Spinoza resumed work on his masterpiece, the *Ethica* (*Ethics*), finishing a five-part version by 1675. The bulk of the *Ethics* is written as a geometric proof in the style of Euclid's *Elements*, though its more direct inspiration was probably Proclus's *Institutio theologica* (*Elements of Theology*), an axiomatic presentation of Neoplatonic metaphysics composed in the 5th century CE.

Spinoza begins by stating a set of definitions of eight terms: *self-caused, finite of its own kind, substance, attribute, mode, God, freedom,* and *eternity*. These definitions are followed by a series of axioms, one of which supposedly guarantees that the results of Spinoza's logical demonstrations will be true about reality. Spinoza quickly establishes that substance must be existent, self-caused, and unlimited. From this he proves that there cannot be two substances with the same attribute, since each would limit the other. This leads to the monumental conclusion of Proposition 11: "God, or substance consisting of infinite attributes, each of which expresses eternal and infinite essence, necessarily exists."

From the definition of God as a substance with infinite attributes and other propositions about substance, it follows that "there can be, or be conceived, no other substance but God" (Proposition 14) and that "whatever is, is in God, and nothing can be or be conceived without God" (Proposition 15). This constitutes the core of Spinoza's pantheism: God is everywhere, and everything that exists is a modification of God. God is known by human beings through only two of his attributes—thought and extension (the quality of having spatial dimensions)—though the number of God's attributes is infinite.

For Spinoza, there is no problem, as there is for Descartes, of explaining the interaction between mind and body. The two are not distinct entities causally interacting with each other but merely different aspects of the same events. Individual physical or mental entities are "modes" of substance: physical entities are modes of substance understood in terms of the attribute of extension; mental entities are modes of substance understood in terms of the attribute of thought. Because God is the only substance, all physical and mental entities are modes of God.

The highest form of knowledge consists of an intellectual intuition of things in their existence as modes and attributes of eternal substance, or God; this is what it means to see the world from the aspect of eternity. This kind of knowledge leads to a deeper understanding of God, who is all things, and ultimately to an intellectual love of God (*amor Dei intellectualis*), a form of blessedness amounting to a kind of rational-mystical experience.

By 1676 Spinoza was in an advanced stage of consumption that was aggravated by the inhaling of glass dust from grinding lenses. He died in 1677, leaving no heir, and his few possessions were sold at auction.

GOTTFRIED WILHELM LEIBNIZ

(b. July 1 [June 21, old style], 1646, Leipzig, Ger.—d. Nov. 14, 1716, Hannover, Hanover)

Gottfried Wilhelm Leibniz was a German philosopher, mathematician, and political adviser who made important contributions to metaphysics and logic and who independently invented the differential and integral calculus.

Leibniz was born into a pious Lutheran family near the end of the Thirty Years' War, which had laid Germany in ruins. As a child, he was educated in the Nicolai School but was largely self-taught in the library of his father, who had died in 1652. At Easter time in 1661, he entered the University of Leipzig as a law student.

After completing his legal studies in 1666, Leibniz applied for the degree of doctor of law. He was refused because of his age and consequently left his native city forever. At Altdorf—the university town of the free city of Nürnberg—his dissertation *De Casibus Perplexis* ("On Perplexing Cases") procured him the doctor's degree at once, as well as the immediate offer of a professor's chair, which, however, he declined. During his stay in Nürnberg, he was introduced into the court of the prince elector, the archbishop of Mainz, Johann Philipp von Schönborn, where he became concerned with questions of law and politics.

In 1672 the elector sent the young jurist on a mission to Paris, where he arrived at the end of March. In search of financial support, he constructed a calculating machine and presented it to the Royal Society during his first journey to London, in 1673.

Late in 1675 Leibniz laid the foundations of both integral and differential calculus. With this discovery, he ceased to consider time and space as substances—another step closer to monadology. He began to develop the notion that the concepts of extension and motion contained an element of the imaginary, so that the basic laws of motion could not be discovered merely from a study of their nature. Nevertheless, he continued to hold that extension and motion could provide a means for explaining and predicting the course of phenomena. If visible movement depends on the imaginary element found in the concept of extension, it can no longer be defined by simple local movement; it must be the result of a force. In criticizing the Cartesian formulation of the laws of motion, known as mechanics, Leibniz became, in 1676, the founder of a new formulation, known as dynamics, which substituted kinetic energy for the conservation of movement.

By October 1676, Leibniz had accepted a position in the employment of John Frederick, the duke of Hanover. He appointed Leibniz librarian, but, beginning in February 1677, Leibniz solicited the post of councillor, which he was finally granted in 1678.

Trying to make himself useful in all ways, Leibniz proposed that education be made more practical, that academies be founded; he worked on hydraulic presses, windmills, lamps, submarines, clocks, and a wide variety of mechanical devices; he devised a means of perfecting carriages and experimented with phosphorus. These many occupations did not stop his work in mathematics: In March 1679 he perfected the binary system of numeration (i.e., using two as a base), and at the end of the same year he proposed the basis for analysis situs, now known as general topology, a branch of mathematics that deals with selected properties of collections of related physical or abstract elements. At this point, Duke John Frederick died on Jan. 7, 1680, and his brother, Ernest Augustus I, succeeded him.

Leibniz noted *Meditationes de Cognitione, Veritate et Ideis* (*Reflections on Knowledge, Truth, and Ideas*) appeared at this time and defined his theory of knowledge: things are not seen in God—as Nicolas Malebranche suggested—but rather there is an analogy, a strict relation, between God's ideas and man's, an identity between God's logic and man's. A further development of Leibniz's views, revealed in a text written in 1686 but long unpublished, was his generalization concerning propositions that in every true affirmative proposition, whether necessary or contingent, the predicate is contained in the notion of the subject. It can be said that, at this time, with the exception of the word monad (which did not appear until 1695), his philosophy of monadology was defined.

In 1691 Leibniz was named librarian at Wolfenbüttel and propagated his discoveries by means of articles in scientific journals. In 1695 he explained a portion of his dynamic theory of motion in the *Système nouveau* ("New System"), which treated the relationship of substances and the preestablished harmony between the soul and the body: God does not need to bring about man's action by means of his thoughts, as Malebranche asserted, or to wind some sort of watch in order to reconcile the two; rather, the Supreme Watchmaker has so exactly matched body and soul that they correspond—they give meaning to each other—from the beginning.

Leibniz was named a foreign member by the Academy of Sciences of Paris in 1700 and was in correspondence with most of the important European scholars of the day. If he was publishing little at this point, it was because he was writing *Théodicée* (1710), in which he set down his ideas on divine justice.

Leibniz returned to Vienna in 1700 and stayed there until September 1714. During this time the Emperor promoted him to the post of *Reichhofrat* ("adviser to the empire") and gave him the title of *Freiherr* ("baron"). About this time he wrote the *Principes de la nature et de la Grâce fondés en raison*, which inaugurated a kind of preestablished harmony between these two orders. Further, in 1714 he wrote the *Monadologia*, which synthesized the philosophy of the *Théodicée*. From June 1716 he suffered greatly from gout and was confined to his bed until his death.

GIAMBATTISTA VICO

(b. June 23, 1668, Naples [Italy] — d. Jan. 23, 1744, Naples)

G iambattista Vico was an Italian philosopher of cultural history and law who is recognized today as a forerunner of cultural anthropology, or ethnology.

Vico was the son of a poor bookseller. He attended various schools, including a Jesuit college, for short periods but was largely self-taught. Despite his life of poverty, he was able to escape occasionally to the countryside; these excursions opened immense horizons beyond his limited early environment. In fact, personal experience, rather than reading, was the primary source of Vico's unique genius, although his reading was extensive, varied, and always distinguished by a personal interpretation.

In December 1699 Vico married a childhood friend, Teresa Destito, who was well intentioned but almost illiterate and incapable of understanding him. In the same year he obtained a chair of rhetoric at the University of Naples. One of the duties of the professor of rhetoric was to open the academic year with a Latin oration, and Vico carried out this responsibility by giving the introductory lectures between 1699 and 1708. The last one, printed in 1709 under the title *De Nostri Temporis Studiorum Ratione* ("On the Method of the Studies of Our Time"), is rich with his reflections about pedagogical methods. This work was followed almost immediately by the publication of Vico's great metaphysical essay *De Antiquissima Italorum Sapientia* ("On the Ancient Wisdom of the Italians"), which was a refutation of the Rationalistic system of Descartes.

The outline of the work that he planned to call *Scienza nuova* first appeared in 1720–21 in a two-volume legal treatise on the "Universal Law." The ideas outlined here were to be fully developed in a version that the powerful cardinal Corsini, the future pope Clement XII, agreed to sponsor. According to contemporary practice, this meant that he would assume the costs of publication. At the last moment the Cardinal withdrew, pleading financial difficulties. It is probable, however, that the Cardinal was alarmed by certain of Vico's propositions, which were bold for that period, such as the notion that human society went through a "bestial" stage and that it is possible for society to revert to this primitive barbarism in which men possess only an obscure form of reason.

According to his autobiography, since he lacked money to publish the full text of his work, Vico sold the only jewel he possessed—a family ring—and reduced his book by two-thirds. It appeared in 1725 under the title *Scienza nuova* but was unsuccessful. Vico complained bitterly of the virtually universal indifference that his masterpiece evoked. He quickly regained his confidence, however, and returned to his work with energy. His mind was crowded with ideas, but ordering and systematizing them was a trying task for him. He thought as a poet, not as a dialectician. Nevertheless, he began a total revision and restructuring of his work.

Vico's effort to restructure his masterpiece was completed as the second edition of the *Scienza nuova*. It was actually the fourth edition, if the outline contained in the legal treatise and the "fragments" written between 1729 and 1732 are taken into account. The definitive edition that appeared posthumously in 1744, however, was marked *terza impressione* ("third edition") and was conceived according to a very different and greatly revised plan.

Vico's contemporaries portray him, in his old age, awakening intermittently from his exhaustion to dash off prophetic lines or to comment on a text from some classical author for the few pupils remaining to him. He found satisfaction in the fact that his eldest son, Gennaro, succeeded him in his chair at the university. Surrounded by the three survivors of his once numerous family (Ignazio had died shortly after his release from prison), Vico died. Since the stairway of his house was too narrow to permit passage of his coffin, it had to be lowered through a window, and then it was unceremoniously borne to the church of the Oratorian priests, where his remains are still kept.

VICO'S VISION

Vico described human societies as passing through stages of growth and decay. The first is a "bestial" condition, from which emerges "the age of the gods," in which man is ruled by fear of the supernatural. "The age of heroes" is the consequence of alliances formed by family leaders to protect against internal dissent and external attack; in this stage, society is rigidly divided into patricians and plebeians. "The age of men" follows, as the result of class conflict in which the plebeians achieve equal rights, but this stage encounters the problems of corruption, dissolution, and a possible reversion to primitive barbarism. Vico affirmed that Providence must right the course of history so that humanity is not engulfed in successive cataclysms.

According to Vico, the origin of unequal social classes, which often retain the rigidity of primitive castes, must be attributed to imperfect forms of religion, not to technological progress. All of Vico's anthropology is based on the affirmation of the absolute primacy of religion, which was no doubt suggested to him by the thought of Giovanni Pico della Mirandola, an Italian Renaissance philosopher.

A second basic notion of Vico is that man has a mixed nature: he remains closer to the beast than to the angel. For Vico the second stage of barbarism, which closes the age of men, arises from an excess of reflection or from the predominance of technology. This stage heralds an imminent new beginning of history. The fundamental perversity of the second stage of barbarism makes it, in fact, more dangerous than the first, which in its excess of strength contains noble impulses that need only to be brought under control. Man becomes a coward, an unbeliever, and an informer, hiding his evil intentions behind "flattery and hypocritical wheedling." This dissolution from the age of men to the bestial state exposes humanity to a fate far worse than arrests or regressions of civilizations. Vico hoped to serve warning to men of the evils that could overtake them if they became worshippers of a materialist ideology or the servants of a science uninformed by conscience.

GEORGE BERKELEY

(b. March 12, 1685, near Dysert Castle, near Thomastown?, County Kilkenny, Ire.—d. Jan. 14, 1753, Oxford, Eng.)

George Berkeley was an Anglo-Irish Anglican bishop, philosopher, and scientist. He is best known for his Empiricist philosophy, which holds that everything save the spiritual exists only insofar as it is perceived by the senses.

Berkeley was the eldest son of William Berkeley, described as a "gentleman" in George's matriculation entry, and as a commissioned officer, a cornet of dragoons, in the entry of a younger brother. Brought up at Dysert Castle, Berkeley entered Kilkenny College in 1696 and Trinity College, Dublin, in 1700, where he was graduated with a B.A. degree in 1704. While awaiting a fellowship vacancy, he made a critical study of time, vision, and the hypothesis that there is no material substance.

Elected fellow of Trinity College in 1707, Berkeley began to "examine and revise" his "first arguings" in his revision notebooks. The revision was drastic and its results revolutionary. His old principle was largely superseded by his new principle; i.e., his original line of argument for immaterialism, based on the subjectivity of colour, taste, and the other sensible qualities, was replaced by a simple, profound analysis of the meaning of "to be" or "to exist." "To be," said of the object, means to be perceived; "to be," said of the subject, means to perceive.

Berkeley called attention to the whole situation that exists when a person perceives something, or imagines it. He argued that, when a person imagines trees or books "and no body by to perceive them," he is failing to appreciate the whole situation: he is "omitting" the perceiver, for imagined trees or books are necessarily imagined as per-ceivable. The situation for him is a two-term relation of perceiver and perceived; there is no third term; there is no "idea of" the object, coming between perceiver and perceived.

For Berkeley, heat and colour (which philosophers had classed as secondary qualities because of their supposed subjectivity) are "as much without the mind" as figure and motion (classed as primary qualities) or as time; for both primary and secondary qualities are *so* in the mind as to be in the thing, and are *so* in the thing as to be in the mind. Colour and extension are not mental qualities for Berkeley: colour can be seen, and extension can be touched; they are "sensible ideas," or sense-data, the direct objects of percipient mind.

Berkeley accepted possible perception as well as actual perception; i.e., he accepted the existence of what a person is not actually perceiving but might perceive if he took the appropriate steps. In his notebook he wrote, "Existence is *percipi* or *percipere*. The horse is in the stable, the Books are in the study as before." Horse and books, when not being actually perceived by man, are still there, still perceivable "still with relation to perception." To a nonphilosophical friend Berkeley wrote, "I question not the existence of anything that we perceive by our senses."

PERIOD OF HIS MAJOR WORKS

Berkeley's golden period of authorship followed the revision. In *An Essay Towards a New Theory of Vision* (1709), he examined visual distance, magnitude, position, and problems of sight and touch, and concluded that "the proper (or real) objects of sight" are not without the mind, though "the contrary be supposed true of tangible objects." In his *Treatise Concerning the Principles of Human Knowledge, Part I* (1710), he brought all objects of sense, including tangibles, within the mind. He rejected material substance, material causes, and abstract general ideas, affirmed spiritual substance, and answered many objections to his theory and drew the consequences, theological and epistemological. His *Three Dialogues between Hylas and Philonous* (1713), by its attractive literary form and its avoidance of technicalities, reinforced the main argument of the *Principles*; the two books speak with one voice about immaterialism.

Berkeley was made a deacon in 1709 and ordained a priest in 1710. He held his fellowship for 17 years, acting as librarian (1709), junior dean (1710–11), and tutor and lecturer in divinity, Greek, and Hebrew.

By 1722 Berkeley had resolved to build a college in Bermuda for the education of young Americans (Indians), publishing the plan in *A Proposal for the better Supplying of Churches* . . . (1724). The scheme caught the public imagination. The King granted a charter, the Archbishop of Canterbury acted as trustee, subscriptions poured in, and Parliament passed a contingent grant of £20,000. But there was opposition. An alternative charity for Georgia was mooted, and the prime minister, Sir Robert Walpole, hesitated.

In 1728 Berkeley married Anne, daughter of Chief Justice Forster, a talented and well-educated woman, who defended her husband's philosophy after his death. Soon after the wedding, they sailed for America, settling at Newport, R.I., where Berkeley bought land, built a house (Whitehall), and waited. Berkeley preached often in Newport and its neighbourhood, and a philosophical study group met at Whitehall. Eventually, word came that the grant would not be paid, and Berkeley returned to London in October 1731.

YEARS AS BISHOP OF CLOYNE

Berkeley was consecrated as bishop of Cloyne in Dublin in 1734. His episcopate, as such, was uneventful. He took a seat in the Irish House of Lords in 1737 and, while in Dublin, published *A Discourse Addressed to Magistrates and Men in Authority* (1738), condemning the Blasters whose Hell-Fire Club, now in ruins, still can be seen near Dublin.

In 1745 Berkeley addressed open letters to his clergy and to the Roman Catholics of his diocese about the Stuart uprising. In letters to the press over his own name or through a friend, he expressed himself on several public questions, political, social, and scientific. Two major works stand out, *The Querist* and *Siris*. *The Querist*, published in three parts from 1735 to 1737, deals with basic economics. *Siris* (1744) is at once a treatise on the medicinal virtues of tar-water, its making and dosage, and a philosopher's vision of a chain of being, "a gradual evolution or ascent" from the world of sense to "the mind, her acts and faculties" and, thence, to the supernatural and God, the three in one.

In August 1752, Berkeley commissioned his brother, Dr. Robert Berkeley, as vicar-general and arranged with the bishop of Cork as to his episcopal duties and, with his wife and his children George and Julia, went to Oxford and took a house in Holywell Street, where he resided until his death. He was buried in Christ Church Chapel.

CHARLES-LOUIS DE SECONDAT, BARON DE LA BRÈDE ET DE MONTESQUIEU

(b. Jan. 18, 1689, Château La Brède, near Bordeaux, France — d. Feb. 10, 1755, Paris)

Montesquieu was a French political philosopher whose major work, *The Spirit of Laws*, was a major contribution to political theory.

His father, Jacques de Secondat, belonged to an old military family of modest wealth that had been ennobled in the 16th century for services to the crown, while his mother, Marie-Françoise de Pesnel, was a pious lady of partial English extraction. When she died in 1696, the barony of La Brède passed to Charles-Louis, who was her eldest child, then aged seven. Educated first at home and then in the village, he was sent away to school in 1700.

Charles-Louis left Juilly in 1705, continued his studies at the faculty of law at the University of Bordeaux, was graduated, and became an advocate in 1708; soon after he appears to have moved to Paris in order to obtain practical experience in law. He was called back to Bordeaux by the death of his father in 1713. Two years later he married Jeanne de Lartigue, a wealthy Protestant, who brought him a respectable dowry of 100,000 livres and in due course presented him with two daughters and a son, Jean-Baptiste.

In 1721 he surprised all but a few close friends by publishing his *Lettres persanes* (*Persian Letters*, 1722), in which he gave a brilliant satirical portrait of French and particularly Parisian civilization, supposedly seen through the eyes of two Persian travellers. This exceedingly successful work mocks the reign of Louis XIV, which had only recently ended; pokes fun at all social classes; discusses, in its allegorical story of the Troglodytes, the theories of Thomas Hobbes relating to the state of nature. The work's anonymity was soon penetrated, and Montesquieu became famous.

Montesquieu now sought to reinforce his literary achievement with social success. Going to Paris in 1722, he was assisted in entering court circles by the Duke of Berwick, the exiled Stuart prince whom he had known when Berwick was military governor at Bordeaux.

In October 1727 he was elected to the Académie Française, taking his seat on Jan. 24, 1728. This official recognition of his talent might have caused him to remain in Paris to enjoy it. On the contrary, though older than most noblemen starting on the grand tour, he resolved to complete his education by foreign travel. Leaving his wife at La Brède with full powers over the estate, he set off for Vienna in April 1728, with Lord Waldegrave, nephew of Berwick and lately British ambassador in Paris, as travelling companion. He wrote an account of his travels as interesting as any other of the 18th century.

Montesquieu had a wide circle of acquaintances in England. He was presented at court, and he was received by the Prince of Wales, at whose request he later made an anthology of French songs. He was elected a Fellow of the Royal Society. He attended parliamentary debates and read the political journals of the day. His stay in England was one of the most formative periods of his life.

MAJOR WORKS

During his travels Montesquieu's serious ambitions were strengthened, and he decided to devote himself to literature. He hastened to La Brède and remained there, working for two years. He was occupied with an essay on the English constitution (not published until 1748, when it became part of his major work) and with his *Considérations sur les causes de la grandeur des Romains et de leur décadence* (1734; *Reflections on the Causes of the Grandeur and Declension of the Romans*, 1734).

Montesquieu's literary ambitions were far from exhausted. He had for some time been meditating the project of a major work on law and politics. By 1740 its main lines were established and a great part of it was written. By 1743 the text was virtually complete, and he began the first of two thorough and detailed revisions, which occupied him until December 1746. In November 1748 the work appeared under the title *De l'esprit des loix, ou du rapport que les loix doivent avoir avec la constitution de chaque gouvernement, les moeurs, le climat, la religion, le commerce, etc. (The Spirit of Laws*, 1750). *L'Esprit des loix* is one of the great works in the history of political theory and in the history of jurisprudence. Its author had acquainted himself with all previous schools of thought but identified himself with none. Of the multiplicity of subjects treated by Montesquieu, none remained unadorned. His treatment of three was particularly memorable.

The first of these is his classification of governments, a subject that was de rigueur for a political theorist. Abandoning the classical divisions of his predecessors into monarchy, aristocracy, and democracy, Montesquieu produced his own analysis and assigned to each form of government an animating principle: the republic, based on virtue; the monarchy, based on honour; and despotism, based on fear.

The second of his most noted arguments, the theory of the separation of powers, is treated differently. Dividing political authority into the legislative, executive, and judicial powers, he asserted that, in the state that most effectively promotes liberty, these three powers must be confided to different individuals or bodies, acting independently. In its own century this doctrine was admired and held authoritative, even in England; it inspired the Declaration of the Rights of Man and the Constitution of the United States.

The third of Montesquieu's most celebrated doctrines is that of the political influence of climate. Basing himself on doctrines met in his reading, on the experience of his travels, and on experiments—admittedly somewhat naive—conducted at Bordeaux, he stressed the effect of climate, primarily thinking of heat and cold, on the physical frame of the individual, and, as a consequence, on the intellectual outlook of society.

After the book was published, praise came to Montesquieu from the most varied headquarters. The philosophers of the Enlightenment accepted him as one of their own, as indeed he was. The work was controversial, however, and a variety of denunciatory articles and pamphlets appeared. Montesquieu's enemies were successful, and the work was placed on the *Index Librorum Prohibitorum* in 1751. This, though it dismayed Montesquieu, was but a momentary setback. He had already published his *Défense de L'Esprit des lois* (1750). His fame was now worldwide.

Renown lay lightly on his shoulders. It was to be expected that the editors of the *Encyclopédie* should wish to have his collaboration, and d'Alembert asked him to write on democracy and despotism. Montesquieu declined, saying that he had already had his say on those themes but would like to write on taste. The resultant *Essai sur le goût* (*Essay on Taste*), first drafted about 25 years earlier, was his last work.

DAVID HUME

(b. May 7 [April 26, Old Style], 1711, Edinburgh, Scot.—d. Aug. 25, 1776, Edinburgh)

David Hume was a Scottish philosopher, historian, economist, and essayist. He is known especially for his philosophical empiricism and skepticism.

Hume was the younger son of Joseph Hume, the modestly circumstanced laird, or lord, of Ninewells, a small estate adjoining the village of Chirnside. David's mother, Catherine, a daughter of Sir David Falconer, president of the Scottish court of session, was in Edinburgh when he was born. In his third year his father died. He entered Edinburgh University when he was about 12 years old and left it at 14 or 15, as was then usual.

In 1734, after trying his hand in a merchant's office in Bristol, he came to the turning point of his life and retired to France for three years. Most of this time he spent at La Flèche on the Loire, in the old Anjou, studying and writing *A Treatise of Human Nature*. The *Treatise* was Hume's attempt to formulate a full-fledged philosophical system. It is divided into three books: book I, on understanding, aims at explaining man's process of knowing, describing in order the origin of ideas, the ideas of space and time, causality, and the testimony of the senses; book II, on the "passions" of man, gives an elaborate psychological machinery to explain the affective, or emotional, order in man and assigns a subordinate role to reason in this mechanism; book III, on morals, describes moral goodness in terms of "feelings" of approval or disapproval that a person has when he considers human behaviour in the light of the agreeable or disagreeable consequences either to himself or to others. Although the *Treatise* is Hume's most thorough exposition of his thought, at the end of his life he vehemently repudiated it as juvenile, avowing that only his later writings presented his considered views.

Returning to England in 1737, he set about publishing the *Treatise*. Books I and II were published in two volumes in 1739; book III appeared the following year. The poor reception of this, his first and very ambitious work, depressed him; but his next venture, *Essays, Moral and Political* (1741–42), won some success. Perhaps encouraged by this, he became a candidate for the chair of moral philosophy at Edinburgh in 1744. Objectors alleged heresy and even atheism, pointing to the *Treatise* as evidence. Unsuccessful, Hume left the city, where he had been living since 1740, and began a period of wandering.

MATURE WORKS

By this time two new studies had already appeared, viz., a further *Three Essays, Moral and Political* (1748) and *Philosophical Essays Concerning Human Understanding* (1748). The latter is a rewriting of book I of the *Treatise* (with the addition of his essay "On Miracles," which became notorious for its denial that a miracle can be proved by any amount or kind of evidence); it is better known as *An Enquiry Concerning Human Understanding*, the title Hume gave to it in a revision of 1758. The *Enquiry Concerning the Principles of Morals* (1751) was a rewriting of book III of the *Treatise*. It was in these works that Hume expressed his mature thought.

An *Enquiry Concerning Human Understanding* is an attempt to define the principles of human knowledge. It poses in logical form significant questions about the nature of reasoning in regard to matters of fact and experience, and it answers them by recourse to the principle of association. The basis of his exposition is a twofold classification of objects of awareness. In the first place, all such objects are either "impressions," data of sensation or of internal consciousness, or "ideas," derived from such data by compounding, transposing, augmenting, or diminishing.

Only on this level of mere meanings, Hume asserts, is there room for demonstrative knowledge. Matters of fact, on the other hand, come before the mind merely as they are, revealing no logical relations; their properties and connections must be accepted as they are given. That primroses are yellow, that lead is heavy, and that fire burns things are facts, each shut up in itself, logically barren. Each, so far as reason is concerned, could be different: the contradictory of every matter of fact is conceivable. Therefore, any demonstrative science of fact is impossible.

From this basis Hume develops his doctrine about causality. The idea of causality is alleged to assert a necessary connection among matters of fact. From what impression, then, is it derived? Hume states that no causal relation among the data of the senses can be observed, for, when a person regards any events as causally connected, all that he does and can observe is that they frequently and uniformly go together. In this sort of togetherness it is a fact that the impression or idea of the one event brings with it the idea of the other. A habitual association is set up in the mind; and, as in other forms of habit, so in this one, the working of the association is felt as compulsion. This feeling, Hume concludes, is the only discoverable impressional source of the idea of causality.

Hume does not claim to prove that the propositions, (1) that events themselves are causally related and (2) that they will be related in the future in the same ways as they were in the past, are false. He firmly believed both of these propositions and insisted that everybody else believed them, will continue to believe them, and must continue to believe them in order to survive. They are natural beliefs, inextinguishable propensities of human nature, madness apart. What Hume claims to prove is that natural beliefs are not obtained and cannot be demonstrated either by empirical observation or by reason, whether intuitive or inferential. Reflection shows that there is no evidence for them and shows both that we are bound to believe them and that it is sensible or sane to do so. This is Hume's skepticism: it is an affirmation of that tension, a denial not of belief but of certainty.

In 1769, somewhat tired of public life and of England too, he again established a residence in his beloved Edinburgh, deeply enjoying the company—at once intellectual and convivial—of friends old and new (he never married), as well as revising the text of his writings. He issued five further editions of his *History* between 1762 and 1773 as well as eight editions of his collected writings (omitting the *Treatise*, *History*, and ephemera) under the title *Essays and Treatises* between 1753 and 1772, besides preparing the final edition of this collection, which appeared posthumously (1777), and *Dialogues Concerning Natural Religion*, held back under pressure from friends and not published until 1779. His curiously detached autobiography, *The Life of David Hume, Esquire, Written by Himself* (1777; the title is his own), is dated April 18, 1776. He died in his Edinburgh house after a long illness and was buried on Calton Hill.

JEAN-JACQUES ROUSSEAU

(b. June 28, 1712, Geneva, Switz.—d. July 2, 1778, Ermenonville, France)

Jean-Jacques Rousseau was a Swiss-born philosopher, writer, and political theorist whose treatises and novels inspired the leaders of the French Revolution and the Romantic generation.

Rousseau's mother died in childbirth and he was brought up by his father, who taught him to believe that the city of his birth was a republic as splendid as Sparta or ancient Rome. Rousseau senior had an equally glorious image of his own importance; after marrying above his modest station as a watchmaker, he got into trouble with the civil authorities by brandishing the sword that his upper-class pretentions prompted him to wear, and he had to leave Geneva to avoid imprisonment. Rousseau, the son, then lived for six years as a poor relation in his mother's family, patronized and humiliated, until he, too, at the age of 16, fled from Geneva to live the life of an adventurer and a Roman Catholic convert in the kingdoms of Sardinia and France.

Rousseau reached Paris when he was 30 and was lucky enough to meet another young man from the provinces seeking literary fame in the capital, Denis Diderot. The two soon became immensely successful as the centre of a group of intellectuals—or "Philosophes"—who gathered round the great French *Encyclopédie*, of which Diderot was appointed editor.

At the age of 37 Rousseau had what he called an "illumination" while walking to Vincennes to visit Diderot, who had been imprisoned there because of his irreligious writings. In the *Confessions*, which he wrote late in life, Rousseau says that it came to him then in a "terrible flash" that modern progress had corrupted instead of improved men. He went on to write his first important work, a prize essay for the Academy of Dijon entitled *Discours sur les sciences et les arts* (1750; *A Discourse on the Sciences and the Arts*), in which he argues that the history of man's life on earth has been a history of decay.

This *Discourse* is by no means Rousseau's best piece of writing, but its central theme was to inform almost everything else he wrote. Throughout his life he kept returning to the thought that man is good by nature but has been corrupted by society and civilization. He did not mean to suggest that society and civilization were inherently bad but rather that both had taken a wrong direction and become more harmful as they had become more sophisticated.

Major Works of Political Philosophy

As part of what Rousseau called his "reform," or improvement of his own character, he began to look back at some of the austere principles that he had learned as a child in the Calvinist republic of Geneva. Indeed he decided to return to that city, repudiate his Catholicism, and seek readmission to the Protestant church. He had in the meantime acquired a mistress, an illiterate laundry maid named Thérèse Levasseur. To the surprise of his friends, he took her with him to Geneva, presenting her as a nurse.

Rousseau had by this time completed a second *Discourse* in response to a question set by the Academy of Dijon: "What is the origin of the inequality among men and is it justified by natural law?" In response to this challenge he produced a masterpiece of speculative anthropology. The argument follows on that of his first *Discourse* by developing the proposition that natural man is good and then tracing the successive stages by which man has descended from primitive innocence to corrupt sophistication.

Rousseau begins his *Discours sur l'origine de l'inegalité* (1755; *Discourse on the Origin of Inequality*) by distinguishing two kinds of inequality, natural and artificial, the first arising from differences in strength, intelligence, and so forth, the second from the conventions that govern societies. It is the inequalities of the latter sort that he sets out to explain. He suggests that original man was not a social being but entirely solitary. But in contrast to the English pessimist's view that the life of man in such a condition must have been "poor, nasty, brutish and short," Rousseau

Portrait of Jean-Jacques Rousseau, painted by the artist Latour c. *1760.*
Hulton Archive/Getty Images

claims that original man, while admittedly solitary, was healthy, happy, good, and free. The vices of men, he argues, date from the time when men formed societies.

Rousseau thus exonerates nature and blames society for the emergence of vices. He says that passions that generate vices hardly exist in the state of nature but begin to develop as soon as men form societies.

The introduction of property marked a further step toward inequality since it made it necessary for men to institute law and government in order to protect property. Rousseau laments the "fatal" concept of property in one of his more eloquent passages, describing the "horrors" that have resulted from men's departure from a condition in which the earth belonged to no one.

Civil society, as Rousseau describes it, comes into being to serve two purposes: to provide peace for everyone and to ensure the right to property for anyone lucky enough to have possessions. It is thus of some advantage to everyone, but mostly to the advantage of the rich, since it transforms their de facto ownership into rightful ownership and keeps the poor dispossessed. It is a somewhat fraudulent social contract that introduces government since the poor get so much less out of it than do the rich.

Like Plato, Rousseau always believed that a just society was one in which everyone was in his right place. And having written the *Discourse* to explain how men had lost their liberty in the past, he went on to write another book, *Du Contrat social* (1762; *The Social Contract*), to suggest how they might recover their liberty in the future. Again Geneva was the model; not Geneva as it had become in 1754 when Rousseau returned there to recover his rights as a citizen, but Geneva as it had once been; i.e., Geneva as Calvin had designed it.

The Social Contract begins with the sensational opening sentence: "Man is born free, and everywhere he is in chains," and proceeds to argue that men need not be in chains. If a civil society, or state, could be based on a genuine social contract, as opposed to the fraudulent social contract depicted in the *Discourse on the Origin of Inequality*, men would receive in exchange for their independence a better kind of freedom, namely true political, or republican, liberty. Such liberty is to be found in obedience to a self-imposed law.

By the year 1762, however, when *The Social Contract* was published, Rousseau had given up any thought of settling in Geneva. After recovering his citizen's rights in 1754, he had returned to Paris and the company of his friends around the *Encyclopédie*. But he became increasingly ill at ease in such worldly society and began to quarrel with his fellow Philosophes.

YEARS OF SECLUSION AND EXILE

By the time his *Lettre à d'Alembert sur les spectacles* (1758; *Letter to Monsieur d'Alembert on the Theatre*) appeared in print, Rousseau had already left Paris to pursue a life closer to nature on the country estate of his friend Mme d'Épinay near Montmorency. When the hospitality of Mme d'Épinay proved to entail much the same social round as that of Paris, Rousseau retreated to a nearby cottage, called Montlouis, under the protection of the Maréchal de Luxembourg. But even this highly placed friend could not save him in 1762 when his treatise on education, *Émile*, was published and scandalized the pious Jansenists of the French Parlements even as *The Social Contract* scandalized the Calvinists of Geneva. In Paris, as in Geneva, they ordered the book to be burned and the author arrested; all the Maréchal de Luxembourg could do was to provide a carriage for Rousseau to escape from France. After formally renouncing his Genevan citizenship in 1763,

Rousseau became a fugitive, spending the rest of his life moving from one refuge to another.

Despite the enthusiasm that some of his writings, and especially *The New Eloise*, excited in the reading public, Rousseau felt himself increasingly isolated, tormented, and pursued. After he had been expelled from France, he was chased from canton to canton in Switzerland. It was in England that Rousseau found refuge after he had been banished from the canton of Bern. The Scottish philosopher David Hume took him there and secured the offer of a pension from King George III; but once in England, Rousseau became aware that certain British intellectuals were making fun of him, and he suspected Hume of participating in the mockery. Various symptoms of paranoia began to manifest themselves in Rousseau, and he returned to France incognito. Believing that Thérèse was the only person he could rely on, he finally married her in 1768, when he was 56 years old.

Rousseau does seem to have recovered his peace of mind in his last years, when he was once again afforded refuge on the estates of great French noblemen, first the Prince de Conti and then the Marquis de Girardin, in whose park at Ermenonville he died.

IMMANUEL KANT

(b. April 22, 1724, Königsberg, Prussia [now Kaliningrad, Russia]—d. Feb. 12, 1804, Königsberg)

Immanuel Kant was a German philosopher whose comprehensive and systematic work in the theory of knowledge, ethics, and aesthetics greatly influenced all subsequent philosophy, especially the various schools of Kantianism and Idealism.

Kant lived in the remote province where he was born for his entire life. His father, a saddler, was, according to

Kant, a descendant of a Scottish immigrant, although scholars have found no basis for this claim; his mother, an uneducated German woman, was remarkable for her character and natural intelligence.

Following the death of his father in 1746 he found employment as a family tutor and, during the nine years that he gave to it, worked for three different families. With them he was introduced to the influential society of the city, acquired social grace, and made his farthest travels from his native city—some 60 miles (96 kilometres) away to the town of Arnsdorf. In 1755, aided by the kindness of a friend, he was able to complete his degree at the university and take up the position of *Privatdozent*, or lecturer.

During the 15 years that he spent as a *Privatdozent*, Kant's renown as a teacher and writer steadily increased. Although he twice failed to obtain a professorship at Königsberg, he refused to accept offers that would have taken him elsewhere—including the professorship of poetry at Berlin that would have brought greater prestige. He preferred the peace and quiet of his native city in which to develop and mature his own philosophy.

Finally, in 1770, Kant was appointed to the chair of logic and metaphysics, a position in which he remained active until a few years before his death. In this period— usually called his critical period, because in it he wrote his great *Critiques*—he published an astounding series of original works on a wide variety of topics, in which he elaborated and expounded his philosophy.

In 1781 the *Kritik der reinen Vernunft* (*Critique of Pure Reason*) was published, followed for the next nine years by great and original works that in a short time brought a revolution in philosophical thought and established the new direction in which it was to go in the years to come.

THE *CRITIQUE OF PURE REASON*

The *Critique of Pure Reason* was the result of some 10 years of thinking and meditation. Yet, even so, Kant published the first edition only reluctantly after many postponements; for although convinced of the truth of its doctrine, he was uncertain and doubtful about its exposition. His misgivings proved well-founded, and Kant complained that interpreters and critics of the work were badly misunderstanding it. To correct these wrong interpretations of his thought he wrote the *Prolegomena zu einer jeden künftigen Metaphysik die als Wissenschaft wird auftreten können* (1783) and brought out a second and revised edition of the first "critique" in 1787. Controversy still continues regarding the merits of the two editions: readers with a preference for an Idealistic interpretation usually prefer the first edition, whereas those with a Realistic view adhere to the second. But with regard to difficulty and ease of reading and understanding, it is generally agreed that there is little to choose between them. Anyone on first opening either book finds it overwhelmingly difficult and impenetrably obscure.

The simplest way of describing the contents of the *Critique* is to say that it is a treatise about metaphysics: it seeks to show the impossibility of one sort of metaphysics and to lay the foundations for another.

As Kant saw it, the problem of metaphysics, as indeed of any science, is to explain how, on the one hand, its principles can be necessary and universal (such being a condition for any knowledge that is scientific) and yet, on the other hand, involve also a knowledge of the real and so provide the investigator with the possibility of more knowledge than is analytically contained in what he already knows; i.e., than is implicit in the meaning alone. To meet these two conditions, Kant maintained, knowledge must rest on judgments that are a priori, for it is only as they are separate from the contingencies of experience that they could be necessary and yet also synthetic; i.e., so that the predicate term contains something more than is analytically contained in the subject. Hence, the basic problem, as Kant formulated it, is to determine "How [i.e., under what conditions] are synthetic a priori judgments possible?"

In the "Transcendental Aesthetic," Kant argued that mathematics necessarily deals with space and time and then claimed that these are both a priori forms of human sensibility that condition whatever is apprehended through the senses. In the "Transcendental Analytic," the most crucial as well as the most difficult part of the book, he maintained that physics is a priori and synthetic because in its ordering of experience it uses concepts of a special sort. These concepts—"categories," he called them—are not so much read out of experience as read into it and, hence, are a priori, or pure, as opposed to empirical. They belong, as it were, to the very framework of knowledge.

In the "Transcendental Dialectic" Kant turned to consideration of a priori synthetic judgments in metaphysics. Here, he claimed, the situation is just the reverse from what it was in mathematics and

Engraved portrait of Immanuel Kant. Kean Collection/Hulton Archive/Getty Images

physics. Metaphysics cuts itself off from sense experience in attempting to go beyond it and, for this very reason, fails to attain a single true a priori synthetic judgment.

THE *CRITIQUE OF PRACTICAL REASON*

The *Kritik der praktischen Vernunft* (1788; *Critique of Practical Reason*) is the standard source book for his ethical doctrines. The earlier *Grundlegung zur Metaphysik der Sitten* (1785) is a shorter and, despite its title, more readily comprehensible treatment of the same general topic.

There are many points of similarity between Kant's ethics and his epistemology, or theory of knowledge. He used the same scaffolding for both—a "Doctrine of Elements," including an "Analytic" and a "Dialectic," followed by a "Methodology"; but the second *Critique* is far shorter and much less complicated. Just as the distinction between sense and intelligence was fundamental for the former, so is that between the inclinations and moral reason for the latter.

In the "Dialectic," Kant took up again the ideas of God, freedom, and immortality. Dismissed in the first *Critique* as objects that men can never know because they transcend human sense experience, he now argued that they are essential postulates for the moral life. Though not reachable in metaphysics, they are absolutely essential for moral philosophy.

Kant is often described as an ethical Rationalist, and the description is not wholly inappropriate. He never espoused, however, the radical Rationalism of some of his contemporaries nor of more recent philosophers for whom reason is held to have direct insight into a world of values or the power to intuit the rightness of this or that moral principle. Thus, practical, like theoretical, reason was for him formal rather than material—a framework of formative principles rather than a content of actual rules. This is why he put such stress on his first formulation of the categorical imperative: "Act only on that maxim through which you can at the same time will that it should become a universal law." Lacking any insight into the moral realm, men can only ask themselves whether what they are proposing to do has the formal character of law—the character, namely, of being the same for all persons similarly circumstanced.

THE *CRITIQUE OF JUDGMENT*

The *Kritik der Urteilskraft* (1790: Critique of Judgment)— one of the most original and instructive of all of Kant's writings—was not foreseen in his original conception of the critical philosophy. Thus it is perhaps best regarded as a series of appendixes to the other two *Critiques*. The work falls into two main parts, called respectively "Critique of Aesthetic Judgment" and "Critique of Teleological Judgment." In the first of these, after an introduction in which he discussed "logical purposiveness," Kant analyzed the notion of "aesthetic purposiveness" in judgments that ascribe beauty to something. Such a judgment, according to him, unlike a mere expression of taste, lays claim to general validity; yet it cannot be said to be cognitive because it rests on feeling, not on argument. The explanation lies in the fact that, when a person contemplates an object and finds it beautiful, there is a certain harmony between his imagination and his understanding, of which he is aware from the immediate delight that he takes in the object. Imagination grasps the object and yet is not restricted to any definite concept; whereas a person imputes the delight that he feels to others because it springs from the free play of his cognitive faculties, which are the same in all men.

In the second part, Kant turned to consider teleology in nature as it is posed by the existence in organic bodies of things of which the parts are reciprocally means and ends to each other. In dealing with these bodies, one cannot be content with merely mechanical principles. Yet if mechanism is abandoned and the notion of a purpose or end of nature is taken literally, this seems to imply that the things to which it applies must be the work of some supernatural designer; but this would mean a passing from the sensible to the suprasensible, a step proved in the first *Critique* to be impossible. Kant answered this objection by admitting that teleological language cannot be avoided in taking account of natural phenomena; but it must be understood as meaning only that organisms must be thought of "as if" they were the product of design, and that is by no means the same as saying that they are deliberately produced.

LAST YEARS

After a gradual decline that was painful to his friends as well as to himself, Kant died in Königsberg, Feb. 12, 1804. His last words were "Es ist gut" ("It is good"). His tomb in the cathedral was inscribed with the words (in German) "The starry heavens above me and the moral law within me," the two things that he declared in the conclusion of the second *Critique* "fill the mind with ever new and increasing admiration and awe, the oftener and the more steadily we reflect on."

MOSES MENDELSSOHN

(b. Sept. 26, 1729, Dessau, Anhalt [Germany] — d. Jan. 4, 1786, Berlin, Prussia)

Moses Mendelssohn was a German-Jewish philosopher, critic, and Bible translator and commentator. He greatly contributed to the efforts of Jews to assimilate to the German bourgeoisie.

The son of an impoverished scribe called Menachem Mendel Dessau, he was known in Jewry as Moses Dessau but wrote as Mendelssohn, from the Hebrew *ben Mendel* ("the Son of Mendel"). His own choice of the German Mendelssohn over the Hebrew equivalent reflected the same acculturation to German life that he sought for other Jews. In 1743 he moved to Berlin, where he studied the thought of the English philosopher John Locke and the German thinkers Gottfried von Leibniz and Christian von Wolff.

In 1750 Mendelssohn became tutor to the children of the silk manufacturer Issak Bernhard, who in 1754 took Mendelssohn into his business. The same year, he met a major German playwright, Gotthold Ephraim Lessing, who had portrayed a noble Jew in his play *Die Juden* (1749; "The Jews") and came to see Mendelssohn as the realization of his ideal. Subsequently, Lessing modeled the central figure of his drama *Nathan der Weise* (1779; *Nathan the Wise*, 1781) after Mendelssohn, whose wisdom had caused him to be known as "the German Socrates." Mendelssohn's first work, praising Leibniz, was printed with Lessing's help as *Philosophische Gespräche* (1755; "Philosophical Speeches"). That year Mendelssohn also published his *Briefe über die Empfindungen* ("Letters on Feeling"), stressing the spiritual significance of feelings.

In 1763 Mendelssohn won the prize of the Prussian Academy of Arts in a literary contest; and as a result King Frederick the Great of Prussia was persuaded to exempt Mendelssohn from the disabilities to which Jews were customarily subjected. Mendelssohn's winning essay compared the demonstrability of metaphysical propositions with that of mathematical ones and was the first to be printed under his own name (1764). His most celebrated work, *Phädon, oder über die Unsterblichkeit der Seele* (1767; "Phaedo, or on the Immortality of the Soul"), defended the immortality of the soul against the materialism prevalent in his day; his title reflects his respect for Plato's *Phaedo*.

In 1771 Mendelssohn experienced a nervous breakdown as the result of an intense dispute over Christianity with the Swiss theologian J.C. Lavater, who two years earlier had sent him his own translation of a work by his compatriot Charles Bonnet. In his dedication, Lavater had challenged Mendelssohn to become a Christian unless he could refute Bonnet's arguments for Christianity. Although Mendelssohn deplored religious controversy, he felt compelled to reaffirm his Judaism. The strain was relaxed only when he began a translation of the Psalms in 1774. He next embarked on a project designed to help Jews relate their own religious tradition to German culture — a version of the Pentateuch, the first five books of the Old Testament, written in German but printed in Hebrew characters (1780–83). At the same time, he became involved in a new controversy that centred on the doctrine of excommunication. The conflict arose when his friend Christian Wilhelm von Dohm agreed to compose a petition for the Jews of Alsace, who originally had sought Mendelssohn's personal intervention for their emancipation. Dohm's *Über die bürgerliche Verbesserung der Juden* (1781; "On the Civil Improvement of the Jews") pleaded for emancipation but, paradoxically, added that the state should uphold the synagogue's right to excommunicate its members. To combat the resulting hostility to Dohm's book, Mendelssohn denounced excommunication in his preface (1782) to a German translation of *Vindiciae Judaeorum* ("Vindication of the Jews") by Manasseh ben Israel. After an anonymous author accused him of subverting an essential part of Mosaic law, Mendelssohn wrote *Jerusalem, oder über religiöse Macht und Judentum* (1783; "Jerusalem, or on Religious Power and Judaism"). This work held that force may be used by the state to control actions only; thoughts are inviolable by both church and state.

A final controversy, revolving around allegations that Lessing had supported the pantheism of Benedict de Spinoza, engaged Mendelssohn in a defense of Lessing, while he wrote his last work, *Morgenstunden* (1785; "Morning Hours"), in support of the theism of Leibniz. His collected works, which fill seven volumes, were published in 1843–45.

MARIE-JEAN-ANTOINE-NICOLAS DE CARITAT, MARQUIS DE CONDORCET
(b. Sept. 17, 1743, Ribemont, France—d. March 29, 1794, Bourg-la-Reine)

Condorcet was a French philosopher of the Enlightenment and an advocate of educational reform. He was also one of the major Revolutionary formulators of the ideas of progress, or the indefinite perfectibility of mankind.

He was descended from the ancient family of Caritat, who took their title from Condorcet, a town in Dauphiné. Condorcet was educated at the Jesuit college in Reims and at the College of Navarre in Paris, where he showed his first promise as a mathematician. In 1769 he became a member of the Academy of Sciences, to which he contributed papers on mathematical and other subjects.

In 1786 he married Sophie de Grouchy (1764–1822), who was said to have been one of the most beautiful women of her time. Her salon at the Hôtel des Monnaies, where Condorcet lived in his capacity as inspector general of the mint, was quite famous.

The outbreak of the French Revolution, which he greeted with enthusiasm, involved him in a great deal of political activity. He was elected to represent Paris in the Legislative Assembly and became its secretary; was active in the reform of the educational system; was chief author of the address to the European powers in 1791; and in 1792 he presented a scheme for a system of state education, which was the basis of that ultimately adopted. Condorcet was one of the first to declare for a republic, and in August 1792 he drew up the declaration justifying the suspension of the king and the summoning of the National Convention. In the trial of Louis XVI he voted against the death penalty. But his independent attitude became dangerous in the wake of the Revolution when Robespierre's radical measures triumphed, and his opposition to the arrest of the Girondins led to his being outlawed.

To occupy his mind while he was in hiding, some of his friends prevailed on him to engage in the work by which he is best known, the *Esquisse d'un tableau historique des progrès de l'esprit humain* (1795; *Sketch for a Historical Picture of the Progress of the Human Mind*). Its fundamental idea is that of the continuous progress of the human race to an ultimate perfection. He represents humans as starting from the lowest stage of savagery with no superiority over the other animals save that of bodily organization and as advancing uninterruptedly in the path of enlightenment, virtue, and happiness. The stages that the human race has already gone through, or, in other words, the great epochs of history, are regarded as nine in number.

Wholly a man of the Enlightenment, an advocate of economic freedom, religious toleration, legal and educational reform, and the abolition of slavery, Condorcet sought to extend the empire of reason to social affairs. Rather than elucidate human behaviour, as had been done thus far, by recourse to either the moral or physical sciences, he sought to explain it by a merger of the two sciences that eventually became transmuted into the discipline of sociology.

JEREMY BENTHAM

(b. Feb. 15, 1748, London, Eng.—d. June 6, 1832, London)

Jeremy Bentham, an English philosopher, economist, and theoretical jurist, was the earliest and chief expounder of Utilitarianism.

At the age of four, Bentham, the son of an attorney, is said to have read eagerly and to have begun the study of Latin. In 1760 he went to Queen's College, Oxford, and took his degree in 1763. In November he entered Lincoln's Inn to study law and took his seat as a student in the King's Bench division of the High Court. On being called to the bar, he "found a cause or two at nurse for him, which he did his best to put to death," to the bitter disappointment of his father, who had confidently looked forward to seeing him become lord chancellor.

Bentham's first book, *A Fragment on Government*, appeared in 1776. The subtitle, "being an examination of what is delivered, on the subject of government in general, in the introduction to Sir William Blackstone's *Commentaries*," indicates the nature of the work. Bentham found the "grand and fundamental" fault of the *Commentaries* to be Blackstone's "antipathy to reform." Bentham's book, written in a clear and concise style different from that of his later works, may be said to mark the beginning of philosophic radicalism.

In 1788, disappointed in the hope of making a political career, he settled down to discovering the principles of legislation. The great work on which he had been engaged for many years, *An Introduction to the Principles of Morals and Legislation*, was published in 1789. In this book he defined the principle of utility as "that property in any object whereby it tends to produce pleasure, good or happiness, or to prevent the happening of mischief, pain, evil or unhappiness to the party whose interest is considered." Mankind, he said, was governed by two sovereign motives, pain and pleasure; and the principle of utility recognized this state of affairs. The object of all legislation must be the "greatest happiness of the greatest number." He deduced from the principle of utility that, since all punishment involves pain and is therefore evil, it ought only to be used "so far as it promises to exclude some greater evil."

Bentham must be reckoned among the pioneers of prison reform. It is true that the particular scheme that he worked out was bizarre and spoiled by the elaborate detail that he loved. "Morals reformed, health preserved, industry invigorated, instruction diffused" and other similar desiderata would, he thought, be the result if his scheme for a model prison, the "Panopticon," were to be adopted; and for many years he tried to induce the government to adopt it. His endeavours, however, came to nothing.

GEORG WILHELM FRIEDRICH HEGEL

(b. Aug. 27, 1770, Stuttgart, Württemberg [Germany] – d. Nov. 14, 1831, Berlin)

Georg Wilhelm Friedrich Hegel was a German philosopher who developed a dialectical scheme that emphasized the progress of history and of ideas from thesis to antithesis and thence to a synthesis.

Hegel was the son of a revenue officer. In 1788 he went as a student to Tübingen with a view to taking religious orders, as his parents wished. Here he studied philosophy and classics for two years and graduated in 1790. On leaving college, Hegel did not enter the ministry; instead, wishing to have leisure for the study of philosophy and Greek literature, he became a private tutor. For the next three years he lived in Berne, with time on his hands and the run of a good library. But Hegel was lonely in Berne and was glad to move, at the end of 1796, to Frankfurt am Main, where Hölderlin had gotten him a tutorship. Hegel worked harder than ever, especially at Greek philosophy and modern history and politics. He read and made clippings from English newspapers, wrote about the internal affairs of his native Wurtemberg, and studied economics.

EMANCIPATION FROM KANTIANISM

Hegel's early theological writings contain hard sayings about Christianity and the churches, but the object of his attack was orthodoxy, not theology itself. All that he wrote at this period throbs with a religious conviction of a kind that is totally absent from Kant and Hegel's other 18th-century teachers. Above all, he was inspired by a doctrine of the Holy Spirit. The spirit of man, his reason, is the candle of the Lord, Hegel held, and therefore cannot be subject to the limitations that Kant had imposed upon it. This faith in reason, with its religious basis, henceforth animated the whole of Hegel's work.

His outlook had also become that of a historian—which again distinguishes him from Kant, who was much more influenced by the concepts of physical science. Every one of Hegel's major works was a history. Indeed, it was among historians and classical scholars rather than among philosophers that his work mainly fructified in the 19th century.

When, in 1798, Hegel turned back to look over the essays that he had written in Berne two or three years earlier, he saw with a historian's eye that, under Kant's influence, he had misrepresented the life and teachings of Jesus and the history of the Christian Church. His newly won insight then found expression in his essay "Der Geist

Georg Wilhelm Friedrich Hegel, portrayed as he appeared c. *1820.* Henry
Guttmann/Hulton Archive/Getty Images

des Christentums und sein Schicksal" ("The Spirit of Christianity and Its Fate"), which went unpublished until 1907. This is one of Hegel's most remarkable works. Its style is often difficult and the connection of thought not always plain, but it is written with passion, insight, and conviction.

Career as Lecturer at Jena

His father's death in 1799 had given Hegel an inheritance, slender, indeed, but sufficient to enable him to surrender a regular income and take the risk of becoming a *Privatdozent*. In January of 1801 he arrived in Jena, where Schelling had been a professor since 1798.

Jena, which had harboured the fantastic mysticism of the Schlegel brothers and their colleagues, as well as the Kantianism and ethical Idealism of Fichte, had already seen its golden age, for these great scholars had all left. The precocious Schelling, who was but 26 on Hegel's arrival, already had several books to his credit. Apt to "philosophize in public," Schelling had been fighting a lone battle in the university against the rather dull followers of Kant. It was suggested that Hegel had been summoned as a new champion to aid his friend. Having obtained a professorship in 1801, Hegel lectured on logic and metaphysics to small numbers of students. Later, in 1804, with a class of about 30, he lectured on his whole system, gradually working it out as he taught. As a result of representations made by himself at Weimar, he was in February 1805 appointed extraordinary professor at Jena.

At this time Hegel published his first great work, the *Phänomenologie des Geistes* (1807; *The Phenomenology of Mind*). This, perhaps the most brilliant and difficult of Hegel's books, describes how the human mind has risen from mere consciousness, through self-consciousness, reason, spirit, and religion, to absolute knowledge. Though man's native attitude toward existence is reliance on the senses, a little reflection is sufficient to show that the reality attributed to the external world is due as much to intellectual conceptions as to the senses and that these conceptions elude a man when he tries to fix them. If consciousness cannot detect a permanent object outside itself, so self-consciousness cannot find a permanent subject in itself. Through aloofness, skepticism, or imperfection, self-consciousness has isolated itself from the world; it has closed its gates against the stream of life. The perception of this is reason. Reason thus abandons its efforts to mold the world and is content to let the aims of individuals work out their results independently.

In spite of the *Phänomenologie*, however, Hegel's fortunes were now at their lowest ebb. He was, therefore, glad to accept the rectorship of the Aegidiengymnasium in Nürnberg, a post he held from December 1808 to August 1816 and one that offered him a small but assured income. In 1811 Hegel married Marie von Tucher (22 years his junior), of Nürnberg. The marriage was entirely happy.

UNIVERSITY PROFESSOR

At Nürnberg in 1812, *Die objektive Logik* appeared, being the first part of his *Wissenschaft der Logik* ("Science of Logic"), which in 1816 was completed by the second part, *Die subjektive Logik*.

This work, in which his system was first presented in what was essentially its ultimate shape, earned him the offer of professorships at Erlangen, at Berlin, and at Heidelberg.

He accepted the chair at Heidelberg. For use at his lectures there, he published his *Encyklopädie der philosophischen Wissenschaften im Grundrisse* (1817; "Encyclopaedia of the Philosophical Sciences in Outline"), an exposition of his system as a whole.

In 1818 Hegel accepted the renewed offer of the chair of philosophy at Berlin, which had been vacant since Fichte's death. There his influence over his pupils was immense, and there he published his *Naturrecht und Staatswissenschaft im Grundrisse*, alternatively titled *Grundlinien der Philosophie des Rechts* (1821, *The Philosophy of Right*).

Hegel seems thereafter to have devoted himself almost entirely to his lectures. Between 1823 and 1827 his activity reached its maximum. During these years hundreds of listeners from all parts of Germany and beyond came under his influence, and his fame was carried abroad by eager or intelligent disciples.

Hegel did not believe, despite some interpretations of the *Philosophy of Right*, the charge of some critics, that history had ended in his lifetime. In particular, he maintained against Kant that to eliminate war is impossible. Each nation-state is an individual; and, as Hobbes had said of relations between individuals in the state of nature, pacts without the sword are but words. Clearly, Hegel's reverence for fact prevented him from accepting Kant's Idealism.

The revolution of 1830 was a great blow to Hegel, and the prospect of mob rule almost made him ill. His last literary work, the first part of which appeared in the *Preussische Staatszeitung* while the rest was censored, was an essay on the English Reform Bill of 1832, considering its probable effects on the character of the new members of Parliament and the measures that they might introduce. In the latter connection he enlarged on several points in which England had done less than many continental states for the abolition of monopolies and abuses.

In 1831 cholera entered Germany. Hegel and his family retired for the summer to the suburbs, and there he finished the revision of the first part of his *Science of Logic*. Home again for the winter session, on November 14, after one day's illness, he died of cholera and was buried, as he had wished, between Fichte and Karl Solger, author of an ironic dialectic.

INFLUENCE

Hegel's system is avowedly an attempt to unify opposites — spirit and nature, universal and particular, ideal and real — and to be a synthesis in which all the partial and contradictory philosophies of his predecessors are alike contained and transcended. It is thus both Idealism and Realism at once; hence, it is not surprising that his successors, emphasizing now one and now another strain in his thought, have interpreted him variously. Conservatives and revolutionaries, believers and atheists alike have professed to draw inspiration from him. In one form or another his teaching dominated German universities for some years after his death and spread to France and to Italy. In the mid-20th century, interest in the early theological writings and in the *Phänomenologie* was increased by the spread of Existenialism. At the same time, the growing importance of Communism encouraged political thinkers to study Hegel's political works, as well as his *Logic*, because of their influence on Karl Marx.

ARTHUR SCHOPENHAUER

(b. Feb. 22, 1788, Danzig, Prussia [now Gdańsk, Pol.]—d. Sept. 21, 1860, Frankfurt am Main)

Arthur Schopenhauer was a German philosopher who was primarily important as the exponent of a metaphysical doctrine of the will in immediate reaction against Hegelian idealism. Often called the "philosopher of pessimism," he influenced later existential philosophy and Freudian psychology.

Schopenhauer was the son of a wealthy merchant, Heinrich Floris Schopenhauer, and his wife, Johanna, who later became famous for her novels, essays, and travelogues. In the fall of 1809 he matriculated as a student of medicine at the University of Göttingen and mainly attended lectures on the natural sciences. As early as his second semester, however, he transferred to the humanities, concentrating first on the study of Plato and Immanuel Kant. From 1811 to 1813 he attended the University of Berlin; and in Rudolstadt, during the summer of 1813, he finished his dissertation, which earned him the doctor of philosophy degree from the University of Jena.

The following winter (1813–14) Schopenhauer spent in Weimar, in intimate association with Goethe, with whom he discussed various philosophical topics. In May 1814 he left for Dresden after a quarrel with his mother over her frivolous way of life, of which he disapproved. His next three years were dedicated exclusively to the preparation and composition of his main work, *Die Welt als Wille und Vorstellung* (1819; *The World as Will and Idea*). The fundamental idea of this work, which is condensed into a short formula in the title itself, is developed in four books composed of two comprehensive series of reflections that include successively the theory of knowledge and the philosophy of nature, aesthetics, and ethics.

In March 1820, after a lengthy first tour of Italy and a triumphant dispute with Hegel, Schopenhauer qualified to lecture at the University of Berlin. Though he remained a member of the university for 24 semesters, only his first lecture was actually held; for he had scheduled (and continued to schedule) his lectures at the same hour when Hegel lectured to a large and ever-growing audience. In May 1825 he made one last attempt in Berlin, but in vain.

Artist Ludwig S. Ruhl painted this portrait of Arthur Schopenhauer in the early 1820s. Hulton Archive/Getty Images

He now occupied himself with secondary works, primarily translations.

During his remaining 28 years, Schopenhauer lived in Frankfurt, which he felt to be free from the threat of cholera, and left the city only for brief interludes. He had finally renounced his career as a university professor and lived henceforth as a recluse, totally absorbed in his studies and his writings.

The second edition of *The World as Will and Idea* (1844) included an additional volume but failed to break what he called "the resistance of a dull world." The little weight that Schopenhauer's name carried became evident when three publishers rejected his latest work. Finally, a rather obscure Berlin bookseller accepted the manuscript without remuneration. In this book, Schopenhauer turned to significant topics hitherto not treated individually within the framework of his writings. The work of six years yielded the essays and comments compiled in two volumes under the title *Parerga und Paralipomena* (1851).

AUGUSTE COMTE

(b. Jan. 19, 1798, Montpellier, France—d. Sept. 5, 1857, Paris)

Auguste Comte was a French philosopher who founded the science of sociology and the philosophical and scientific movement known as Positivism.

Comte's father, Louis Comte, was a tax official. Comte was intellectually precocious and in 1814 entered the École Polytechnique. The school was temporarily closed in 1816, but Comte soon took up permanent residence in Paris, earning a precarious living there by the occasional teaching of mathematics and by journalism.

In 1826 Comte began a series of lectures on his "system of positive philosophy" for a private audience, but he soon suffered a serious nervous breakdown. He made an almost complete recovery from his symptoms the following year, and in 1828/29 he again took up his projected lecture series. This was so successfully concluded that he redelivered it at the Royal Athenaeum during 1829–30. The following 12 years were devoted to his publication (in six volumes) of his philosophy in a work entitled *Cours de philosophie positive* (1830–42, "Course of Positive Philosophy").

From 1832 to 1842, Comte was a tutor and then an examiner at the revived École Polytechnique. In the latter year he quarreled with the directors of the school and lost his post, along with much of his income. During the remainder of his life he was supported in part by English admirers such as John Stuart Mill and by French disciples, especially the philologist and lexicographer Maximilien Littré. Comte married Caroline Massin in 1825, but the marriage was unhappy and they separated in 1842.

Comte's other major work was the *Système de politique positive*, (1851–54, *System of Positive Polity*), in which he completed his formulation of sociology. The entire work emphasized morality and moral progress as the central preoccupation of human knowledge and effort and gave an account of the polity, or political organization, that this required. His other writings include *Catéchisme positiviste* (1852; *The Catechism of Positive Religion*) and *Synthèse subjective* (1856; "Subjective Synthesis"). In general, his writing was well organized, and its exposition proceeded in impressively orderly fashion, but his style was heavy, laboured, and rather monotonous. His chief works are notable mainly because of the scope, magnitude, and importance of his project and the conscientious persistence with which he developed and expressed his ideas.

Comte lived to see his writings widely scrutinized throughout Europe. Many English intellectuals were influenced by him, and they translated and promulgated his work. His French devotees had also increased, and a large correspondence developed with positivist societies throughout the world. Comte died of cancer in 1857.

JOHN STUART MILL

(b. May 20, 1806, London, Eng.—d. May 8, 1873, Avignon, France)

John Stuart Mill was an English philosopher, economist, and exponent of Utilitarianism.

The eldest son of the British historian, economist, and philosopher James Mill, he was born in his father's house in Pentonville, London. An extremely precocious boy, he was educated exclusively by his father, who was a strict disciplinarian. By his eighth year he had read in the original Greek Aesop's *Fables*, Xenophon's *Anabasis*, and the whole of the historian Herodotus.

From May 1820 until July 1821, Mill was in France with the family of Sir Samuel Bentham, brother of Jeremy Bentham, the English Utilitarian philosopher, economist, and theoretical jurist. In 1823, when he had just completed his 17th year, he entered the examiner's office of the India House. He was promoted to assistant examiner in 1828. For 20 years, from 1836 (when his father died) to 1856, Mill had charge of the British East India Company's relations with the Indian states, and in 1856 he became chief of the examiner's office.

In 1835 Sir William Molesworth founded *The London Review*, with Mill as editor. It was amalgamated with *The Westminster* (as *The London and Westminster Review*) in 1836, and Mill continued as editor (latterly as proprietor, also) until 1840. In and after 1840 he published several important articles in *The Edinburgh Review*. The twin essays on Bentham and Coleridge show Mill's powers at their splendid best and indicate very clearly the new spirit that he tried to breathe into English radicalism.

During these years Mill also wrote his great systematic works on logic and on political economy. His reawakened enthusiasm for humanity had taken shape as an aspiration to supply an unimpeachable method of proof for conclusions in moral and social science. But he was determined that the new logic should not simply oppose the old logic. He required his inductive logic to "supplement and not supersede." *A System of Logic*, in two volumes, was published in 1843.

Mill distinguished three stages in his development as a political economist. In 1844 he published the *Essays on Some Unsettled Questions of Political Economy*, which he had written several years earlier, and four out of five of these essays are solutions of perplexing technical problems. In his second stage, originality and independence become more conspicuous as he struggles toward the standpoint from which he wrote his *Principles of Political Economy* (1848). Thereafter, he made a more thorough study of Socialist writers. He did not come to a Socialist solution, but he had the great merit of having considered afresh the foundations of society.

During the seven years of his marriage Mill became increasingly absorbed in the work of the British East India Company and in consequence published less than at any other period of his life. On the dissolution of the company in 1858, Mill was offered a seat in the new council but declined it and retired with a pension of £1,500. His retirement from official life was followed almost immediately by his wife's death at Avignon, France. He spent most of the rest of his life at a villa at Saint-Véran, near Avignon, returning to his house at Blackheath only for a short period in each year.

Mill sought relief by publishing a series of books on ethics and politics that he had meditated upon and partly

John Stuart Mill, carte de visite, 1884. Library of Congress, Neg. Co. LC-USZ62-76491

written in collaboration with his wife. The essay *On Liberty* appeared in 1859 with a touching dedication to her and the *Thoughts on Parliamentary Reform* in the same year. In his *Considerations on Representative Government* (1861) he systematized opinions already put forward in many casual articles and essays. His *Utilitarianism* (in *Fraser's Magazine*, 1861; separate publication, 1863) was a closely reasoned attempt to answer objections to his ethical theory and to remove misconceptions about it.

Mill died in 1873, and his *Autobiography* and *Three Essays on Religion* (1874) were published posthumously.

A bronze statue of Mill stands on the Thames embankment in London, and G.F. Watts's copy of his original portrait of Mill hangs in the National Gallery there.

SØREN KIERKEGAARD

(b. May 5, 1813, Copenhagen, Den.—d. Nov. 11, 1855, Copenhagen)

Søren Kierkegaard, a Danish philosopher, theologian, and cultural critic, was a major influence on existentialism and Protestant theology in the 20th and 21st centuries.

Kierkegaard's father, Michael Pedersen Kierkegaard, was a prosperous but retired businessman who devoted the later years of his life to raising his children. His domineering presence stimulated young Søren's imaginative and intellectual gifts but, as his son would later bear witness, made a normal childhood impossible.

Kierkegaard enrolled at the University of Copenhagen in 1830 but did not complete his studies until 1841. Like the German philosopher Georg Wilhelm Friedrich Hegel (1770–1831), whose system he would severely criticize, Kierkegaard entered university in order to study theology but devoted himself to literature and philosophy instead.

A Life of Conflicts

During his student days, he became estranged both from his father and from the faith in which he had been brought up, and he moved out of the family home. But by 1838, just before his father's death, he was reconciled both to his father and to the Christian faith; the latter became the idea for which he would live and die. However, it should not be assumed that his conversion was instantaneous. On the one hand, he often seemed to be moving away from the faith of his father and back toward it at virtually the same time. On the other hand, he often stressed that conversion is a long process. He saw becoming a Christian as the task of a lifetime. Accordingly, he decided to publish *Sygdomme til døden* (1849; *Sickness unto Death*) under a pseudonym (as he had done with several previous works), lest anyone think he lived up to the ideal he there presented. Likewise, the pseudonymous authors of his other works often denied they possessed the faith they talked about.

After his father's death, Kierkegaard became serious about finishing his formal education. He took his doctoral exams and wrote his dissertation, *Om begrebet ironi med stadigt hensyn til Socrates* (*On the Concept of Irony, with Constant Reference to Socrates*), completing it in June of 1841 and defending it in September. In between, he broke his engagement with Regine Olsen. They had met in 1837, when she was only 15 years old, and had become engaged in 1840. The reasons for this action are far from clear. What is clear is that this relationship haunted him for the rest of his life.

It is also clear that this crisis triggered a period of astonishing literary productivity, during which Kierkegaard published many of the works for which he is best known. Even after acknowledging that he had written these works, however, he insisted that they continue to be attributed to their pseudonymous authors.

Stages on Life's Way

In the pseudonymous works of Kierkegaard's early literary career, three stages on life's way, or three spheres of existence, are distinguished: the aesthetic, the ethical, and the religious. These are not developmental stages in a biological or psychological sense. But there is a directionality in the sense that the earlier stages have the later ones as their telos, or goal, while the later stages both presuppose and include the earlier ones as important but subordinate moments.

What the various goals of aesthetic existence have in common is that they have nothing to do with right and wrong. The criteria by which the good life is defined are premoral, unconcerned with good and evil. A stage or sphere of existence, then, is a fundamental project, a form of life, a mode of being-in-the-world that defines success in life by its own distinctive criteria.

Judge William, the representative of the ethical in *Either/Or*, argues that the aesthete fails to become a self at all but becomes, by choice, what David Hume (1711–76) said the self inevitably is: a bundle of events without an inner core to constitute identity or cohesion over time. Moreover, the aesthete fails to see that in the ethical the aesthetic is not abolished but ennobled. Judge William presents marriage as the scene of this transformation, in which, through commitment, the self acquires temporal continuity and, following Hegel, the sensuous is raised to the level of spirit.

In *Fear and Trembling* this ethical stage is teleologically suspended in the religious, which means not that it is abolished but that it is reduced to relative validity in relation to something absolute, which is its proper goal. By retelling the story of Abraham, *Fear and Trembling* presents the religious stage as the choice not to allow the laws and customs of one's people to be one's highest norm—not to equate socialization with sanctity and salvation but to be open to a voice of greater authority, namely God.

This higher normativity does not arise from reason, as Plato and Kant would have it, but is, from reason's point of view, absurd, paradoxical, even mad. These labels do not bother Kierkegaard, because he interprets reason as human, all too human—as the rationale of the current social order, which knows nothing higher than itself.

Kierkegaard said that his writings as a whole are religious. They are best seen as belonging to the prophetic traditions, in which religious beliefs become the basis for a critique of the religious communities that profess them. The modern theologies that were influenced by Kierkegaard go beyond the tasks of metaphysical affirmation and ethical instruction to a critique of complacent piety. In existential philosophies—which are often less overtly theological and sometimes entirely secular—this element of critique is retained but is directed against forms of personal and social life that do not take the tasks of human existence seriously enough. Thus, Friedrich Nietzsche (1844–1900) complains that his secular contemporaries do not take the death of God seriously enough, just as Kierkegaard complains that his Christian contemporaries do not take God seriously enough.

LATER YEARS

Kierkegaard had intended to cease writing and become a country pastor. But it was not to be. The first period of literary activity (1843–46) was followed by a second (1847–55). Instead of retiring, he picked a quarrel with *The Corsair*, a newspaper known for its liberal political sympathies but more famous as a scandal sheet that used satire to skewer the establishment. For months Kierkegaard was the target of raucous ridicule, the greatest butt of jokes in Copenhagen. Better at giving than at taking, he was deeply wounded, and indeed he never fully recovered.

In December 1854 he began to publish dozens of short, shrill pieces insisting that what passed as Christianity in Denmark was counterfeit and making clear that the leaders of the Church of Denmark (Lutheran), the bishops J.P. Mynster and H.L. Martensen, were responsible for reducing the religion to "leniency." The last of these pieces was found on Kierkegaard's desk after he collapsed in the street in October 1855 and died.

KARL MARX

(b. May 5, 1818, Trier, Rhine province, Prussia [Germany]—d. March 14, 1883, London, Eng.)

Karl Marx was a German philosopher, economist, sociologist, historian, and revolutionary. He published (with Friedrich Engels) *Manifest der Kommunistischen Partei* (1848), commonly known as *The Communist Manifesto*, the most celebrated pamphlet in the history of the socialist movement.

Karl Heinrich Marx was the oldest surviving boy of nine children. His father, Heinrich, a successful lawyer, was a man of the Enlightenment, devoted to Kant and Voltaire, who took part in agitations for a constitution in Prussia. His mother, born Henrietta Pressburg, was from Holland. Both parents were Jewish and were descended from a long line of rabbis, but, a year or so before Karl was born, his father—probably because his professional career required it—was baptized in the Evangelical Established Church. Karl was baptized when he was six years old.

Marx was educated from 1830 to 1835 at the high school in Trier. In October 1835 he matriculated at the University of Bonn. He left Bonn after a year and in October 1836 enrolled at the University of Berlin to study law and philosophy.

Marx's crucial experience at Berlin was his introduction to Hegel's philosophy, regnant there, and his adherence to the Young Hegelians. Marx joined a society called the Doctor Club, whose members were intensely involved in the new literary and philosophical movement. The Young Hegelians began moving rapidly toward atheism and also talked vaguely of political action.

The Prussian government, fearful of the subversion latent in the Young Hegelians, soon undertook to drive them from the universities. By 1841 the Young Hegelians had become left republicans. Marx's studies, meanwhile, were lagging. Urged by his friends, he submitted a doctoral dissertation to the university at Jena, which was known to be lax in its academic requirements, and received his degree in April 1841.

In 1841 Marx, together with other Young Hegelians, was much influenced by the publication of *Das Wesen des Christentums* (1841; *The Essence of Christianity*) by Ludwig Feuerbach. Its author, to Marx's mind, successfully criticized Hegel, an idealist who believed that matter or existence was inferior to and dependent upon mind or spirit, from the opposite, or materialist, standpoint, showing how the "Absolute Spirit" was a projection of "the real man standing on the foundation of nature."

In June 1843 Marx, after an engagement of seven years, married Jenny von Westphalen. Four months after their marriage, the young couple moved to Paris, which was then the centre of socialist thought and of the more extreme sects that went under the name of communism.

The "German-French Yearbooks" proved short-lived, but through their publication Marx befriended Friedrich Engels, a contributor who was to become his lifelong collaborator, and in their pages appeared Marx's article "Zur Kritik der Hegelschen Rechtsphilosophie" ("Toward the Critique of the Hegelian Philosophy of Right") with its oft-quoted assertion that religion is the "opium of the people." It was there, too, that he first raised the call for an "uprising of the proletariat" to realize the conceptions of philosophy. Marx was expelled from France and left for Brussels—followed by Engels—in February 1845.

BRUSSELS PERIOD

The next two years in Brussels saw the deepening of Marx's collaboration with Engels. Engels had seen at firsthand in Manchester, Eng., where a branch factory of his father's textile firm was located, all the depressing aspects of the Industrial Revolution. Now he and Marx, finding that they shared the same views, combined their intellectual resources.

Marx and Engels wrote their pamphlet *The Communist Manifesto* in 1847–48. It enunciated the proposition that all history had hitherto been a history of class struggles, summarized in pithy form their materialist conception of history, which stated that the course of history is dependent on economic

Karl Marx. Courtesy of the trustees of the British Museum; photograph, J.R. Freeman & Co. Ltd.

developments, and asserted that the forthcoming victory of the proletariat would put an end to class society forever. It closed with the words, "The proletarians have nothing to lose but their chains. They have a world to win. Workingmen of all countries, unite!"

Revolution suddenly erupted in Europe in the first months of 1848, in France, Italy, and Austria. Marx had been invited to Paris by a member of the provisional government just in time to avoid expulsion by the Belgian government. As the revolution gained in Austria and Germany, Marx returned to the Rhineland. When the king of Prussia dissolved the Prussian Assembly in Berlin, Marx was indicted on several charges, including advocacy of the nonpayment of taxes. The jury acquitted him unanimously and with thanks. Nevertheless, he was ordered banished as an alien on May 16, 1849.

EARLY YEARS IN LONDON

Expelled once more from Paris, Marx went to London in August 1849. It was to be his home for the rest of his life.

From 1850 to 1864 Marx lived in material misery and spiritual pain. His funds were gone, and except on one occasion he could not bring himself to seek paid employment. In March 1850 he and his wife and four small children were evicted and their belongings seized. Several of his children died—including a son Guido, "a sacrifice to bourgeois misery," and a daughter Franziska, for whom his wife rushed about frantically trying to borrow money for a coffin.

In 1859 Marx published his first book on economic theory, *Zur Kritik der politischen Ökonomie* (*A Contribution to the Critique of Political Economy*). At this time, however, Marx regarded his studies in economic and social history at the British Museum as his main task. He was busy producing the drafts of his magnum opus, which was to be published later as *Das Kapital*. Some of these drafts, including the *Outlines* and the *Theories of Surplus Value*, are important in their own right and were published after Marx's death.

Role in the First International

Marx's political isolation ended in 1864 with the founding of the International Working Men's Association. Although he was neither its founder nor its head, he soon became its leading spirit. Marx was assiduous in attendance at its meetings, which were sometimes held several times a week.

When the Franco-German War broke out in 1870, Marx and Engels disagreed with followers in Germany who refused to vote in the Reichstag in favour of the war. After the defeat of the French armies, however, they felt that the German terms amounted to aggrandizement at the expense of the French people. When an insurrection broke out in Paris and the Paris Commune was proclaimed, Marx gave it his unswerving support.

The advent of the Commune, however, exacerbated the antagonisms within the International Working Men's Association and thus brought about its downfall. The Reform Bill of 1867, which had enfranchised the British working class, had opened vast opportunities for political action by the trade unions. English labour leaders found they could make many practical advances by cooperating with the Liberal Party and, regarding Marx's rhetoric as an encumbrance, resented his charge that they had "sold themselves" to the Liberals. A left opposition also developed under the leadership of the famed Russian revolutionary Mikhail Alexandrovich Bakunin. A veteran of tsarist prisons and Siberian exile, Bakunin admired Marx's intellect but strongly opposed several of Marx's theories, especially

Marx's support of the centralized structure of the International.

At the congress of the International at The Hague in 1872, the only one he ever attended, Marx managed to defeat the Bakuninists. Then, to the consternation of the delegates, Engels moved that the seat of the General Council be transferred from London to New York City. The Bakuninists were expelled, but the International languished and was finally disbanded in Philadelphia in 1876.

LAST YEARS

During the next and last decade of his life, Marx's creative energies declined. He was beset by what he called "chronic mental depression," and his life turned inward toward his family. When his own followers and those of the German revolutionary Ferdinand Lassalle coalesced in 1875 to found the German Social Democratic Party, Marx wrote a caustic criticism of their program (the so-called Gotha Program), claiming that it made too many compromises with the status quo.

Marx was broken by the death of his wife on Dec. 2, 1881, and of his eldest daughter, Jenny Longuet, on Jan. 11, 1883. He died in London, evidently of a lung abscess, in the following year.

HERBERT SPENCER

(b. April 27, 1820, Derby, Derbyshire, Eng.—d. Dec. 8, 1903, Brighton, Sussex)

Herber Spencer was an English sociologist and philosopher and an early advocate of the theory of evolution. He is known for coining the phrase "survival of the fittest."

Spencer's father, William George Spencer, was a schoolmaster. Spencer declined an offer from his uncle, the Rev. Thomas Spencer, to send him to Cambridge, and in consequence his higher education was largely the result of his own reading, which was chiefly in the natural sciences.

In 1842 he contributed some letters (republished later as a pamphlet, *The Proper Sphere of Government*, 1843) to *The Nonconformist*, in which he argued that it is the business of governments to uphold natural rights and that they do more harm than good when they go beyond this. In 1848 he became a subeditor of *The Economist*. In 1851 he published *Social Statics*, which contained in embryo most of his later views, including his argument in favour of an extreme form of economic and social laissez-faire. In 1853 Spencer, having received a legacy from his uncle, resigned his position with *The Economist*.

Having published the first part of *The Principles of Psychology* in 1855, Spencer in 1860 issued a prospectus and accepted subscriptions for a comprehensive work, *The Synthetic Philosophy*, which was to include, besides the already published *Principles of Psychology*, volumes on first principles and on biology, sociology, and morality. *First Principles* was published in 1862, and between then and 1896, when the third volume of *The Principles of Sociology* appeared, the task was completed. In order to prepare the ground for *The Principles of Sociology*, Spencer started in 1873 a series of works called *Descriptive Sociology*, in which information was provided about the social institutions of various societies, both primitive and civilized. Spencer died in 1903, at Brighton, leaving a will by which trustees were set up to complete the publication of the *Descriptive Sociology*. The series comprised 19 parts (1873–1934).

THE SYNTHETIC PHILOSOPHY IN OUTLINE

Spencer saw philosophy as a synthesis of the fundamental principles of the special sciences, a sort of scientific summa to replace the theological systems of the Middle Ages. He thought of unification in terms of development, and his whole scheme was in fact suggested to him by the evolution of biological species. In *First Principles* he argued that there is a fundamental law of matter, which he called the law of the persistence of force, from which it follows that nothing homogeneous can remain as such if it is acted upon, because any external force must affect some part of it differently from other parts and cause difference and variety to arise. From this, he continued, it would follow that any force that continues to act on what is homogeneous must bring about an increasing variety.

This "law of the multiplication of effects," due to an unknown and unknowable absolute force, is in Spencer's view the clue to the understanding of all development, cosmic as well as biological. It should be noted that Spencer published his idea of the evolution of biological species before the views of Charles Darwin and the British naturalist Alfred Russel Wallace were known, but Spencer at that time thought that evolution was caused by the inheritance of acquired characteristics, whereas Darwin and Wallace attributed it to natural selection. Spencer later accepted the theory that natural selection was one of the causes of biological evolution, and he himself coined the phrase "survival of the fittest."

That Spencer first derived his general evolutionary scheme from reflection on human society is seen in *Social Statics*, in which social evolution is held to be a process of increasing "individuation." He saw human societies as evolving by means of increasing division of labour from undifferentiated hordes into complex civilizations. Spencer believed that the fundamental sociological classification was between military societies, in which cooperation was secured by force, and industrial societies, in which cooperation was voluntary and spontaneous.

WILHELM DILTHEY

(b. Nov. 19, 1833, Biebrich, near Wiesbaden, Nassau—d. Oct. 1, 1911, Seis am Schlern, near Bozen, South Tirol, Austria-Hungary)

Wilhelm Dilthey was a German philosopher who made important contributions to the methodology of the humanities and other human sciences.

Dilthey was the son of a Reformed Church theologian. After he finished grammar school in Wiesbaden, he began to study theology, first at Heidelberg, then at Berlin, where he soon transferred to philosophy. After completing exams in theology and philosophy, he taught for some time at secondary schools in Berlin.

In 1864 he took his doctorate at Berlin and obtained the right to lecture. In 1882 he succeeded R.H. Lotze at the University of Berlin, where he spent the remainder of his life.

Opposed to the trend in the historical and social sciences to approximate the methodological ideal of the natural sciences, Dilthey tried to establish the humanities as interpretative sciences in their own right. In the course of this work he broke new philosophical ground by his study of the relations between personal experience, its realization in creative expression, and the reflective understanding of this experience; the interdependence of self-knowledge and knowledge of other persons; and, finally, the logical development from these to the understanding of social groups and historical processes.

Dilthey held that historical consciousness—i.e., the consciousness of the historical relativity of all ideas, attitudes, and institutions—is the most characteristic and challenging fact in the intellectual life of the modern world. It shakes all belief in absolute principles, but it thereby sets people free to understand and appreciate all the diverse possibilities of human experience. Dilthey did not have the ability for definitive formulation; he was suspicious of rationally constructed systems and preferred to leave questions unsettled, realizing that they involved complexity. For a long time, therefore, he was regarded primarily as a sensitive cultural historian who lacked the power of systematic thought. Only posthumously, through the editorial and interpretative work of his disciples, did the significance of the methodology of his historical philosophy of life emerge.

WILLIAM JAMES

(b. Jan. 11, 1842, New York, N.Y., U.S.—d. Aug. 26, 1910, Chocorua, N.H.)

William James, an American philosopher and psychologist, was a leader of the philosophical movement of Pragmatism and of the psychological movement of functionalism.

James was the eldest son of Henry James, an idiosyncratic and voluble man. One of William's brothers was the novelist Henry James. When William James was 19 years of age he entered the Lawrence Scientific School of Harvard University. From courses in chemistry, anatomy, and similar subjects there, he went to the study of medicine in the Harvard Medical School; but he interrupted this study in order to accompany the eminent naturalist Louis Agassiz, in the capacity of assistant, on an expedition to the Amazon.

There James's health failed, and his duties irked him. He returned to the medical school for a term and then during 1867–68 went to Germany for courses with the physicist and physiologist Hermann von Helmholtz and others. After taking the degree of M.D. at the Harvard Medical School in June 1869, he lived in a state of semi-invalidism in his father's house as he recovered from a nervous breakdown he had suffered in Germany.

In 1872 James was appointed instructor in physiology at Harvard College, in which capacity he served until 1876. With his marriage in 1878, to Alice H. Gibbens of Cambridge, Mass., a new life began for James. His neurasthenia practically disappeared, and he went at his tasks with a zest and an energy of which his earlier record had given no hint. He contracted to produce a textbook of psychology by 1880. But the work grew under his hand, and when it finally appeared in 1890, as *The Principles of Psychology*, it was not a textbook but a monumental work in two great volumes, from which the textbook was condensed two years later. The *Principles*, which was recognized at once as both definitive and innovating in its field, established the functional point of view in psychology.

The *Principles* completed, James seems to have lost interest in the subject. His studies, which were now of the nature and existence of God, the immortality of the soul, free will and determinism, the values of life, were empirical, not dialectical; James went directly to religious experience for the nature of God, to psychical research for survival after death, to fields of belief and action for free will and determinism. His views on these topics were set forth in the period between 1893 and 1903 in various essays and lectures, afterward collected into works, of which the most notable is *The Will to Believe and Other Essays in Popular Philosophy* (1897).

His natural interest in religion was reinforced by the practical stimulus of an invitation to give the Gifford

Lectures on natural religion at the University of Edinburgh. Published as *The Varieties of Religious Experience* (1902), they had an even greater acclaim as a book than as articles.

James now explicitly turned his attention to the ultimate philosophic problems that had been at least marginally present along with his other interests. Already in 1898 he had formulated the theory of method known as Pragmatism. He showed how the meaning of any idea whatsoever—scientific, religious, philosophical, political, social, personal—can be found ultimately in nothing save in the succession of experiential consequences that it leads through and to; that truth and error, if they are within the reach of the mind at all, are identical with these consequences. He used the pragmatic rule in his polemic against monism and the "block universe," which held that all of reality is of one piece (cemented, as it were, together); and he used this rule against internal relations (i.e., the notion that you cannot have one thing without having everything), against all finalities, staticisms, and complete-nesses. His classes rang with the polemic against absolutes, and a new vitality flowed into the veins of American philosophers.

Later essays in the extension of the empirical and pragmatic method, which were collected after James's death and published as *Essays in Radical Empiricism* (1912). The fundamental point of these writings is that the relations between things, holding them together or separating them, are at least as real as the things themselves; that their function is real; and that no hidden substrata are necessary to account for the clashes and coherences of the world.

James was now the centre of a new life for philosophy in the English-speaking world. After 1909 James found himself working, against growing physical trouble, upon the material that was partially published after his death as *Some Problems of Philosophy* (1911). Finally, his physical discomfort exceeded even his remarkable voluntary endurance. After a fruitless trip to Europe in search of a cure, he returned, going straight to the country home in New Hampshire, where he died in 1910.

FRIEDRICH NIETZSCHE

(b. Oct. 15, 1844, Röcken, Saxony, Prussia [now in Germany] — d. Aug. 25, 1900, Weimar, Thuringian States)

Friedrich Nietzsche, a German classical scholar, philosopher, and critic of culture, was one of the most influential of all modern thinkers. His attempts to unmask the motives that underlie traditional Western religion, morality, and philosophy deeply affected generations of theologians, philosophers, psychologists, poets, novelists, and playwrights.

THE EARLY YEARS

Nietzsche's father, Carl Ludwig Nietzsche, was appointed pastor at Röcken by order of King Friedrich Wilhelm IV of Prussia, after whom Friedrich Nietzsche was named. His father died in 1849, before Nietzsche's fifth birthday, and he spent most of his early life in a household consisting of five women: his mother Franziska, his younger sister Elisabeth, his maternal grandmother, and two maiden aunts.

In 1864 he went to the University of Bonn to study theology and classical philology. In 1865 he transferred to the University of Leipzig, joining Friedrich Wilhelm Ritschl, who had accepted an appointment there.

Nietzsche prospered under Ritschl's tutelage in Leipzig. During the years in Leipzig, Nietzsche discovered Arthur Schopenhauer's philosophy, met the great operatic composer Richard Wagner, and began his lifelong friendship with fellow classicist Erwin Rohde (author of *Psyche*).

THE BASEL YEARS

When a professorship in classical philology fell vacant in 1869 in Basel, Switz., Ritschl recommended Nietzsche with unparalleled praise. He had completed neither his doctoral thesis nor the additional dissertation required for a German degree; yet Ritschl assured the University of Basel that he had never seen anyone like Nietzsche in 40 years of teaching and that his talents were limitless. In 1869 the University of Leipzig conferred the doctorate without examination or dissertation on the strength of his published writings, and the University of Basel appointed him extraordinary professor of classical philology. The following year Nietzsche became a Swiss citizen and was promoted to ordinary professor.

Nietzsche obtained a leave to serve as a volunteer medical orderly in August 1870, after the outbreak of the Franco-Prussian War. Within a month, while accompanying a transport of wounded, he contracted dysentery and diphtheria, which ruined his health permanently. He returned to Basel in October to resume a heavy teaching load, but as early as 1871 ill health prompted him to seek relief from the stultifying chores of a professor of classical philology.

Nietzsche's first book, *Die Geburt der Tragödie aus dem Geiste der Musik* (1872; *The Birth of Tragedy from the Spirit of Music*), marked his emancipation from the trappings of classical scholarship. A speculative rather than exegetical work, it argued that Greek tragedy arose out of the fusion of what he termed Apollonian and Dionysian elements — the former representing measure, restraint, harmony, and the latter representing unbridled passion — and that Socratic rationalism and optimism spelled the death of Greek tragedy.

By October 1876 Nietzsche requested and received a year's sick leave. In 1877 he set up house with his sister and

Peter Gast, and in 1878 his aphoristic *Menschliches, Allzumenschliches* (*Human, All-Too-Human*) appeared. Because his health deteriorated steadily he resigned his professorial chair on June 14, 1879.

NIETZSCHE'S MATURE PHILOSOPHY

Nietzsche's writings fall into three well-defined periods. The early works, *The Birth of Tragedy*, and the four *Unzeitgemässe Betrachtungen* (1873; *Untimely Meditations*), are dominated by a Romantic perspective influenced by Schopenhauer and Wagner. The middle period, from *Human, All-Too-Human* up to *The Gay Science*, reflects the tradition of French aphorists. It extols reason and science, experiments with literary genres, and expresses Nietzsche's emancipation from his earlier Romanticism and from Schopenhauer and Wagner. Nietzsche's mature philosophy emerged after *The Gay Science*.

In his mature writings Nietzsche was preoccupied by the origin and function of values in human life. If, as he believed, life neither possesses nor lacks intrinsic value and yet is always being evaluated, then such evaluations can usefully be read as symptoms of the condition of the evaluator. He was especially interested, therefore, in a probing analysis and evaluation of the fundamental cultural values of Western philosophy, religion, and morality, which he characterized as expressions of the ascetic ideal.

Nietzsche's critique of traditional morality centred on the typology of "master" and "slave" morality. Nietzsche maintained that the distinction between good and bad was originally descriptive, that is, a nonmoral reference to those who were privileged, the masters, as opposed to those who were base, the slaves. The good/evil contrast arose when slaves avenged themselves by converting

Friedrich Nietzsche, photographed c. *1885.* Hulton Archive/Getty Images

attributes of mastery into vices. Crucial to the triumph of slave morality was its claim to being the only true morality. Although Nietzsche gave a historical genealogy of master and slave morality, he maintained that it was an ahistorical typology of traits present in everyone.

"Nihilism" was the term Nietzsche used to describe the devaluation of the highest values posited by the ascetic ideal. He thought of the age in which he lived as one of passive nihilism, that is, as an age that was not yet aware that religious and philosophical absolutes had dissolved in the emergence of 19th-century Positivism. With the collapse of metaphysical and theological foundations and sanctions for traditional morality only a pervasive sense of purposelessness and meaninglessness would remain. And the triumph of meaninglessness is the triumph of nihilism: "God is dead."

Nietzsche often identified life itself with "will to power," that is, with an instinct for growth and durability. This concept provides yet another way of interpreting the ascetic ideal, since it is Nietzsche's contention "that all the supreme values of mankind *lack* this will—that values which are symptomatic of decline, *nihilistic* values, are lording it under the holiest names." Thus, traditional philosophy, religion, and morality have been so many masks a deficient will to power wears. The sustaining values of Western civilization have been sublimated products of decadence in that the ascetic ideal endorses existence as pain and suffering.

The doctrine of eternal recurrence, the basic conception of *Thus Spoke Zarathustra*, asks the question "How well disposed would a person have to become to himself and to life to crave nothing more fervently than the infinite repetition, without alteration, of each and every moment?" Presumably most men would, or should, find such a thought shattering because they should always find it possible to prefer the eternal repetition of their lives in an edited version rather than to crave nothing more fervently than the eternal recurrence of each of its horrors. The person who could accept recurrence without self-deception or evasion would be a superhuman being (*Übermensch*), a superman whose distance from the ordinary man is greater than the distance between man and ape, Nietzsche says.

ISOLATION, COLLAPSE, AND MISUSE

Apart from the books Nietzsche wrote between 1879 and 1889, it is doubtful that his life held any intrinsic interest. Seriously ill, half-blind, in virtually unrelenting pain, he lived in boarding houses in Switzerland, the French Riviera, and Italy, with only limited human contact.

Nietzsche collapsed in the streets of Turin, Italy, in January 1889, having lost control of his mental faculties completely. Bizarre but meaningful notes he sent immediately after his collapse brought Franz Overbeck to Italy to return Nietzsche to Basel. Nietzsche spent the last 11 years of his life in total mental darkness, first in a Basel asylum, then in Naumburg under his mother's care and, after her death in 1897, in Weimar in his sister's care. He died in 1900. Informed opinion favours a diagnosis of atypical general paralysis caused by dormant tertiary syphilis.

The association of Nietzsche's name with Adolf Hitler and fascism owes much to the use made of his works by his sister Elisabeth. She had married a leading chauvinist and anti-Semite, Bernhard Förster, and after his suicide in 1889 she worked diligently to refashion Nietzsche in Förster's image. Elisabeth maintained ruthless control over Nietzsche's literary estate and, dominated by greed, produced collections of his "works" consisting of discarded notes. She also committed petty forgeries. Generations of commentators were misled. Equally important, her enthusiasm for Hitler linked Nietzsche's name with that of the dictator in the public mind.

FRIEDRICH LUDWIG GOTTLOB FREGE

(b. Nov. 8, 1848, Wismar, Mecklenburg-Schwerin, Ger.—d. July 26, 1925, Bad Kleinen)

Gottlob Frege was a German philosopher, logician, and mathematician who founded modern mathematical logic. Frege discovered, on his own, the fundamental ideas that have made possible the whole modern development of logic and thereby invented an entire discipline.

Frege was the son of Alexander Frege, a principal of a girls' high school in Wismar. His mother, Auguste Frege, *née* Bialloblotzky, who was perhaps of Polish origin, outlived her husband, who died in 1866. Frege entered the University of Jena in 1869, where he studied for two years, and then went to the University of Göttingen for a further two—in mathematics, physics, chemistry, and philosophy. Frege spent the whole of his working life as a teacher of mathematics at Jena: he became a *Privatdozent* in May 1871, was made an *ausserordentlicher Professor* (associate professor) in July 1879, and became statutory professor of mathematics in May 1896.

Frege had a vivid awareness of his own genius and a belief that it would one day be recognized; but he became increasingly embittered at the failure of scholars to recognize it during his lifetime. He delighted in controversy and polemic; but the originality of his own work, the almost total independence of his own ideas from other influences, past or present, was quite exceptional and, indeed, astonishing.

SYSTEM OF MATHEMATICAL LOGIC

In 1879 Frege published his *Begriffsschrift* ("Conceptscript"), in which, for the first time, a system of mathematical logic in the modern sense was presented. There followed a period of intensive work on the philosophy of logic and of mathematics, embodied initially in his first book, *Die Grundlagen der Arithmetik* (1884; *The Foundations of Arithmetic*). Frege returned to the philosophy of mathematics with the first volume of *Grundgesetze der Arithmetik* (1893; partial Eng. trans., *Basic Laws of Arithmetic*), in which he presented, in a modified version of the symbolic system of the *Begriffsschrift*, a rigorous development of the theory of *Grundlagen*.

CONTRADICTIONS IN FREGE'S SYSTEM

While volume 2 of the *Grundgesetze* was at the printer's, Frege received a letter from one of the few contemporaries who had read and admired his works—Bertrand Russell. The latter pointed out, modestly but correctly, the possibility of deriving a contradiction in Frege's logical system—the celebrated Russell paradox.

At this point Frege's productive life effectively ceased. He never published the projected third volume of the *Grundgesetze*, and he took no part in the development of the subject, mathematical logic, that he had founded, though it had progressed considerably by the time of his death. In 1912 he declined, in terms expressing deep depression, an invitation by Russell to address a mathematical congress in Cambridge.

Frege's system of mathematical logic frequently was not comprehended clearly when first presented. Some decades later, however, when the subject began to get under way, his ideas reached others mostly as filtered through the minds of other men, such as Peano. In his lifetime there were very few—one was Russell—to give Frege the credit due him.

EDMUND HUSSERL

(b. April 8, 1859, Prossnitz, Moravia, Austrian Empire [now Prostějov, Czech Republic]—d. April 27, 1938, Freiburg im Breisgau, Ger.)

Edmund Husserl was a German philosopher and the founder of phenomenology, a method for the description and analysis of consciousness through which philosophy attempts to gain the character of a strict science.

Husserl was born into a Jewish family and completed his qualifying examinations in 1876 at the German public gymnasium in the neighbouring city of Olmütz (Olomouc). He then studied physics, mathematics, astronomy, and philosophy at the universities of Leipzig, Berlin, and Vienna. In Vienna he received his doctor of philosophy degree in 1882 with a dissertation entitled *Beiträge zur Theorie der Variationsrechnung* ("Contributions to the Theory of the Calculus of Variations").

In the autumn of 1883, Husserl moved to Vienna to study with the philosopher and psychologist Franz Brentano. In Vienna Husserl converted to the Evangelical Lutheran faith, and one year later, in 1887, he married Malvine Steinschneider, the daughter of a secondary-school professor from Prossnitz.

LECTURER AT HALLE

In 1886 Husserl went—with a recommendation from Brentano—to Carl Stumpf, the oldest of Brentano's students, who had further developed his psychology and who was professor of philosophy and psychology at the University of Halle. In 1887 Husserl qualified as a lecturer at the University of Halle with a *Habilitation* thesis—*Über den*

Begriff der Zahl: Psychologische Analysen ("On the Concept of Number: Psychological Analyses")—that showed him in the transition from his mathematical research to a reflection upon the psychological source of the basic concepts of mathematics.

The years of his teaching in Halle (1887–1901) were later seen by Husserl to have been his most difficult. The problem of uniting a psychological analysis of consciousness with a philosophical grounding of formal mathematics and logic seemed insoluble. But from this crisis there emerged the insight that the philosophical grounding of logic and mathematics must commence with an analysis of the experience that lies before all formal thinking.

The fruits of this realization were presented in the *Logische Untersuchungen* (1900–01; "Logical Investigations"), which employed a method of analysis that Husserl now designated as "phenomenological." The revolutionary significance of this work was only gradually recognized, for its method could not be subsumed under any of the philosophical orientations well known at that time.

PHENOMENOLOGY AS THE UNIVERSAL SCIENCE

As a university lecturer at the University of Göttingen (1901–16) Husserl drafted the outline of phenomenology as a universal philosophical science. Its fundamental methodological principle was what Husserl called the phenomenological reduction. It focuses the philosopher's attention on uninterpreted basic experience and the quest, thereby, for the essences of things. In this sense, it is "eidetic" reduction. On the other hand, it is also the reflection on the functions by which essences become conscious. As such, the reduction reveals the ego for which everything has meaning. Hence, phenomenology took on the character of a new style of transcendental philosophy, which repeats and improves Kant's mediation between Empiricism and Rationalism in a modern way. Husserl presented its program and its systematic outline in the *Ideen zu einer reinen Phänomenologie und phänomenologischen Philosophie* (1913; *Ideas; General Introduction to Pure Phenomenology*), of which, however, only the first part was completed.

THE RENEWAL OF SPIRITUAL LIFE

His call in 1916 to the position of *ordentlicher Professor* (university professor) at the University of Freiburg meant a new beginning for Husserl in every respect. His inaugural lecture on "Die reine Phänomenologie, ihr Forschungsgebiet und ihre Methode" ("Pure Phenomenology, Its Area of Research and Its Method") circumscribed his program of work. He had understood World War I as the collapse of the old European world, in which spiritual culture, science, and philosophy had held an incontestable position. In this situation, the epistemological grounding that he had previously provided for phenomenology no longer satisfied him; after this, his reflections were directed with special emphasis upon philosophy's task in the renewal of life.

In this sense he had set forth in his lectures on *Erste Philosophie* (1923–24; "First Philosophy") the thesis that phenomenology, with its method of reduction, is the way to the absolute vindication of life—i.e., to the realization of the ethical autonomy of man. Upon this basis, he continued his clarification of the relation between a psychological and a phenomenological analysis of consciousness and his research into the grounding of logic, which he published as the *Formale und transzendentale Logik: Versuch einer Kritik der logischen Vernunft* (1929; *Formal and Transcendental Logic*, 1969).

When he retired in 1928, Martin Heidegger, who was destined to become a leading Existentialist and one of Germany's foremost philosophers, became his successor. Husserl had looked upon him as his legitimate heir. Only later did he see that Heidegger's chief work, *Sein und Zeit* (1927; *Being and Time*, 1962), had given phenomenology a turn that would lead down an entirely different path. Husserl's disappointment led to a cooling of their relationship after 1930.

LATER YEARS

Adolf Hitler's seizure of power in 1933 did not break Husserl's ability to work. Rather, the experience of this upheaval was, for him, the occasion for concentrating more than ever upon phenomenology's task of preserving the freedom of the mind. He was excluded from the university; but the loneliness of his study was broken through his daily philosophical walks with his research assistant, Eugen Fink, through his friendships with a few colleagues who belonged to the circles of the resistance and the "Denominational Church," and through numerous visits by foreign philosophers and scholars.

In the summer of 1937, the illness that made it impossible for him to continue his work set in. From the beginning of 1938 he saw only one remaining task: to be able to die in a way worthy of a philosopher. He died in April 1938, and his ashes were buried in the cemetery in Günterstal near Freiburg.

HENRI BERGSON

(b. Oct. 18, 1859, Paris, France—d. Jan. 4, 1941, Paris)

Henri Bergson, a French philosopher, was the first to elaborate what came to be called a process philosophy. He was awarded the Nobel Prize for Literature in 1927.

Through his father, a talented musician, Bergson was descended from a rich Polish Jewish family. His mother came from an English Jewish family. Bergson's upbringing, training, and interests were typically French, and his professional career, as indeed all of his life, was spent in France, most of it in Paris.

Bergson received a doctorate in 1889 for his *Essai sur les données immédiates de la conscience* (*Time and Free Will: An Essay on the Immediate Data of Consciousness*). This work was primarily an attempt to establish the notion of duration, or lived time, as opposed to what he viewed as the spatialized conception of time, measured by a clock, that is employed by science. He proceeded by analyzing the awareness that man has of his inner self to show that psychological facts are qualitatively different from any other, charging psychologists in particular with falsifying the facts by trying to quantify and number them. Once the confusions were cleared away that confounded duration with extension, succession with simultaneity, and quality with quantity, he maintained that the objections to human liberty made in the name of scientific determinism could be seen to be baseless.

Philosophical Triumphs

The publication of the *Essai* found Bergson returned to Paris, teaching at the Lycée Henri IV. In 1891 he married Louise Neuburger, a cousin of the French novelist Marcel Proust. Meanwhile, he had undertaken the study of the relation between mind and body. Though he was convinced that he had refuted the argument for determinism, his own work, in the doctoral dissertation, had not attempted to explain how mind and body are related. The findings of his research into this problem were published in 1896 under the title *Matière et mémoire: essai sur la relation du corps à l'esprit* (*Matter and Memory*).

The *Essai* had been widely reviewed in the professional journals, but *Matière et mémoire* attracted the attention of a wider audience and marked the first step along the way that led to Bergson's becoming one of the most popular and influential lecturers and writers of the day. *L'Évolution créatrice* (1907; *Creative Evolution*), the greatest work of these years and Bergson's most famous book, reveals him most clearly as a philosopher of process at the same time that it shows the influence of biology upon his thought. In examining the idea of life, Bergson accepted evolution as a scientifically established fact. But he proposed that the whole evolutionary process should be seen as the endurance of an *élan vital* ("vital impulse") that is continually developing and generating new forms.

LATER YEARS

In 1914 Bergson retired from all active duties at the Collège de France, although he did not formally retire from the chair until 1921. Having received the highest honours that France could offer him, including membership, since 1915, among the "40 immortals" of the Académie Française, he was awarded the Nobel Prize for Literature in 1927.

In 1932 he published *Les Deux Sources de la morale et de la religion* (*The Two Sources of Morality and Religion*). Here he came much closer to the orthodox religious notion of God than he had in the vital impulse of *L'Évolution créatrice*. He acknowledged in his will of 1937, "My reflections have led me closer and closer to Catholicism, in which I see the complete fulfillment of Judaism." Yet, although declaring his "moral adherence to Catholicism," he never went beyond that. In explanation, he wrote: "I would have become a convert, had I not foreseen for years a formidable wave of anti-Semitism about to break upon the world. I wanted to remain among those who tomorrow were to be persecuted." To confirm this conviction, only a few weeks before his death, he arose from his sickbed and stood in line in order to register as a Jew, in accord with the law just imposed by the Vichy government and from which he refused the exemption that had been offered him.

JOHN DEWEY

(b. Oct. 20, 1859, Burlington, Vt., U.S.—d. June 1, 1952, New York, N.Y.)

John Dewey, an American philosopher and educator, was one of the founders of the philosophical school of pragmatism, a pioneer in functional psychology, and a leader of the progressive movement in education in the United States.

The son of a grocer in Vermont, Dewey attended the public schools of Burlington and there entered the University of Vermont. After being awarded the Ph.D. degree by Johns Hopkins University in 1884, Dewey, in the fall of that year, went to the University of Michigan, where he had been appointed an instructor in philosophy and psychology. With the exception of the academic year 1888–89, when he served as professor of philosophy at the University of Minnesota, Dewey spent the next 10 years at Michigan.

PHILOSOPHICAL THOUGHT

Dewey left Michigan in 1894 to become professor of philosophy and chairman of the department of philosophy, psychology, and pedagogy at the University of Chicago. Dewey's achievements there brought him national fame. The increasing dominance of evolutionary biology and psychology in his thinking led him to abandon the Hegelian theory of ideas, which views them as somehow mirroring the rational order of the universe, and to accept instead an instrumentalist theory of knowledge, which conceives of ideas as tools or instruments in the solution of problems encountered in the environment. Dewey found more acceptable a theory of reality holding that nature, as encountered in scientific and ordinary experience, is the ultimate reality and that man is a product of nature who finds his meaning and goals in life here and now.

Dewey's philosophical orientation has been labeled a form of pragmatism, though Dewey himself seemed to favour the term "instrumentalism," or "experimentalism." William James's *The Principles of Psychology* early stimulated Dewey's rethinking of logic and ethics by directing his attention to the practical function of ideas and concepts, but Dewey and the Chicago school of pragmatists went farther than James had gone in that they conceived of ideas as instruments for transforming the uneasiness connected with the experience of having a problem into the satisfaction of some resolution or clarification of it.

Dewey developed from these views a philosophical ground for democracy and liberalism. He conceived of democracy not as a mere form of government, but rather as a mode of association which provides the members of a society with the opportunity for maximum experimentation and personal growth. The ideal society, for Dewey, was one that provided the conditions for ever enlarging the experience of all its members.

Dewey's writings on education, notably his *The School and Society* (1899) and *The Child and the Curriculum* (1902), presented and defended what were to remain the chief underlying tenets of the philosophy of education he originated. These tenets were that the educational process must begin with and build upon the interests of the child; that it must provide opportunity for the interplay of thinking and doing in the child's classroom experience; that the teacher should be a guide and coworker with the pupils, rather than a taskmaster assigning a fixed set of lessons and recitations; and that the school's goal is the growth of the child in all aspects of its being.

Dewey's ideas and proposals strongly affected educational theory and practice in the United States. Aspects of his views were seized upon by the "progressive movement" in education, which stressed the student-centred rather than the subject-centred school, education through activity rather than through formal learning, and laboratory, workshop, or occupational education rather than the mastery of traditional subjects. But though Dewey's own faith in progressive education never wavered, he came to realize that the zeal of his followers introduced a number of excesses and defects into progressive education. Indeed, in *Experience and Education* (1938) he sharply criticized educators who sought merely to interest or amuse students, disregarded organized subject matter in favour of mere activity on the part of students, and were content with mere vocational training.

CAREER AT COLUMBIA UNIVERSITY

Disagreements between President William Rainey Harper of the University of Chicago and Dewey led, in 1904, to Dewey's resignation of his posts and to his acceptance of a professorship of philosophy at Columbia University in New York City. Dewey was associated with Columbia for 47 years, first as professor and then as professor emeritus of philosophy.

His interest in current affairs prompted Dewey to contribute regularly to liberal periodicals, especially *The New Republic*. His articles focused on domestic, foreign, and international developments and were designed to reach a wide reading public. Because of his skill in analyzing and interpreting events, he soon was rated as among the best of American commentators and social critics.

ALFRED NORTH WHITEHEAD

(b. Feb. 15, 1861, Ramsgate, Isle of Thanet, Kent, Eng.—d. Dec. 30, 1947, Cambridge, Mass., U.S.)

Alfred North Whitehead was an English philosopher and mathematician who developed a comprehensive metaphysical theory from the mid-1920s. He also collaborated with Bertrand Russell on *Principia Mathematica* (1910–13).

Whitehead's father, Alfred Whitehead, an Anglican clergyman, later became vicar of St. Peter's in Thanet. His mother, born Maria Sarah Buckmaster, was the daughter of a prosperous military tailor. Alfred North Whitehead was their youngest child.

In 1880 Whitehead entered Trinity College, Cambridge, on a scholarship. He attended only mathematical lectures, and his interests in literature, religion, philosophy, and politics were nourished solely by conversation. It was not until May 1884, however, that he was elected to an elite discussion society known as the "Apostles." Whitehead did well in the Mathematical Tripos (honours examination) of 1883–84, won a Trinity fellowship, and was appointed to the mathematical staff of the college. Stimulated by pioneering works in modern algebra, he envisaged a detailed comparative study of systems of symbolic reasoning allied to ordinary algebra. He did not begin to write his *Treatise on Universal Algebra* (1898), however, until January 1891, one month after his marriage to Evelyn Willoughby Wade.

Whitehead was at work on a second volume of his *Universal Algebra*, from 1898 to 1903, when he abandoned it because he was busy on a related, large investigation with Bertrand Russell. By the end of 1900 he had written the first draft of his brilliant *Principles of Mathematics* (1903). Whitehead agreed with its main thesis—that all pure mathematics follows from a reformed formal logic so that, of the two, logic is the fundamental discipline. By 1901 Russell had secured his collaboration on volume 2 of the *Principles*, in which this thesis was to be established by strict symbolic reasoning. The task turned out to be enormous. Their work had to be made independent of Russell's book; they called it *Principia Mathematica*. The project occupied them until 1910, when the first of its three volumes was published.

CAREER IN LONDON

Whitehead's future was uncertain because he had not made the sort of discoveries that cause a man to be counted an outstanding mathematician. There was, thus, little prospect of a Cambridge professorship in mathematics for him at the expiration of his Trinity lectureship. He did not wait for it to expire but moved to London in 1910, even though he had no position waiting for him there. In that first London year, Whitehead wrote the first of his books for a wide audience, *An Introduction to Mathematics* (1911), still one of the best books of its kind. In 1911 he was appointed to the staff of University College (London), and in 1914 he became professor of applied mathematics at the Imperial College of Science and Technology.

During those years, Whitehead was also constructing philosophical foundations for physics. He was led to this by the way in which he wanted to present geometry—not as deduced from hypothetical premises about assumed though imperceptible entities (e.g., points) but as the science of actual space, which is a complex of relations between extended things. From perceivable elements and relations, he logically constructed entities that are related to each other just as points are in geometry. That was only the beginning of his task, for Albert Einstein had revised the ideas of space, time, and motion. Whitehead was convinced that these three concepts should be based upon the general character of men's perception of the external world. In 1919 he published his *Enquiry Concerning the Principles of Natural Knowledge*; it was both searching and constructive but too philosophical and too complicated to influence physicists.

CAREER IN THE UNITED STATES

In the early 1920s Whitehead was clearly the most distinguished philosopher of science writing in English. When a friend of Harvard University, the historical scholar Henry Osborn Taylor, pledged the money for his salary, Harvard offered Whitehead a five-year appointment as professor of philosophy.

Early in 1925, he gave a course of eight lectures in Boston, published that same year (with additions—among them his earliest writing about God) as *Science and the Modern World*. In it he dramatically described what had long engaged his meditation; namely, the rise, triumph, and impact of "scientific Materialism"—i.e., the view that nature consists of nothing else but matter in motion, or a flux of purely physical energy. He criticized this Materialism as mistaking an abstract system of mathematical physics for the concrete reality of nature. The importance of this book was immediately recognized.

Adventures of Ideas (1933) was Whitehead's last big philosophical book and the most rewarding one for the general reader. It offered penetrating, balanced reflections on the parts played by brute forces and by general ideas about humanity, God, and the universe in shaping the course of Western civilization. Whitehead emphasized the impulse of life toward newness and the absolute need for societies stable enough to nourish adventure that is fruitful rather than anarchic. In this book he also summarized his metaphysics and used it to elucidate the nature of beauty, truth, art, adventure, and peace. By "peace" he meant a religious attitude that is "primarily a trust in the efficacy of beauty."

A Fellow of the Royal Society since 1903, Whitehead was elected to the British Academy in 1931. In 1945 he received the Order of Merit. His unpublished manuscripts and correspondence were destroyed by his widow, as he had wanted.

BENEDETTO CROCE

(b. Feb. 25, 1866, Pescasseroli, Italy—d. Nov. 20, 1952, Naples)

B enedetto Croce was a historian, a humanist, and the foremost Italian philosopher of the first half of the 20th century.

Croce belonged to a family of landed proprietors with estates in the Abruzzi region of central Italy but chiefly resident in Naples. His background was religious, monarchical, and conservative. Croce spent almost his whole life in Naples, becoming intimately identified with and a keen observer of its life and a biographer of its heroes.

FOUNDING OF LA CRITICA

In 1903 he founded *La Critica*, a journal of cultural criticism, in which, during the course of the next 41 years, he published nearly all his writings and reviewed all of the most important historical, philosophical, and literary work that was being produced in Europe at the time. At this same time he began the systematic exposition of his "Philosophy of the Spirit," his chief intellectual achievement. This term designates two distinct, but related, aspects of his thought. In the first aspect, philosophy of spirit designates the construction of a philosophical system on the remote pattern of the Rationalism of classical Romantic philosophy. Its principle is the "circularity" of spirit within the structure of the system and in historical time. The phases, or moments, of spirit in this system are theoretical and practical; they are distinguished, respectively, into aesthetic, logical, and economic and ethical. In the second aspect, Croce gradually abandoned, without explicitly renouncing, this schematism in response primarily to methodological considerations in history. Its moments are not dissolved but are concretized into the flow of historical action and thought. History becomes the unique mediational principle for all the moments of spirit, while spirit—i.e., human consciousness—is completely spontaneous, without a predetermined structure.

STRUGGLE WITH FASCISM

Croce confessed that he first saw in fascism a movement to the right of the political spectrum that might restrain and counteract the leftist tendencies toward unrestricted individual freedom released by World War I. But as the character of the Benito Mussolini regime revealed itself, his opposition hardened, becoming absolute, beyond compromise. He became, within and without Italy, the symbol of the opposition to fascism, the rallying point of the lovers of liberty.

In the maelstrom of conflict and ambiguity that followed Italy's defeat in World War II, a voice of moral authority that could speak for the true Italy was demanded. Croce's was unanimously recognized as that voice. And with authority that voice recalled Italy to the inner spiritual resources through which it might renew itself. It matters little that Croce's own project for the rebuilding of Italy—the retention of the monarchy with certain dynastic changes, the return to the principles of a revived Liberal Party in government—was not the one realized in history. More important is the fact that the new Italy, in its democratic form, was inspired by his spirit.

This last public duty fulfilled, Croce returned to his studies. In his own library—one of the finest collections in Europe within its own scope—he established the Italian Institute for Historical Studies as a research centre. Asked his state of health, he replied with true stoic equanimity, "I am dying at my work." He died at age 86.

NISHIDA KITARŌ

(b. June 17, 1870, near Kanazawa, Ishikawa prefecture, Japan—d. June 7, 1945, Kamakura)

Nishida Kitarō was a Japanese philosopher who exemplified the attempt by his country to assimilate Western philosophy into the East Asian spiritual tradition.

Nishida's father, Nishida Yasunori, was for a time a teacher of an elementary school among whose few pupils was Kitarō. His mother, Tosa, was a pious devotee of the Jōdo, or True Pure Land, school of Buddhism. In his boyhood, Nishida took traditional lessons in Chinese from an excellent Confucian teacher, and in his higher school days he was taught by another scholar erudite in Chinese. Another important teacher of Nishida's was Hōjō Takiyoshi, a professor of mathematics of the Fourth Higher School, under whom Nishida had studied mathematics even before he entered high school. This exposure to Chinese culture enriched his life with a lasting Confucian quality and worldview. Later, when Western philosophy and Buddhism (especially Zen Buddhism) were merged in his mature mind, there remained deep within him an undercurrent of Confucian conviction with regard to "the ideal person," "the Way" to good and truth, sincerity, self-cultivation, and detachment.

After graduation Nishida became a teacher in a middle school near his home (1895). In the following year, he was appointed a lecturer in the Fourth Higher School at Kanazawa, and, after two years as a lecturer and later as a professor at the Yamaguchi Higher School in Yamaguchi, he was again appointed as a professor of the Fourth Higher School, teaching psychology, logic, ethics, and German (1899–1909). During his Yamaguchi and Kanazawa teaching periods, he was much engaged in the practice of Zen meditation. Remarks about Zen practice are overwhelmingly conspicuous in his diary of this period.

After one year as professor at Gakushūin University (Tokyo) in 1909, he was appointed associate professor of ethics at Kyōto Imperial University. In 1913 he was appointed professor of philosophy of religion and in 1914 professor of philosophy, a post he held until his retirement in 1928. About the end of his professorship in Kyōto Imperial University, Nishida's philosophy attained its maturity, which can be defined as "the philosophy of the *topos* (place) of Nothingness." In his latter years he delved most deeply into philosophical problems and endeavoured to explain more concrete facts by his logic. Thus his idea of the true reality that overcomes the dichotomy of subjectivity and objectivity (the mind and its objects) in the *topos* of Nothingness became significant, he emphasized, for "historical reality in the historical world." Nishida developed this implication of absolute Nothingness in his *Tetsugakuron bunshū* ("Philosophical Essays"; 7 vol.), which he wrote after his retirement.

BERTRAND RUSSELL

(b. May 18, 1872, Trelleck, Monmouthshire, Wales — d. Feb. 2, 1970, Penrhyndeudraeth, Merioneth)

B ertrand Russell, a British philosopher, logician, and social reformer, was a founding figure in the analytic movement in Anglo-American (analytic) philosophy and the recipient of the Nobel Prize for Literature in 1950.

Russell was born in Ravenscroft, the country home of his parents, Lord and Lady Amberley. His grandfather, Lord John Russell, was the youngest son of the 6th Duke of Bedford. In 1861, after a long and distinguished political career in which he served twice as prime minister, Lord Russell was ennobled by Queen Victoria, becoming the 1st Earl Russell. Bertrand Russell became the 3rd Earl Russell in 1931, after his elder brother, Frank, died childless.

Russell's early life was marred by tragedy and bereavement. By the time he was age six, his sister, Rachel, his parents, and his grandfather had all died. He and Frank were left in the care of their grandmother, Countess Russell. Though Frank was sent to Winchester School, Bertrand was educated privately at home, and his childhood, to his later great regret, was spent largely in isolation from other children.

In 1890 Russell's isolation came to an end when he entered Trinity College, University of Cambridge, to study mathematics. There he made lifelong friends through his membership in the famously secretive student society the Apostles, whose members included some of the most influential philosophers of the day. Inspired by his discussions with this group, Russell abandoned mathematics for philosophy.

Analysis and Logicism

Russell flirted with idealism but soon abandoned it. His development is customarily attributed to the influence of his friend and fellow Apostle G.E. Moore. A much greater influence on his thought at this time, however, was a group of German mathematicians that included Karl Weierstrass, Georg Cantor, and Richard Dedekind, whose work was aimed at providing mathematics with a set of logically rigorous foundations. For Russell, their success in this endeavour was of enormous philosophical as well as mathematical significance; indeed, he described it as "the greatest triumph of which our age has to boast." After becoming acquainted with this body of work, Russell adopted the view, which he was to hold for the rest of his life, that analysis rather than synthesis was the surest method of philosophy, and that therefore all the grand system building of previous philosophers was misconceived.

Inspired by the work of the mathematicians whom he so greatly admired, Russell conceived the idea of demonstrating that mathematics not only had logically rigorous foundations but also that it was in its entirety nothing but logic. The philosophical case for this point of view—subsequently known as logicism—was stated at length in *The Principles of Mathematics* (1903). Near the end of his work on *The Principles of Mathematics*, Russell discovered that he had been anticipated in his logicist philosophy of mathematics by the German mathematician Gottlob Frege, whose book *The Foundations of Arithmetic* (1884) contained, as Russell put it, "many things . . . which I believed I had invented." Russell quickly added an appendix to his book that discussed Frege's work, acknowledged Frege's earlier discoveries, and explained the differences in their respective understandings of the nature of logic.

RUSSELL'S PARADOX

The tragedy of Russell's intellectual life is that the deeper he thought about logic, the more his exalted conception of its significance came under threat. He himself described his philosophical development after *The Principles of Mathematics* as a "retreat from Pythagoras." The first step in this retreat was his discovery of a contradiction—now known as Russell's Paradox—at the very heart of the system of logic upon which he had hoped to build the whole of mathematics. The contradiction arises from the following considerations: Some classes are members of themselves (e.g., the class of all classes), and some are not (e.g., the class of all men), so we ought to be able to construct the class of all classes that are not members of themselves. But now, if we ask of this class "Is it a member of itself?" we become enmeshed in a contradiction. If it is, then it is not, and if it is not, then it is. This is rather like defining the village barber as "the man who shaves all those who do not shave themselves" and then asking whether the barber shaves himself or not.

At first this paradox seemed trivial, but the more Russell reflected upon it, the deeper the problem seemed, and eventually he was persuaded that there was something fundamentally wrong with the notion of class as he had understood it in *The Principles of Mathematics*. Frege saw the depth of the problem immediately. When Russell wrote to him to tell him of the paradox, Frege replied, "arithmetic totters." The foundation upon which Frege and Russell had hoped to build mathematics had, it seemed, collapsed. Whereas Frege sank into a deep depression, Russell set about repairing the damage by attempting to construct a theory of logic immune to the paradox. Like a malignant cancerous growth, however, the contradiction reappeared in different guises whenever Russell thought that he had eliminated it.

Eventually, Russell's attempts to overcome the paradox resulted in a complete transformation of his scheme of logic, as he added one refinement after another to the basic theory. In the process, important elements of his "Pythagorean" view of logic were abandoned. In particular, Russell came to the conclusion that there were no such things as classes and propositions and that therefore, whatever logic was, it was not the study of them. In their place he substituted a bewilderingly complex theory known as the ramified theory of types, which, though it successfully avoided contradictions such as Russell's Paradox, was (and remains) extraordinarily difficult to understand. By the time he and his collaborator, Alfred North Whitehead, had finished the three volumes of *Principia Mathematica* (1910–13), the theory of types and other innovations to the basic logical system had made it unmanageably complicated.

Despite their differences, Russell and Frege were alike in taking an essentially Platonic view of logic. Indeed, the passion with which Russell pursued the project of deriving mathematics from logic owed a great deal to what he would later somewhat scornfully describe as a "kind of mathematical mysticism." As he put it in his more disillusioned old age, "I disliked the real world and sought refuge in a timeless world, without change or decay or the will-o'-the-wisp of progress." Russell, like Pythagoras and Plato before him, believed that there existed a realm of truth that, unlike the messy contingencies of the everyday world of sense-experience, was immutable and eternal. This realm was accessible only to reason, and knowledge of it, once attained, was not tentative or corrigible but certain and irrefutable. Logic, for Russell, was the means by which one

Bertrand Russell (second from left), *photographed entering a courthouse to face charges stemming from a peace demonstration in 1961.* Evening Standard/ Hulton Archive/Getty Images

gained access to this realm, and thus the pursuit of logic was, for him, the highest and noblest enterprise life had to offer.

THEORY OF DESCRIPTIONS AND LATER DOCTRINES

In philosophy, the greatest impact of *Principia Mathematica* has been through its so-called theory of descriptions. This method of analysis, first introduced by Russell in his article "On Denoting" (1905), translates propositions containing definite descriptions (e.g., "the present king of France") into expressions that do not—the purpose being to remove the logical awkwardness of appearing to refer to things (such as the present king of France) that do not exist. Originally developed by Russell as part of his efforts to overcome the contradictions in his theory of logic, this method of analysis has since become widely influential even among philosophers with no specific interest in mathematics. The general idea at the root of Russell's theory of descriptions—that the grammatical structures of ordinary language are distinct from, and often conceal, the true "logical forms" of expressions—has become his most enduring contribution to philosophy.

Russell later said that his mind never fully recovered from the strain of writing *Principia Mathematica*, and he never again worked on logic with quite the same intensity. In 1918 he wrote *An Introduction to Mathematical Philosophy*, which was intended as a popularization of *Principia*, but, apart from this, his philosophical work tended to be on epistemology rather than logic. In 1914, in *Our Knowledge of the External World*, Russell argued that the world is "constructed" out of sense-data, an idea that he refined in *The Philosophy of Logical Atomism* (1918–19). In *The Analysis of Mind* (1921) and *The Analysis of Matter* (1927), he abandoned this notion in favour of what he called neutral monism, the view that the "ultimate stuff" of the world is neither mental nor physical but something "neutral" between the two. Although treated with respect, these works had markedly less impact upon subsequent philosophers than his early works in logic and the philosophy of mathematics, and they are generally regarded as inferior by comparison.

A TURBULENT LIFE

Connected with the change in his intellectual direction after the completion of *Principia* was a profound change in his personal life. Throughout the years that he worked single-mindedly on logic, Russell's private life was bleak and joyless. He had fallen out of love with his first wife, Alys, though he continued to live with her. In 1911, however, he fell passionately in love with Lady Ottoline Morrell. Doomed from the start (because Morrell had no intention of leaving her husband), this love nevertheless transformed Russell's entire life. He left Alys and began to hope that he might, after all, find fulfillment in romance.

In the same year that he began his affair with Morrell, Russell met Ludwig Wittgenstein, a brilliant young Austrian who arrived at Cambridge to study logic with Russell. Fired with intense enthusiasm for the subject, Wittgenstein made great progress, and within a year Russell began to look to him to provide the next big step in philosophy and to defer to him on questions of logic. However, Wittgenstein's own work, eventually published in 1921 as *Logisch-philosophische Abhandlung* (*Tractatus Logico-Philosophicus*, 1922), undermined the entire approach to logic that had inspired Russell's great contributions to the philosophy of mathematics. It persuaded Russell that there were no "truths" of logic at all, that logic consisted entirely of tautologies, the truth of which was not guaranteed by eternal facts in the Platonic realm of ideas but lay, rather, simply in the nature of language. This was to be the final step in the retreat from Pythagoras and a further incentive for Russell to abandon technical philosophy in favour of other pursuits.

During World War I Russell was for a while a full-time political agitator, campaigning for peace and against conscription. He was twice taken to court, the second time to receive a sentence of six months in prison, which he served at the end of the war. In 1916, as a result of his antiwar campaigning, Russell was dismissed from his lectureship at Trinity College. The war had had a profound effect on Russell's political views, causing him to abandon his inherited liberalism and to adopt a thorough-going socialism.

In 1921 Russell married his second wife, Dora Black, a young graduate of Girton College, Cambridge, with whom he had two children, John and Kate. In the interwar years Russell and Dora acquired a reputation as leaders of a progressive socialist movement that was stridently anticlerical, openly defiant of conventional sexual morality, and dedicated to educational reform. Russell's published work during this period consists mainly of journalism and popular books written in support of these causes. His public lecture "Why I Am Not a Christian," delivered in 1927 and printed many times, became a popular locus classicus of atheistic rationalism. In 1927 Russell and Dora set up their own school, Beacon Hill, as a pioneering experiment in primary education.

In 1932 Russell left Dora for Patricia ("Peter") Spence, a young University of Oxford undergraduate, and for the next three years his life was dominated by an extraordinarily acrimonious and complicated divorce from

Dora, which was finally granted in 1935. In the following year he married Spence, and in 1937 they had a son, Conrad.

RETURN TO ACADEMIA

Worn out by years of frenetic public activity and desiring, at this comparatively late stage in his life (he was then age 66), to return to academic philosophy, Russell gained a teaching post at the University of Chicago. From 1938 to 1944 Russell lived in the United States, where he taught at Chicago and the University of California at Los Angeles, but he was prevented from taking a post at the City College of New York because of objections to his views on sex and marriage. On the brink of financial ruin, he secured a job teaching the history of philosophy at the Barnes Foundation in Philadelphia. Although he soon fell out with its founder, Albert C. Barnes, and lost his job, Russell was able to turn the lectures he delivered at the founda-tion into a book, *A History of Western Philosophy* (1945), which proved to be a best seller and was for many years his main source of income.

In 1944 Russell returned to Trinity College, where he lectured on the ideas that formed his last major contribution to philosophy, *Human Knowledge: Its Scope and Limits* (1948). During this period Russell, for once in his life, found favour with the authorities, and he received many official tributes, including the Order of Merit in 1949 and the Nobel Prize for Literature in 1950. His private life, how-ever, remained as turbulent as ever, and he left his third wife in 1949.

In 1952 Russell married his fourth wife, Edith Finch, and finally, at the age of 80, found lasting marital harmony. Russell devoted his last years to campaigning against nuclear weapons and the Vietnam War, assuming once again the role of gadfly of the establishment.

G.E. MOORE

(b. Nov. 4, 1873, London, Eng.—d. Oct. 24, 1958, Cambridge, Cambridgeshire)

G.E. (George Edward) Moore was an influential British Realist philosopher and professor whose systematic approach to ethical problems and remarkably meticulous approach to philosophy made him an outstanding modern British thinker.

Elected to a fellowship at Trinity College, Cambridge, in 1898, Moore remained there until 1904, during which time he published several journal articles, including "The Nature of Judgment" (1899) and "The Refutation of Idealism" (1903), as well as his major ethical work, *Principia Ethica* (1903). These writings were important in helping to undermine the influence of Hegel and Kant on British philosophy. After residence in Edinburgh and London, he returned to Cambridge in 1911 to become a lecturer in moral science. From 1925 to 1939 he was professor of philosophy there, and from 1921 to 1947 he was editor of the philosophical journal *Mind*.

A friend of Bertrand Russell, who first directed him to the study of philosophy, Moore was also a leading figure in the Bloomsbury group, a coterie that included the economist John Keynes and the writers Virginia Woolf and E.M. Forster. Because of his view that "the good" is knowable by direct apprehension, he became known as an "ethical intuitionist." He claimed that other efforts to decide what is "good," such as analyses of the concepts of approval or desire, which are not themselves of an ethical nature, partake of a fallacy that he termed the "naturalistic fallacy."

Moore was also preoccupied with such problems as the nature of sense perception and the existence of other minds and material things. He was not as skeptical as those philosophers who held that we lack sufficient data to prove that objects exist outside our own minds, but he did believe that proper philosophical proofs had not yet been devised to overcome such objections.

Although few of Moore's theories achieved general acceptance, his unique approaches to certain problems and his intellectual rigour helped change the texture of philosophical discussion in England. His other major writings include *Philosophical Studies* (1922) and *Some Main Problems of Philosophy* (1953); posthumous publications were *Philosophical Papers* (1959) and the *Commonplace Book, 1919–1953* (1962).

MARTIN BUBER

(b. Feb. 8, 1878, Vienna, Austria-Hungary [now in Austria] — d. June 13, 1965, Jerusalem, Israel)

German-Jewish Martin Buber was a religious philosopher, biblical translator and interpreter, and master of German prose style. His philosophy was centred on the encounter, or dialogue, of the individual with other beings, particularly exemplified in the relation with other persons but ultimately resting on and pointing to the relation with God. This thought reached its fullest dialogical expression in *Ich und Du* (1923; *I and Thou*).

FROM VIENNA TO JERUSALEM

Buber was the son of Carl Buber, an agronomist, and his wife—both assimilated Jews. When Martin was three his mother left his father, and the boy was brought up by his grandparents in Lemberg (now Lviv, Ukraine). The search after the lost mother became a strong motive for his dialogical thinking—his I-Thou philosophy.

Buber's grammar-school education provided him with an excellent grounding in the classics. During his adolescence he ceased to participate in Jewish religious observances. In his university days—he attended the universities of Vienna, Berlin, Leipzig, and Zürich—Buber studied philosophy and art. His doctoral dissertation (*Vienna*, 1904) dealt with the theories of individuation in the thought of two great mystics, Nicholas of Cusa and Jakob Böhme, but it was Friedrich Nietzsche's proclamation of heroic nihilism and his criticism of modern culture that exerted the greatest influence on Buber at that time. The Nietzschean influence was reflected in Buber's turn to Zionism and its call for a return to roots and a more wholesome culture.

In 1916 Buber founded the influential monthly *Der Jude* ("The Jew"), which he edited until 1924 and which became the central forum for practically all German-reading Jewish intellectuals. In its pages he advocated the unpopular cause of Jewish-Arab cooperation in the formation of a binational state in Palestine.

After his marriage (1901) to a non-Jewish, pro-Zionist author, Paula Winckler, who converted to Judaism, Buber took up the study of Hasidism. His *Chassidischen Bücher* (1927) made the legacy of this popular 18th-century eastern European Jewish pietistic movement a part of Western literature. In Hasidism Buber saw a healing power for the malaise of Judaism and mankind in an age of alienation that had shaken three vital human relationships: those between man and God, man and man, and man and nature. They can be restored, he asserted, only by man's again meeting the other person or being who stands over against him, on all three levels—the divine, human, and natural. Buber maintained that early Hasidism accomplished this encounter and that Zionism should follow its example.

Buber's pedagogical work reached a climax under the new conditions created by the Nazi assumption of power. In November 1933 he became head of the newly reopened Freies Jüdisches Lehrhaus for Jewish adult education in Frankfurt am Main. In 1934 he became director of the whole organization of Jewish adult education and retraining of Jewish teachers in Nazi Germany, where Jewish teachers and students were being progressively excluded from the educational system. He was a courageous spokesman of spiritual resistance.

After the Nazi secret police forbade his public lectures and then all of his teaching activities, he emigrated as a man of 60 to Palestine. He was appointed to a professorship in social philosophy at Hebrew University in Jerusalem, a post he held until 1951. He was the first president of the Israeli Academy of Sciences and Arts. After the establishment of the State of Israel, Buber initiated the founding of the Teachers Training College for Adult Education in Jerusalem and became its head (1949).

FROM MYSTICISM TO DIALOGUE

Buber's manifold activities were inspired by his philosophy of encounter—of man's meeting with other beings. An early mystical period culminated in *Daniel* (1913), five dialogues on orientation and realization, man's two basic stances toward the world. Orientation takes the world as a static state of affairs governed by comprehensible laws. It is a receptive, analytical, or systematizing attitude. Realization, on the other hand, is a creative, participative attitude that realizes the possibilities in things, experiencing through one's own full reality the full reality of the world. It operates within an open horizon of possibilities.

The *Reden über das Judentum* (1923; "Talks on Judaism") mark another step in his development. The early "Talks" were delivered in 1909–11 before large Zionist student audiences in Prague; each of the speeches tries to answer its opening question: "Jews, why do we call ourselves Jews?" To half-assimilated Zionists in search of a rationale for their Jewish existence, Buber offered his theories regarding the essence of Judaism, basing his quest for it on his listeners' assumed identity as Jews. In some of the "Talks," as well as in *Daniel*, the mystic element still prevails, but Buber later abandoned the notion of a mystical union between man and God and embraced instead the notion of their encounter, which presupposes and preserves their separate existence.

This basic view underlies Buber's mature thinking; it was expressed with great philosophic and poetic power in his famous work *Ich und Du* (1923; *I and Thou*). According to this view, God, the great Thou, enables human I–Thou relations between man and other beings. Their measure of mutuality is related to the levels of being: it is almost nil on the inorganic and botanic levels, rare on the animal level, but always possible and sometimes actual between human beings.

Martin Buber. Consulate General of Israel in New York.

A true relationship with God, as experienced from the human side, must be an I–Thou relationship, in which God is truly met and addressed, not merely thought of and expressed.

Between man and man, the I–Thou relationship into which both parties enter in the fullness of their being—as in a great love at its highest moment or in an ideal friendship—is an exception. Generally, we enter into relationships not with the fullness of our being but only with some fraction of it. This is the I–It relationship, as in scholarly pursuits in which other beings are reduced to mere objects of thought or in social relations (e.g., boss and worker) wherein persons are treated largely as tools or conveniences. This form of relationship enables the creation of pure and applied science as well as the manipulation of man by man. Buber's ethical concept of the demarcation line—to be drawn anew every day between the maximum of good that can be done in a concrete situation and the minimum of evil that must be done in it—calls for an I–Thou relation whenever possible and settles for an I–It relation whenever necessary—e.g., for the purpose of human survival.

FINAL YEARS

In his last years a group of kibbutz members turned to him with their personal and communal problems. *Siḥot loḥamin* (1967; *The Seventh Day*, 1970), published by them shortly after the Six-Day War, testifies to Buber's living spirit by its self-searching attitude on ethical questions of war and peace and on Arab–Jewish relations.

An unprecedented event occurred at Buber's funeral in Jerusalem, a high state function. A delegation of the Arab Students' Organization placed a wreath on the grave of one who strove mightily for peace between Israel's and Palestine's two peoples.

LUDWIG WITTGENSTEIN

(b. April 26, 1889, Vienna, Austria-Hungary [now in Austria]—d. April 29, 1951, Cambridge, Cambridgeshire, Eng.)

L udwig Wittgenstein was an Austrian-born English philosopher who has been regarded by many as the greatest philosopher of the 20th century. His charismatic personality has, in addition, exerted a powerful fascination upon artists, playwrights, poets, novelists, musicians, and even filmmakers, so that his fame has spread far beyond the confines of academic life.

Wittgenstein was born into one of the wealthiest and most remarkable families of Habsburg Vienna. His father, Karl Wittgenstein, was an industrialist of extraordinary talent and energy who rose to become one of the leading figures in the Austrian iron and steel industry. Although his family was originally Jewish, Karl Wittgenstein had been brought up as a Protestant, and his wife, Leopoldine, also from a partly Jewish family, had been raised as a Catholic. Karl and Leopoldine had eight children, of whom Ludwig was the youngest. The family possessed both money and talent in abundance, and their home became a centre of Viennese cultural life during one of its most dynamic phases. Leopoldine Wittgenstein played the piano to a remarkably high standard, as did many of her children. One of them, Paul, became a famous concert pianist, and another, Hans, was regarded as a musical prodigy comparable to Mozart. But the family also was beset with tragedy. Three of Ludwig's brothers—Hans, Rudolf, and Kurt—committed suicide, the first two after rebelling against their father's wish that they pursue careers in industry.

Although he shared his family's veneration for music, Wittgenstein's deepest interest as a boy was in engineering. In 1908 he went to Manchester, England, to study the then-nascent subject of aeronautics. While engaged on a project to design a jet propeller, Wittgenstein became increasingly absorbed in purely mathematical problems. After reading *The Principles of Mathematics* (1903) by Bertrand Russell and *The Foundations of Arithmetic* (1884) by Gottlob Frege, he developed an obsessive interest in the philosophy of logic and mathematics. In 1911 Wittgenstein went to Trinity College, University of Cambridge, in order to make Russell's acquaintance. From the moment he met Russell, Wittgenstein's aeronautical studies were forgotten in favour of a ferociously intense preoccupation with questions of logic.

Wittgenstein worked with such intensity on logic that within a year Russell declared that he had nothing left to teach him. Wittgenstein evidently thought so too and left Cambridge to work on his own in remote isolation in a wooden hut that he built by the side of a fjord in Norway. There he developed, in embryo, what became known as the picture theory of meaning, a central tenet of which is that a proposition can express a fact by virtue of sharing with it a common structure or "logical form." This logical form, however, precisely because it is what makes "picturing" possible, cannot itself be pictured. It follows both that logic is inexpressible and that there are—pace Frege and Russell—no logical facts or logical truths. Logical form has to be shown rather than stated, and, though some languages and methods of symbolism might reveal their structure more perspicuously than others, there is no symbolism capable of representing its own structure.

THE TRACTATUS LOGICO-PHILOSOPHICUS

In the summer of 1914, at the outbreak of World War I, Wittgenstein was staying with his family in Vienna. Unable to return to Norway to continue his work on logic, he enlisted in the Austrian army. Wittgenstein spent the first two years of the war behind the lines, relatively safe from harm and able to continue his work on logic. In 1916, however, at his own request, he was sent to a fighting unit at the Russian front. His surviving manuscripts show that during this time his philosophical work underwent a profound change. Whereas previously he had separated his thoughts on logic from his thoughts on ethics, aesthetics, and religion by writing the latter remarks in code, at this point he began to integrate the two sets of remarks, applying to all of them the distinction he had earlier made between that which can be said and that which must be shown. Ethics, aesthetics, and religion, in other words, were like logic: their "truths" were inexpressible; insight in these areas could be shown but not stated.

Near the end of the war, while he was on leave in Salzburg, Austria, Wittgenstein finally finished the book that was later published as *Tractatus Logico-Philosophicus*. In the preface he announced that he considered himself to have found "on all essential points" the solution to the problems of philosophy. For the most part, the book consists of an austerely compressed exposition of the picture theory of meaning. It ends, however, with some remarks about ethics, aesthetics, and the meaning of life, stressing that, if its view about how propositions can be meaningful is correct, then, just as there are no meaningful propositions about logical form, so there can be no meaningful propositions concerning these subjects either. This point, of course, applies to Wittgenstein's own remarks in the book itself, so Wittgenstein is forced to conclude that whoever understands his remarks "finally recognizes them as senseless"; they offer, so to speak, a ladder that one must throw away after using it to climb.

Consistent with his view that he had solved all the essential problems of philosophy, Wittgenstein abandoned the subject after World War I and instead trained to be an elementary school teacher. Meanwhile, the *Tractatus* was published and attracted the attention of two influential groups of philosophers, one based in Cambridge and including R.B. Braithwaite and Frank Ramsey and the other based in Vienna and including Moritz Schlick, Friedrich Waismann, and other logical positivists later collectively known as the Vienna Circle. Both groups tried to make contact with Wittgenstein. Frank Ramsey made two trips to Puchberg — the small Austrian village in which Wittgenstein was teaching — to discuss the *Tractatus* with him, and Schlick invited him to join the discussions of the Vienna Circle. Stimulated by these contacts, Wittgenstein's interest in philosophy revived, and, after his brief and unsuccessful career as a schoolteacher came to an end, he returned to the discipline, persuaded, largely by Ramsey, that the views he had expressed in his book were not, after all, definitively correct.

A NEW UNDERSTANDING OF PHILOSOPHY

In 1929 Wittgenstein returned to Trinity College, initially to work with Ramsey. The following year Ramsey died at the tragically young age of 26, after a spell of severe jaundice. Wittgenstein stayed on at Cambridge as a lecturer, spending his vacations in Vienna. During this time his ideas changed rapidly as he abandoned altogether the notion of logical form as it appeared in the *Tractatus*, along with the theory of meaning that it had seemed to require. Indeed, he adopted a view of philosophy that rejected entirely the construction of theories of any sort and that viewed philosophy rather as an activity, a method of clearing up the confusions that arise through misunderstandings of language.

Philosophers, Wittgenstein believed, had been misled into thinking that their subject was a kind of science, a search for theoretical explanations of the things that puzzled them: the nature of meaning, truth, mind, time, justice, and so on. But philosophical problems are not amenable to this kind of treatment, he claimed. What is required is not a correct doctrine but a clear view, one that dispels the confusion that gives rise to the problem. Many of these problems arise through an inflexible view of language that insists that if a word has a meaning there must be some kind of object corresponding to it. If we remind ourselves that language has many uses and that words can be used quite meaningfully without corresponding to things, the problem disappears.

Wittgenstein thought that he himself had succumbed to an overly narrow view of language in the *Tractatus*, concentrating on the question of how propositions acquired their meaning and ignoring all other aspects of meaningful language use. A proposition is something that is either true or false, but we do not use language only to say things that are true or false, and thus a theory of propositions is not—pace the *Tractatus*—a general theory of meaning nor even the basis of one.

Wittgenstein found the proper arrangement of his later book, *Philosophical Investigations*, enormously difficult. For the last 20 years of his life, he tried again and again to produce a version of the book that satisfied him, but he never felt he had succeeded, and he would not allow the book to be published in his lifetime. What became known as the works of the later Wittgenstein are the discarded attempts at a definitive expression of his new approach to philosophy.

The themes addressed by Wittgenstein in these post-humously published manuscripts and typescripts are so various as to defy summary. The two focal points are the traditional problems in the philosophy of mathematics (e.g., "What is mathematical truth?" and "What are numbers?") and the problems that arise from thinking about the mind (e.g., "What is consciousness?" and "What is a soul?"). Wittgenstein's method is not to engage directly in polemics against specific philosophical theories but rather to trace their source in confusions about language.

To dispel these confusions, Wittgenstein developed a method of describing and imagining what he called "language games." Language games, for Wittgenstein, are concrete social activities that crucially involve the use of specific forms of language. By describing the countless variety of language games—the countless ways in which language is actually used in human interaction—Wittgenstein meant to show that "the speaking of a language is part of an activity, or of a form of life." The meaning of a word, then, is not the object to which it corresponds but rather the use that is made of it in "the stream of life."

LAST YEARS

Wittgenstein himself several times considered leaving his academic job in favour of training to become a psychiatrist. In 1935 he even thought seriously of moving to the Soviet Union to work on a farm. When he was offered the prestigious chair of philosophy at Cambridge in 1939, he accepted, but with severe misgivings. During World War II he worked as a porter in Guy's Hospital in London and then as an assistant in a medical research team.

In 1947 he finally resigned his academic position and moved to Ireland to work on his own, as he had done in Norway before World War I. In 1949 he discovered that he had cancer of the prostate, and in 1951 he moved into his doctor's house in Cambridge, knowing that he had only a few months to live. He died on April 29, 1951. His last words were: "Tell them I've had a wonderful life."

MARTIN HEIDEGGER

(b. Sept. 26, 1889, Messkirch, Schwarzwald, Ger.—d. May 26, 1976, Messkirch, W. Ger.)

Martin Heidegger, a German philosopher, was one of the main exponents of Existentialism. His groundbreaking work in ontology and metaphysics determined the course of 20th-century philosophy on the European continent and exerted an enormous influence in virtually every other humanistic discipline, including literary criticism, hermeneutics, psychology, and theology.

BACKGROUND AND YOUTH

The son of a Roman Catholic sexton, Heidegger showed an early interest in religion. Intending to become a priest, he began theological studies at the University of Freiburg in 1909 but switched to philosophy and mathematics in 1911.

Franz Brentano's work in ontology helped to inspire Heidegger's lifelong conviction that there is a single, basic sense of the verb "to be" that lies behind all its varied usages. From Brentano Heidegger also developed his enthusiasm for the ancient Greeks—especially the pre-Socratics. In addition to these philosophers, Heidegger's work is obviously influenced by Plato, Aristotle, the Gnostic philosophers of the 2nd century CE, and several 19th- and early 20th-century thinkers, including the early figures of Existentialism, Søren Kierkegaard and Friedrich Nietzsche; Wilhelm Dilthey, who was noted for directing the attention of philosophers to the human and historical sciences; and Edmund Husserl, the founder of the phenomenological movement in philosophy.

While still in his 20s, Heidegger studied at Freiburg with Heinrich Rickert, the leading figure of the axiological school of neo-Kantianism, and with Husserl, who was then already famous. Husserl's phenomenology, and especially his struggle against the intrusion of psychologism into traditionally philosophical studies of man, determined the background of the young Heidegger's doctoral dissertation, *Die Lehre vom Urteil im Psychologismus: Ein kritisch-positiver Beitrag zur Logik* ("The Doctrine of Judgment in Psychologism: A Critical-Positive Contribution to Logic"; 1914).

PHILOSOPHY

Heidegger began teaching at the University of Freiburg during the winter semester of 1915 and wrote his habilitation thesis on the 13th-century English Franciscan philosopher Duns Scotus. As a colleague of Husserl, Heidegger was expected to carry the phenomenological movement forward in the spirit of his former master. As a religiously inclined young man, however, he went his own way instead. While serving as a professor ordinarius at Marburg University (1923–28), he astonished the German philosophical world with *Being and Time* (1927). Although almost unreadable, it was immediately felt to be of prime importance, whatever its relation to Husserl might be. In spite of—and perhaps partly because of—its intriguingly difficult style, *Being and Time* was acclaimed as a masterpiece not only in German-speaking countries but also in Latin ones, where phenomenology was well established. It strongly influenced Jean-Paul Sartre and other existentialists in France, and on the basis of this work Heidegger came to be regarded as the leading atheistic Existentialist, though he always rejected that label. The reception of *Being and Time* in the English-speaking world was chilly, however, and its influence there was negligible for several decades.

Heidegger's declared purpose in *Being and Time* is to show what it means for a person to be—or, more accurately, how it is for a person to be. This task leads to a more fundamental question: what does it mean to ask, "What is the meaning of Being?" These questions lie behind the obviousness of everyday life and, therefore, also behind the empirical questions of natural science. They are usually overlooked, because they are too near to everyday life to be grasped. One might say that Heidegger's entire prophetic mission amounts to making each person ask this question with maximum involvement. Whether one arrives at a definite answer is, in the present crisis of mankind, of secondary importance.

The wealth of ideas in *Being and Time* is best discussed in conjunction with those developed in another, shorter work, *What Is Metaphysics?* (1929), which was originally delivered as an inaugural lecture when Heidegger succeeded Husserl at Freiburg in 1928. As Heidegger learned from Husserl, it is the phenomenological and not the scientific method that unveils man's ways of Being. Thus, in pursuing this method, Heidegger comes into conflict with the dichotomy of the subject-object relation, which has traditionally implied that man, as knower, is something (some-thing) within an environment that is against him. This relation, however, must be transcended. The deepest knowing, on the contrary, is a matter of *phainesthai* (Greek: "to show itself" or "to be in the light"), the word from which phenomenology, as a method, is derived. Something is just "there" in the light. Thus, the distinction between subject and object is not immediate but comes only later through conceptualization, as in the sciences.

In the early 1930s Heidegger's thought underwent a change that scholars call his *Kehre* ("turning around"). Although some specialists regard the *Kehre* as a turning away from the central problem of *Being and Time*, Heidegger himself denied this, insisting that he had been asking the same basic question since his youth. Nevertheless, in his later years he clearly became more reluctant to offer an answer, or even to indicate a way in which an answer might be found.

HEIDEGGER AND NAZISM

In the months after the appointment of Adolf Hitler as chancellor of Germany in January 1933, German universities came under increasing pressure to support the "national revolution" and to eliminate Jewish scholars and the teaching of "Jewish" doctrines, such as the theory of relativity. After the rector of Freiburg resigned to protest these policies, the university's teaching staff elected Heidegger as his successor in April 1933. One month later, Heidegger became a member of the Nazi Party, and until he resigned as rector in April 1934 he helped to institute Nazi educational and cultural programs at Freiburg and vigorously promoted the domestic and foreign policies of the Nazi regime. In the fall of 1933, Heidegger began a speaking tour on behalf of Hitler's national referendum to withdraw Germany from the League of Nations. As he proclaimed in one speech: "Let not doctrines and ideas be your guide. The Führer is Germany's only reality and law." Heidegger continued to support Hitler in the years after his rectorship, though with somewhat less enthusiasm than he had shown in 1933–34.

At the end of the war in 1945, a favourably disposed university de-Nazification commission found Heidegger guilty of having "consciously placed the great prestige of his scholarly reputation . . . in the service of the National Socialist Revolution," and he was banned from further teaching. (The ban was lifted in 1950.) In later years, despite pleas from friends and associates to disavow publicly his Nazi past, Heidegger declined to do so. In his book *Introduction to Metaphysics*, published in 1953, Heidegger retrospectively praised "the inner truth and greatness of National Socialism." Beginning in the 1980s, there was considerable controversy among Heidegger scholars regarding the alleged connection between Heidegger's philosophy and his political views in the 1930s and '40s.

RUDOLF CARNAP

(b. May 18, 1891, Ronsdorf, Ger.—d. Sept. 14, 1970, Santa Monica, Calif., U.S.)

Rudolf Carnap was a German-born U.S. philosopher of Logical Positivism. He made important contributions to logic, the analysis of language, the theory of probability, and the philosophy of science.

From 1910 to 1914, Carnap studied mathematics, physics, and philosophy at the universities of Jena and Freiburg im Breisgau. At Jena he attended the lectures of Gottlob Frege, now widely acknowledged as the greatest logician of the 19th century, whose ideas exerted a deep influence on Carnap.

After serving in World War I, Carnap earned his doctorate in 1921 at Jena with a dissertation on the concept of space. He argued that the conflicts among the various theories of space then held by scholars resulted from the fact that those theories actually dealt with quite different subjects; he called them, respectively, formal space, physical space, and intuitive space and exhibited their principal characteristics and fundamental differences.

For several years afterward Carnap was engaged in private research in logic and the foundations of physics and wrote a number of essays on problems of space, time, and causality, as well as a textbook in symbolic, or mathematical, logic (*Abriss der Logistik*, 1929; a considerably different later German version appeared in English translation: *Introduction to Symbolic Logic and Its Applications*, 1958).

LOGICAL EMPIRICISM

In 1926 Moritz Schlick, the founder of the Vienna Circle — a small group of philosophers, mathematicians, and other scholars who met regularly to discuss philosophical issues — invited Carnap to join the faculty of the University of Vienna, where he soon became an influential member of the Circle. Out of their discussions developed the initial ideas of Logical Positivism, or Logical Empiricism. This school of thought shared its basic Empiricist orientation with David Hume, a Scottish Empiricist, and Ernst Mach, an Austrian physicist and philosopher. Its leading members, informed and inspired by the methods and theories of contemporary mathematics and science, sought to develop a "scientific world view" by bringing to philosophical inquiry the precision and rigour of the exact sciences. As one means to this end, Carnap made extensive use of the concepts and techniques of symbolic logic in preference to the often inadequate analytic devices of traditional logic.

Carnap and his associates established close connections with like-minded scholars in other countries, among them a group of Empiricists that had formed in Berlin under the leadership of Hans Reichenbach, an eminent philosopher of science. With Reichenbach, Carnap founded a periodical, *Erkenntnis* (1930–40), as a forum for the new "scientific philosophy."

The basic thesis of Empiricism, in a familiar but quite vague formulation, is that all of man's concepts and beliefs concerning the world ultimately derive from his immediate experience. In some of his most important writings, Carnap sought, in effect, to give this idea a clear and precise interpretation. Setting aside, as a psychological rather than a philosophical problem, the question of how human beings arrive at their ideas about the world, he proceeded to construe Empiricism as a systematic-logical thesis about the evidential grounding of empirical knowledge. To this end, he gave the issue a characteristically linguistic turn by asking how the terms and sentences that, in scientific or in everyday language, serve to express assertions about the world are related to those terms and sentences by which the data of immediate experience can be described. The Empiricist thesis, as construed and defended by Carnap, then asserts that the terms and sentences of the first kind are "reducible" to those of the second kind in a clearly specifiable sense. Carnap's conception of the relevant sense of reducibility, which he always stated in precise logical terms, was initially rather narrow but gradually became more liberal.

WORKS ON EMPIRICISM

In his first great work, *Der logische Aufbau der Welt* (1928; *The Logical Structure of the World: Pseudoproblems in Philosophy*), Carnap developed, with unprecedented rigour, a version of the Empiricist reducibility thesis according to which all terms suited to describe actual or possible empirical facts are fully definable by terms referring exclusively to aspects of immediate experience, so that all empirical statements are fully translatable into statements about immediate experiences.

Prompted by discussions with his associates in Vienna, Carnap soon began to develop a more liberal version of

Empiricism, which he elaborated while he was professor of natural philosophy at the German University in Prague (1931–35). He eventually presented it in full detail in his essay "Testability and Meaning" (*Philosophy of Science*, vol. 3 [1936] and 4 [1937]). Carnap argued that the terms of empirical science are not fully definable in purely experiential terms but can at least be partly defined by means of "reduction sentences," which are logically much-refined versions of operational definitions, and "observation sentences," whose truth can be checked by direct observation. Carnap stressed that usually such tests cannot provide strict proof or disproof but only more or less strong "confirmation" for an empirical statement.

Sentences that do not thus yield observational implications and therefore cannot possibly be tested and confirmed by observational findings were said to be empirically meaningless. By reference to this testability criterion of empirical significance, Carnap and other Logical Empiricists rejected various doctrines of speculative metaphysics and of theology, not as being false but as making no significant assertions at all.

Carnap argued that the observational statements by reference to which empirical statements can be tested may be construed as sentences describing directly and publicly observable aspects of physical objects, such as the needle of a measuring instrument turning to a particular point on the scale or a subject in a psychological test showing a change in pulse rate. All such sentences, he noted, can be formulated in terms that are part of the vocabulary of physics. This was the basic idea of his "physicalism," according to which all terms and statements of empirical science—from the physical to the social and historical disciplines—can be reduced to terms and statements in the language of physics.

In later writings, Carnap liberalized his conception of reducibility and of empirical significance even further so as to give a more adequate account of the relation between scientific theories and scientific evidence.

CAREER IN THE UNITED STATES

By the time "Testability and Meaning" appeared in print, Carnap had moved to the United States, mainly because of the growing threat of German National Socialism. From 1936 to 1952 he served on the faculty of the University of Chicago. During the 1940–41 school year, Carnap was a visiting professor at Harvard University and was an active participant in a discussion group that included Bertrand Russell, Alfred Tarski, and W.V.O. Quine.

Soon after going to Chicago, Carnap joined with the sociologist Otto Neurath, a former fellow member of the Vienna Circle, and with an academic colleague, the Pragmatist philosopher Charles W. Morris, in founding the *International Encyclopedia of Unified Science*, which was published, beginning in 1938, as a series of monographs on general problems in the philosophy of science and on philosophical issues concerning mathematics or particular branches of empirical science.

Since his Vienna years, Carnap had been much concerned also with problems in logic and in the philosophy of language. He held that philosophical perplexities often arise from a misunderstanding or misuse of language and that the way to resolve them is by "logical analysis of language." On this point, he agreed with the "ordinary language" school of Analytic Philosophy, which had its origins in England. He differed from it, however, in insisting that more technical issues—e.g., those in the philosophy of science or of mathematics—cannot be adequately dealt with by considerations of ordinary linguistic usage but require clarification by reference to artificially constructed languages that are formulated in logical symbolism and that have their structure and interpretation precisely specified by so-called syntactic and semantic rules. Carnap developed these ideas and the theoretical apparatus for their implementation in a series of works, including *Logische Syntax der Sprache* (1934; *The Logical Syntax of Language*) and *Meaning and Necessity* (1947; 2nd enlarged ed., 1956).

Carnap's interest in artificial languages included advocacy of international auxiliary languages such as Esperanto and Interlingua to facilitate scholarly communication and to further international understanding.

One idea in logic and the theory of knowledge that occupied much of Carnap's attention was that of analyticity. In contrast to the 19th-century radical Empiricism of John Stuart Mill, Carnap and other Logical Empiricists held that the statements of logic and mathematics, unlike those of empirical science, are analytic—i.e., true solely by virtue of the meanings of their constituent terms—and that they can therefore be established a priori (without any empirical test). Carnap repeatedly returned to the task of formulating a precise characterization and theory of analyticity. His ideas were met with skepticism by some, however—among them Quine, who argued that the notion of analytic truth is inherently obscure and the attempt to delimit a class of statements that are true a priori should be abandoned as misguided.

From about 1945 onward, Carnap turned his efforts increasingly to problems of inductive reasoning and of rational belief and decision. His principal aim was to construct a formal system of inductive logic; its central concept, corresponding to that of deductive implication, would be that of probabilistic implication—or, more precisely, a concept representing the degree of rational credibility or of probability that a given body of evidence may be said to confer upon a proposed hypothesis. Carnap presented a rigorous theory of this kind in his *Logical Foundations of Probability* (1950).

Carnap spent the years from 1952 to 1954 at the Institute for Advanced Study in Princeton, where he continued his work in probability theory. Subsequently, he accepted a professorship at the University of California at Los Angeles. During those years and indeed until his death, Carnap was occupied principally with modifications and considerable extensions of his inductive logic.

SIR KARL POPPER

(b. July 28, 1902, Vienna, Austria—d. Sept. 17, 1994, Croydon, Greater London, Eng.)

Karl Popper was an Austrian-born British philosopher of natural and social science. He subscribed to an antideterminist metaphysics, believing that knowledge evolves from experience of the mind.

Although his first book, *Logik der Forschung* (1934; *The Logic of Scientific Discovery*), was published by the Vienna Circle of logical positivists, Popper rejected their inductive empiricism and developmental historicism. After studying mathematics, physics, and psychology at the University of Vienna, he taught philosophy at Canterbury University College, New Zealand (1937–45). In 1945 he became a reader in logic at the London School of Economics, and he served there as professor of logic and scientific method from 1949 until his retirement in 1969.

Popper's principal contribution to the philosophy of science rests on his rejection of the inductive method in the empirical sciences. According to this traditional view, a scientific hypothesis may be tested and verified by

obtaining the repeated outcome of substantiating observations. As the Scottish empiricist David Hume had shown,
however, only an infinite number of such confirming
results could prove the theory correct. Popper argued
instead that hypotheses are deductively validated by what
he called the "falsifiability criterion." Under this method,
a scientist seeks to discover an observed exception to his
postulated rule. The absence of contradictory evidence
thereby becomes corroboration of his theory. According
to Popper, such pseudosciences as astrology, metaphysics,
Marxist history, and Freudian psychoanalysis are not
empirical sciences, because of their failure to adhere to
the principle of falsifiability.

Popper's later works include *The Open Society and Its
Enemies* (1945), *The Poverty of Historicism* (1957), and
Postscript to the Logic of Scientific Discovery, 3 vol. (1981–82).
He was knighted in 1965.

THEODOR WIESENGRUND ADORNO
(b. Sept. 11, 1903, Frankfurt am Main, Ger.—d. Aug. 6, 1969, Visp, Switz.)

Theodor Wiesengrund Adorno was a German philosopher who also wrote on sociology, psychology, and
musicology. Adorno obtained a degree in philosophy from
Johann Wolfgang Goethe University in Frankfurt in 1924.
His early writings, which emphasize aesthetic development
as important to historical evolution, reflect the influence
of Walter Benjamin's application of Marxism to cultural
criticism.

After teaching two years at the University of Frankfurt,
Adorno immigrated to England in 1934 to escape the Nazi
persecution of the Jews. He taught at the University of
Oxford for three years and then went to the United States
(1938), where he worked at Princeton (1938–41) and then

was codirector of the Research Project on Social Discrimination at the University of California, Berkeley (1941–48). Adorno and his colleague Max Horkheimer returned to the University of Frankfurt in 1949. There they rebuilt the Institute for Social Research and revived the Frankfurt school of critical theory, which contributed to the German intellectual revival after World War II.

One of Adorno's themes was civilization's tendency to self-destruction, as evinced by Fascism. In their widely influential book *Dialektik der Aufklärung* (1947; *Dialectic of Enlightenment*), Adorno and Horkheimer located this impulse in the concept of reason itself, which the Enlightenment and modern scientific thought had transformed into an irrational force that had come to dominate not only nature but humanity itself. The rationalization of human society had ultimately led to Fascism and other totalitarian regimes that represented a complete negation of human freedom. Adorno concluded that rationalism offers little hope for human emancipation, which might come instead from art and the prospects it offers for preserving individual autonomy and happiness. Adorno's other major publications are *Philosophie der neuen Musik* (1949; *Philosophy of Modern Music*), *The Authoritarian Personality* (1950, with others), *Negative Dialektik* (1966; *Negative Dialectics*), and *Ästhetische Theorie* (1970; "Aesthetic Theory").

JEAN-PAUL SARTRE

(b. June 21, 1905, Paris, France — d. April 15, 1980, Paris)

Jean-Paul Sartre was a French exponent of Existentialism — a philosophy acclaiming the freedom of the individual human being. Also a novelist and a playwright, he was awarded the Nobel Prize for Literature in 1964, but he declined it.

Early Life and Writings

Sartre lost his father at an early age and grew up in the home of his maternal grandfather, Carl Schweitzer, uncle of the medical missionary Albert Schweitzer and himself professor of German at the Sorbonne. The boy, who wandered in the Luxembourg Gardens of Paris in search of playmates, was small in stature and cross-eyed.

Sartre went to the Lycée Henri IV in Paris and, later on, after the remarriage of his mother, to the lycée in La Rochelle. From there he went to the prestigious École Normale Supérieure, from which he was graduated in 1929. Sartre resisted what he called "bourgeois marriage," but while still a student he formed with Simone de Beauvoir a union that remained a settled partnership in life. From 1931 until 1945 Sartre taught in the lycées of Le Havre, Laon, and, finally, Paris. Twice this career was interrupted, once by a year of study in Berlin and the second time when Sartre was drafted in 1939 to serve in World War II. He was made prisoner in 1940 and released a year later.

During his years of teaching in Le Havre, Sartre published *La Nausée* (1938; *Nausea*, 1949), his first claim to fame. This novel, written in the form of a diary, narrates the feeling of revulsion that a certain Roquentin undergoes when confronted with the world of matter—not merely the world of other people but the very awareness of his own body.

Sartre took over the phenomenological method, which proposes careful, unprejudiced description rather than deduction, from the German philosopher Edmund Husserl and used it with great skill in three successive publications: *L'Imagination* (1936; *Imagination: A Psychological Critique*, 1962), *Esquisse d'une théorie des émotions* (1939; *Sketch for a Theory of the Emotions*, 1962), and *L'Imaginaire: Psychologie phénoménologique de l'imagination* (1940; *The Psychology of Imagination*, 1950). But it was above all in *L'Être et le néant* (1943; *Being and Nothingness*, 1956) that Sartre revealed himself as a master of outstanding talent. Sartre places human consciousness, or no-thingness (*néant*), in opposition to being, or thingness (*être*). Consciousness is not-matter and by the same token escapes all determinism. The message, with all the implications it contains, is a hopeful one; yet the incessant reminder that human endeavour is and remains useless makes the book tragic as well.

POST-WORLD WAR II WORK

Having written his defense of individual freedom and

Jean-Paul Sartre, photographed in the 1940s. Hulton Archive/Getty Images

human dignity, Sartre turned his attention to the concept of social responsibility. For many years he had shown great concern for the poor and the disinherited of all kinds. While a teacher, he had refused to wear a tie, as if he could shed his social class with his tie and thus come closer to the worker. Freedom itself, which at times in his previous writings appeared to be a gratuitous activity that needed no particular aim or purpose to be of value, became a tool for human struggle in his brochure *L'Existentialisme est un humanisme* (1946; *Existentialism and Humanism*, 1948). Freedom now implied social responsibility.

In his novels and plays Sartre began to bring his ethical message to the world at large. He started a four-volume novel in 1945 under the title *Les Chemins de la liberté*, of which three were eventually written: *L'Âge de raison* (1945; *The Age of Reason*, 1947), *Le Sursis* (1945; *The Reprieve*, 1947), and *La Mort dans l'âme* (1949; *Iron in the Soul*, 1950; U.S. title, *Troubled Sleep*, 1950).

After the publication of the third volume, Sartre changed his mind concerning the usefulness of the novel as a medium of communication and turned back to plays. All the plays, in their emphasis upon the raw hostility of man toward man, seem to be predominantly pessimistic; yet, according to Sartre's own confession, their content does not exclude the possibility of a morality of salvation. Other publications of the same period include a book, *Baudelaire* (1947), a vaguely ethical study on the French writer and poet Jean Genet entitled *Saint Genet, comédien et martyr* (1952; *Saint Genet, Actor and Martyr*, 1963), and innumerable articles that were published in *Les Temps Modernes*, the monthly review that Sartre and Simone de Beauvoir founded and edited.

POLITICAL ACTIVITIES

After World War II, Sartre took an active interest in French political movements, and his leanings to the left became more pronounced. He became an outspoken admirer of the Soviet Union, although he did not become a member of the Communist Party. Upon the entry of Soviet tanks into Budapest in 1956, however, Sartre's hopes for communism were sadly crushed. He wrote in *Les Temps*

Modernes a long article, "Le Fantôme de Staline," that condemned both the Soviet intervention and the submission
of the French Communist Party to the dictates of Moscow.
Over the years this critical attitude opened the way to a
form of "Sartrian Socialism" that would find its expression
in a new major work, *Critique de la raison dialectique* (1960;
Eng. trans., of the introduction only, under the title *The
Problem of Method*, 1963; U.S. title, *Search for a Method*).

LAST YEARS

From 1960 until 1971 most of Sartre's attention went into
the writing of a four-volume study called *Flaubert*. Two
volumes with a total of some 2,130 pages appeared in the
spring of 1971. This huge enterprise aimed at presenting
the reader with a "total biography" of Gustave Flaubert, the
famous French novelist, through the use of a double tool:
on the one hand, Karl Marx's concept of history and class
and, on the other, Sigmund Freud's illuminations of the
dark recesses of the human soul through explorations into
his childhood and family relations.

As if he himself were saturated by the prodigal abundance of his writings, Sartre moved away from his desk
during 1971 and did very little writing. Under the motto
that "commitment is an act, not a word," Sartre often went
into the streets to participate in rioting, in the sale of
left-wing literature, and in other activities that in his
opinion were the way to promote "the revolution." Paradoxically enough, this same radical Socialist published in
1972 the third volume of the work on Flaubert, *L'Idiot de
la famille*, another book of such density that only the
bourgeois intellectual can read it.

The enormous productivity of Sartre came herewith
to a close. Sartre became blind and his health deteriorated.

In April 1980 he died of a lung tumour. His very impressive funeral, attended by some 25,000 people, was reminiscent of the burial of Victor Hugo, but without the official recognition that his illustrious predecessor had received.

HANNAH ARENDT

(b. Oct. 14, 1906, Hannover, Ger.—d. Dec. 4, 1975, New York, N.Y., U.S.)

Hannah Arendt was a German-born American political scientist and philosopher who is known for her critical writing on Jewish affairs and her study of totalitarianism.

Arendt grew up in Hannover, Germany, and in Königsberg, Prussia (now Kaliningrad, Russia). Beginning in 1924 she studied philosophy at the Universities of Marburg, Freiburg, and Heidelberg; she received a doctoral degree in philosophy at Heidelberg in 1928. At Marburg she began a romantic relationship with her teacher, Martin Heidegger, that lasted until 1928. In 1933, when Heidegger joined the Nazi Party and began implementing Nazi educational policies as rector of Freiburg, Arendt, who was Jewish, was forced to flee to Paris. She married Heinrich Blücher, a philosophy professor, in 1940. She again became a fugitive from the Nazis in 1941, when she and her husband immigrated to the United States.

Settling in New York City, she became research director of the Conference on Jewish Relations (1944–46), chief editor of Schocken Books (1946–48), and executive director (1949–52) of Jewish Cultural Reconstruction, Inc., which sought to salvage Jewish writings dispersed by the Nazis. She was naturalized as an American citizen in 1951. She taught at the University of Chicago from 1963 to 1967 and thereafter at the New School for Social Research in New York City.

An informal photographic portrait of Hannah Arendt, taken in 1972. New York Times Co./Hulton Archive/Getty Images

Arendt's reputation as a major political thinker was established by her *Origins of Totalitarianism* (1951), which also treated 19th-century anti-Semitism, imperialism, and racism. Arendt viewed the growth of totalitarianism as the outcome of the disintegration of the traditional nation-state. She argued that totalitarian regimes, through their pursuit of raw political power and their neglect of material or utilitarian considerations, had revolutionized the social structure and made contemporary politics nearly impossible to predict.

The Human Condition, published in 1958, was a wide-ranging and systematic treatment of what Arendt called the *vita activa* (Latin: "active life"). She defended the classical ideals of work, citizenship, and political action against what she considered a debased obsession with mere welfare. Like most of her work, it owed a great deal to the philosophical style of Heidegger.

In a highly controversial work, *Eichmann in Jerusalem* (1963), based on her reportage of the trial of the Nazi war criminal Adolf Eichmann in 1961, Arendt argued that Eichmann's crimes resulted not from a wicked or depraved character but from sheer "thoughtlessness": he was simply an ambitious bureaucrat who failed to reflect on the enormity of what he was doing. His role in the mass extermination of Jews epitomized "the fearsome, word-and-thought-defying banality of evil" that had spread across Europe at the time. Arendt's refusal to recognize Eichmann as "inwardly" evil prompted fierce denunciations from both Jewish and non-Jewish intellectuals.

Arendt resumed contact with Heidegger in 1950, and in subsequent essays and lectures she defended him by claiming that his Nazi involvement had been the "mistake" of a great philosopher. In the late 20th century, following the publication of a volume of letters between Arendt and Heidegger written between 1925 and 1975, some scholars suggested that Arendt's personal and intellectual attachment to her former teacher had led her to adopt a lenient assessment of him that was inconsistent with her condemnation of the collaboration of others and with her insistence in various writings that any act of compromise with evil is wholly immoral.

Arendt's other works include *Between Past and Future* (1961), *On Revolution* (1963), *Men in Dark Times* (1968), *On Violence* (1970), and *Crises of the Republic* (1972). Her unfinished manuscript *The Life of the Mind* was edited by her friend and correspondent Mary McCarthy and published in 1978. *Responsibility and Judgment*, published in 2003, collects essays and lectures on moral topics from the years following publication of *Eichmann in Jerusalem*.

SIMONE DE BEAUVOIR

(b. Jan. 9, 1908, Paris, France—d. April 14, 1986, Paris)

Simone de Beauvoir, a French writer and feminist, was a member of the intellectual fellowship of philosopher-writers who gave literary expression to the themes of Existentialism. She is known primarily for her treatise *Le Deuxième Sexe*, 2 vol. (1949; *The Second Sex*), a scholarly and passionate plea for the abolition of what she called the myth of the "eternal feminine." This seminal work became a classic of feminist literature.

Schooled in private institutions, de Beauvoir attended the Sorbonne, where, in 1929, she passed her *agrégation* in philosophy and met Jean-Paul Sartre, beginning a lifelong association with him. She taught at a number of schools (1931–43) before turning to writing for her livelihood. In 1945 she and Sartre founded and began editing *Le Temps Modernes*, a monthly review.

Jean-Paul Sartre walks with Simone de Beauvoir in Paris in 1970. Hulton Archive/Getty Images

Her novels expound the major Existential themes, demonstrating her conception of the writer's commitment to the times. *L'Invitée* (1943; *She Came to Stay*) describes the subtle destruction of a couple's relationship brought about by a young girl's prolonged stay in their home; it also treats the difficult problem of the relationship of a conscience to "the other," each individual conscience being fundamentally a predator to another. Of her other works of fiction, perhaps the best known is *Les Mandarins* (1954; *The Mandarins*), for which she won the Prix Goncourt. It is a chronicle of the attempts of post-World War II intellectuals to leave their "mandarin" (educated elite) status and engage in political activism. She also wrote four books of philosophy, including *Pour une Morale de l'ambiguité* (1947; *The Ethics of Ambiguity*); travel books on China (*La Longue Marche: essai sur la Chine* [1957]; *The Long March*) and the United States (*L'Amérique au jour de jour* [1948]; *America Day by Day*); and a number of essays, some of them book-length, the best known of which is *The Second Sex*.

Several volumes of her work are devoted to autobiography. These include *Mémoires d'une jeune fille rangée* (1958; *Memoirs of a Dutiful Daughter*), *La Force de l'âge* (1960; *The Prime of Life*), *La Force des choses* (1963; *Force of Circumstance*), and *Tout compte fait* (1972; *All Said and Done*). This body of work, beyond its personal interest, constitutes a clear and telling portrait of French intellectual life from the 1930s to the 1970s.

In addition to treating feminist issues, de Beauvoir was concerned with the issue of aging, which she addressed in *Une Mort très douce* (1964; *A Very Easy Death*), on her mother's death in a hospital, and in *La Vieillesse* (1970; *Old Age*), a bitter reflection on society's indifference to the elderly. In 1981 she wrote *La Cérémonie des adieux* (*Adieux: A Farewell to Sartre*), a painful account of Sartre's last years. *Simone de Beauvoir: A Biography*, by Deirdre Bair, appeared in 1990.

Simone de Beauvoir revealed herself as a woman of formidable courage and integrity, whose life supported her thesis: the basic options of an individual must be made on the premises of an equal vocation for man and woman founded on a common structure of their being, independent of their sexuality.

WILLARD VAN ORMAN QUINE
(b. June 25, 1908, Akron, Ohio, U.S.—d. Dec. 25, 2000, Boston, Mass.)

Willard Van Orman Quine, an American philosopher and logician, is widely considered one of the dominant figures in Anglo-American (analytic) philosophy in the last half of the 20th century.

After studying mathematics and logic at Oberlin College (1926–30), Quine won a scholarship to Harvard University, where he completed his Ph.D. in 1932. On a travelling fellowship to Europe in 1932–33, he met some of the leading philosophers and logicians of the day, including Rudolf Carnap and Alfred Tarski. After three years as a junior fellow at Harvard, Quine joined the faculty in 1936. From 1942 to 1945 he served as a naval intelligence officer in Washington, D.C. Promoted to full professor at Harvard in 1948, he remained there until 1978, when he retired.

Quine produced highly original and important work in several areas of philosophy, including logic, ontology, epistemology, and the philosophy of language. By the 1950s he had developed a comprehensive and systematic philosophical outlook that was naturalistic, empiricist, and behaviourist. Conceiving of philosophy as an extension of science, he rejected epistemological foundationalism, the attempt to ground knowledge of the external world in allegedly transcendent and self-validating mental experience. The proper task of a "naturalized epistemology," as he saw it, was simply to give a psychological account of how scientific knowledge is actually obtained.

Although much influenced by the Logical Positivism of Carnap and other members of the Vienna Circle, Quine famously rejected one of that group's cardinal doctrines, the analytic-synthetic distinction. According to this doctrine, there is a fundamental difference between statements such as "All bachelors are unmarried," which are true or false solely by virtue of the meanings of the terms they contain, and statements such as "All swans are white," which are true or false by virtue of nonlinguistic facts about the world. Quine argued that no coherent definition of analyticity had ever been proposed. One consequence of his view was that the truths of mathematics and logic, which the positivists had regarded as analytic, and the empirical truths of science differed only in "degree" and not kind. In keeping with his empiricism, Quine held that both the former and the latter were known through experience and were thus in principle revisable in the face of countervailing evidence.

In ontology, Quine recognized only those entities that it was necessary to postulate in order to assume that our best scientific theories are true—specifically, concrete physical objects and abstract sets, which were required by the mathematics used in many scientific disciplines. He rejected notions such as properties, propositions, and meanings as ill-defined or scientifically useless.

In the philosophy of language, Quine was known for his behaviourist account of language learning and for his thesis of the "indeterminacy of translation." This is the view that there are always indefinitely many possible translations of one language into another, each of which is equally compatible with the totality of empirical evidence available to linguistic investigators. There is thus no "fact of the matter" about which translation of a language is correct. The indeterminacy of translation is an instance of a more general view, which Quine called "ontological relativity," that claims that for any given scientific theory there are always indefinitely many alternatives entailing different ontological assumptions but accounting for all available evidence equally well. Thus, it does not make sense to say that one theory rather than another gives a true description of the world.

Among Quine's many books are *Word and Object* (1960), *The Roots of Reference* (1974), and his autobiography, *The Time of My Life* (1985).

SIR A.J. AYER

(b. Oct. 29, 1910, London, Eng.—d. June 27, 1989, London)

A.J. Ayer was a British philosopher and educator and a leading representative of Logical Positivism through his widely read work *Language, Truth, and Logic* (1936).

Although Ayer was raised in London, both his father, a French Swiss businessman, and his mother, a Dutch citizen of Jewish ancestry, were born abroad, and Ayer grew up speaking French fluently. An extremely able, though sensitive, boy, he won a scholarship to Eton College (1923), where he excelled in classics but had no opportunity to study science, an omission that he would always regret. In 1929 he won a classics scholarship to the University of Oxford, where he also studied philosophy. His tutor, Gilbert Ryle (1900–76), soon described Ayer as "the best student I have yet been taught by."

LANGUAGE, TRUTH, AND LOGIC

Having secured a fellowship at the college of Christ Church, Ayer spent part of 1933 in Vienna, where he attended meetings of the Vienna Circle, a group of mostly German and Austrian philosophers and scientists who were just then beginning to attract the attention of philosophers in England and the United States. Although Ayer spoke poor German and was hardly able to take part in the discussions, he became convinced that the doctrine of Logical Positivism that the group was developing marked an important advance in the empiricist tradition, and he returned home an ardent convert. Within two and a half years he had written a manifesto for the movement, *Language, Truth, and Logic.*

In this work, following Wittgenstein and the members of the Vienna Circle, Ayer defended a verificationist theory of meaning (also called the verifiability principle), according to which an utterance is meaningful only if it expresses a proposition the truth or falsehood of which can be verified (at least in principle) through experience. He used this theory to argue that metaphysical talk about God, the cosmos, or "transcendent values" was not merely, as earlier empiricists had maintained, excessively conjectural but literally meaningless. Ayer's specific contribution was to develop this argument with unusual clearheadedness and rigour, showing how statements about the external world, other minds, and the past could be accorded sense through an analysis in verificationist terms. His argument that statements of moral evaluation, because they are unverifiable, are not descriptions of fact but merely "emotive" expressions of feeling aroused particular controversy.

Although Ayer claimed that *Language, Truth, and Logic* answered all major philosophical questions, the problems he had so confidently "solved" soon came back to haunt him. In a series of important papers and a book, *The Foundations of Empirical Knowledge* (1940), he wrestled with critics who doubted that all meaningful discourse could be analyzed in terms of sense experience.

In the years surrounding the publication of *Language, Truth, and Logic*, philosophy had to compete with more pressing concerns. Like many young men of the period,

Ayer was critical of what he saw as the British government's do-nothing approach to the rise of unemployment at home and of fascism abroad. After briefly considering joining the British Communist Party, Ayer instead joined the Labour Party. An early and forthright critic of Neville Chamberlain's policy of appeasement, Ayer volunteered for the Welsh Guards as soon as war broke out. After completing officer training, he joined an intelligence unit, eventually becoming a specialist on France and the French Resistance and gaining the rank of major. His war assignments took him to New York, to Algeria, and, after the liberation of France, to the southern part of that country and to Paris.

THE PROBLEM OF KNOWLEDGE

At the end of the war, Ayer at last secured an Oxford fellowship. One year later, in 1946, he was appointed Grote Professor of Mental Philosophy at University College, London. Although little philosophy had been published in England during the war, Ayer found that the philosophical climate was now very different. Influenced by the ideas of the later Wittgenstein, which were only then becoming known outside Cambridge, a group of philosophers at Oxford, led by Gilbert Ryle and J.L. Austin (1911–60), were arguing persuasively that most philosophical problems were simply conceptual confusions resulting from philosophers' insufficient attention to the complex ways in which philosophically loaded terms and their cognates were used in ordinary speech. Although Ayer well understood the Oxford philosophers' weariness with metaphysical speculation and supported their commitment to careful conceptual analysis, he did not share their hostility toward philosophical theorizing.

The next decade and a half, until the early 1960s, was perhaps the most fruitful of Ayer's life. He transformed the University College philosophy department into one of the best in the country, rivaling those of Cambridge and even Oxford. He edited several series of books, presided over various discussion groups, developed a friendship with his hero Bertrand Russell, lectured around the world, and made lively contributions to literary journals and radio broadcasts. At the same time, he produced a series of influential papers and what was probably his most philosophically successful book, *The Problem of Knowledge* (1956).

In this work the great combative proclamations of *Language, Truth, and Logic* were replaced by a quieter treatment of skepticism. Whereas Ayer previously had in effect pursued a "reductionism" of all meaningful propositions to the sense-data by which they are verified, he now admitted that not everything can be translated into the language of the senses; instead, the constructions made on the basis of experience have their own inherent validity.

Later Years

Ayer was metropolitan in his tastes, enjoying the company of writers, actors, and politicians as much as that of philosophers. It was with some misgivings, then, that in 1959 Ayer returned to Oxford to become Wykeham Professor of Logic. As it was, his tenure there, until his retirement in 1978, proved extremely happy. In 1973 he published *The Central Questions of Philosophy*, in which he returned to familiar topics in the theory of knowledge and presented a commonsense conception of the world as a theory founded on the basis of sense-data.

The last decade of Ayer's life was troubled. In 1980 his first wife, Renee Lees, whom he had divorced in 1945, died, and one year later their daughter Valerie died suddenly of Hodgkin's disease. In 1982 he divorced his second wife, the writer Dee Wells. His third wife, Vanessa Lawson (formerly married to Nigel Lawson, the chancellor of the Exchequer), died in 1984, leaving him bereft. Suffering from emphysema, he collapsed in 1988 and underwent a remarkable near-death experience, in which, as he later described, he seemed to encounter the "Master of the Universe" and his ministers for space and time. (His account was misunderstood by some critics as a recantation of his atheism.)

Just before his real death in 1989, Ayer remarried Dee Wells and was united with his daughter born to the Hollywood gossip columnist Sheilah Graham. It was an end in keeping with his colourful, eventful private life.

WILFRID SELLARS

(b. May 20, 1912, Ann Arbor, Mich., U.S.—d. July 2, 1989, Pittsburgh, Pa.)

Wilfrid Sellars, an American philosopher, is best known for his critique of traditional philosophical conceptions of mind and knowledge and for his uncompromising effort to explain how human reason and thought can be reconciled with the vision of nature found in science. Although he was one of the most original and influential American philosophers of the second half of the 20th century, he remains largely unknown outside academic circles.

Sellars's father, Roy Sellars, was a distinguished Canadian philosopher. After studying at the University of Michigan and the University of Buffalo, the younger Sellars was awarded a Rhodes scholarship to the University of Oxford, where he earned bachelor's (1936) and master's (1940) degrees in philosophy, politics, and economics. He was appointed assistant professor of philosophy at the

University of Iowa in 1938. After serving as an intelligence officer in the U.S. Navy (1943–46), he was appointed assistant professor of philosophy at the University of Minnesota. He was professor of philosophy at Yale University from 1959 to 1963 and University Professor of Philosophy and Research Professor of Philosophy at the University of Pittsburgh from 1963 until his death.

Sellars came to prominence in 1956 with the publication of his essay *Empiricism and the Philosophy of Mind*, a critique of a conception of mind and knowledge inherited from René Descartes (1596–1650). Sellars there attacked what he called the "myth of the given," the Cartesian idea that one can have immediate and indubitable perceptual knowledge of one's own sense experiences. Sellars's ideas anticipated and contributed to the development of theories of mind, knowledge, and science that played significant roles in later debates on these topics.

Sellars was an articulate exponent of the modernist enterprise of reconciling the comprehensive picture of reality emerging from the theoretical activities of natural science with the traditional conception of human beings as morally accountable agents and subjective centres of experience. In *Philosophy and the Scientific Image of Man* (1960), he characterized this project as bringing together into one "synoptic view" two competing images of "man-in-the-world": the "scientific" image derived from the fruits of theory construction and the "manifest" image, the "framework in terms of which man encountered himself."

Sellars subscribed to a form of philosophical naturalism according to which science is the final arbiter of what exists. Entities exist if and only if they would be invoked in a complete scientific explanation of the world. His synoptic project, however, required him to develop ways of accommodating dimensions of human experience that seem initially to resist incorporation into the "scientific image." Science describes how humans do think and act, for example, but not how they ought to think and act, and this latter element therefore requires explanation if it is to be reconciled with Sellars's naturalism. His fundamental response to these challenges was to develop a sophisticated theory of conceptual roles, concretely instantiated in human conduct and transmitted by modes of social interaction, including language. He used this theory in turn to defend a form of linguistic nominalism, the denial of the real existence of universals or irreducibly mentalistic entities as the referents or meanings of linguistic expressions. Sellars also introduced the functionalist idea of explaining semantic meaning in terms of the inferential and ultimately behavioral roles played by particular linguistic expressions, a view later known as conceptual-role semantics.

Sellars's major published works, in addition to the essays mentioned above, include *Science, Perception, and Reality* (1963), *Philosophical Perspectives* (1967), *Science and Metaphysics: Variations on Kantian Themes* (1968), *Naturalism and Ontology* (1979), and *Foundations for a Metaphysics of Pure Process* (1981).

JOHN RAWLS

(b. Feb. 21, 1921, Baltimore, Md., U.S.—d. Nov. 24, 2002, Lexington, Mass.)

John Rawls was an American political and ethical philosopher. He is widely considered the most important political philosopher of the 20th century.

Rawls was the second of five children of William Lee Rawls and Anna Abell Stump. After attending an Episcopalian preparatory school, Kent School, in Connecticut, he entered Princeton University, where he earned a bachelor's degree in 1943. He enlisted in the army later that year and served with the infantry in the South Pacific until his discharge in 1945. He returned to Princeton in 1946 and earned a Ph.D. in moral philosophy in 1950. He taught at Princeton (1950–52), Cornell University (1953–59), the Massachusetts Institute of Technology (1960–62), and finally Harvard University, where he was appointed James Bryant Conant University Professor in 1979.

In *A Theory of Justice*, Rawls defends a conception of "justice as fairness." He holds that an adequate account of justice cannot be derived from utilitarianism, because that doctrine is consistent with intuitively undesirable forms of government in which the greater happiness of a majority is achieved by neglecting the rights and interests of a minority. Reviving the notion of a social contract, Rawls argues that justice consists of the basic principles of government that free and rational individuals would agree to in a hypothetical situation of perfect equality. In order to ensure that the principles chosen are fair, Rawls imagines a group of individuals who have been made ignorant of the social, economic, and historical circumstances from which they come, as well as their basic values and goals, including their conception of what constitutes a "good life." Situated behind this "veil of ignorance," they could not be influenced by self-interested desires to benefit some social groups (i.e., the groups they belong to) at the expense of others. Thus they would not know any facts about their race, sex, age, religion, social or economic class, wealth, income, intelligence, abilities, talents, and so on.

In this "original position," as Rawls characterizes it, any group of individuals would be led by reason and self-interest to agree to the following principles: (1) Each person is to have an equal right to the most extensive basic liberty compatible with a similar liberty for others, and (2) Social and economic inequalities are to be arranged so that they are both (*a*) to the greatest benefit of the least advantaged and (*b*) attached to offices and positions open to all under conditions of fair equality of opportunity.

The "basic liberty" mentioned in principle 1 comprises most of the rights and liberties traditionally associated with liberalism and democracy: freedom of thought and conscience, freedom of association, the right to representative government, the right to form and join political parties, the right to personal property, and the rights and liberties necessary to secure the rule of law. Economic rights and liberties, such as freedom of contract or the right to own means of production, are not among the basic liberties as Rawls construes them. Basic liberties cannot be infringed under any circumstances, even if doing so would increase the aggregate welfare, improve economic efficiency, or augment the income of the poor.

Clause *b* of principle 2 provides that everyone has a fair and equal opportunity to compete for desirable public or private offices and positions. This entails that society must provide all citizens with the basic means necessary to participate in such competition, including appropriate education and health care. Clause *a* of principle 2 is known as the "difference principle": it requires that any unequal distribution of wealth and income be such that those who are worst off are better off than they would be under any other distribution consistent with principle 1, including an equal distribution. (Rawls holds that some inequality of wealth and income is probably necessary in order to maintain high levels of productivity.)

In Rawls's view, Soviet-style communism is unjust because it is incompatible with most basic liberties and because it does not provide everyone with a fair and equal opportunity to obtain desirable offices and positions. Pure laissez-faire capitalism is also unjust, because it tends to produce an unjust distribution of wealth and income (concentrated in the hands of a few), which in turn effectively deprives some (if not most) citizens of the basic means necessary to compete fairly for desirable offices and positions. A just society, according to Rawls, would be a "property-owning democracy" in which ownership of the means of production is widely distributed and those who are worst off are prosperous enough to be economically independent.

THOMAS S. KUHN

(b. July 18, 1922, Cincinnati, Ohio, U.S.—d. June 17, 1996, Cambridge, Mass.)

Thomas S. Kuhn was an American philosopher and historian of science who is noted for *The Structure of Scientific Revolutions* (1962), one of the most influential works of history and philosophy written in the 20th century.

Kuhn earned bachelor's (1943) and master's (1946) degrees in physics at Harvard University but obtained his Ph.D. (1949) there in the history of science. He taught the history or philosophy of science at Harvard (1951–56), the University of California at Berkeley (1956–64), Princeton University (1964–79), and the Massachusetts Institute of Technology (1979–91).

In his first book, *The Copernican Revolution* (1957), Kuhn studied the development of the heliocentric theory of the solar system during the Renaissance. In his landmark second book, *The Structure of Scientific Revolutions*, he argued that scientific research and thought are defined by "paradigms," or conceptual world-views, that consist of formal theories, classic experiments, and trusted methods. Scientists typically accept a prevailing paradigm and try to extend its scope by refining theories, explaining puzzling data, and establishing more precise measures of standards and phenomena. Eventually, however, their efforts may generate insoluble theoretical problems or experimental anomalies that expose a paradigm's inadequacies or contradict it altogether. This accumulation of difficulties triggers a crisis that can only be resolved by an intellectual revolution that replaces an old paradigm with a new one. The overthrow of Ptolemaic cosmology by Copernican heliocentrism, and the displacement of Newtonian mechanics by quantum physics and general relativity, are both examples of major paradigm shifts.

Kuhn questioned the traditional conception of scientific progress as a gradual, cumulative acquisition of knowledge based on rationally chosen experimental frameworks. Instead, he argued that the paradigm determines the kinds of experiments scientists perform, the types of questions they ask, and the problems they consider important. A shift in the paradigm alters the fundamental concepts underlying research and inspires new standards of evidence, new research techniques, and new pathways of theory and experiment that are radically incommensurate with the old ones.

Kuhn's book revolutionized the history and philosophy of science, and his concept of paradigm shifts was extended to such disciplines as political science, economics, sociology, and even to business management. Kuhn's later works were a collection of essays, *The Essential Tension* (1977), and the technical study *Black-Body Theory and the Quantum Discontinuity* (1978).

MICHEL FOUCAULT

(b. Oct. 15, 1926, Poitiers, France — d. June 25, 1984, Paris)

M ichel Foucault was a French philosopher and historian and one of the most influential and controversial scholars of the post-World War II period.

The son and grandson of a physician, Michel Foucault was born to a solidly bourgeois family. A distinguished but sometimes erratic student, Foucault gained entry at the age of 20 to the École Normale Supérieure (ENS) in Paris in 1946. After graduating in 1952, Foucault first taught at the University of Lille, then spent five years (1955–60) as a cultural attaché in Uppsala, Sweden; Warsaw, Poland; and Hamburg, West Germany (now Germany). He defended his doctoral dissertation at the ENS in 1961. Circulated under the title *Folie et déraison: histoire de la folie à l'âge classique* ("Madness and Unreason: A History of Madness in the Classical Age"), it won critical praise but a limited audience. (An abridged version was translated into English and published in 1965 as *Madness and Civilization: A History of Insanity in the Age of Reason.*)

Foucault's other early monographs, written while he taught at the University of Clermont-Ferrand in France (1960–66), had much the same fate. Not until the appearance of *Les Mots et les choses* ("Words and Things"; Eng. trans. *The Order of Things*) in 1966 did Foucault begin to attract wide notice as one of the most original and controversial thinkers of his day. He chose to watch his reputation grow from a distance—at the University of Tunis in Tunisia (1966–68). In 1969 he published *L'Archéologie du savoir* (*The Archaeology of Knowledge*). In 1970, after a brief tenure as director of the philosophy department at the University of Paris, Vincennes, he was awarded a chair in the history of systems of thought at the Collège de France, France's most prestigious postsecondary institution.

Between 1971 and 1984 Foucault wrote several works, including *Surveiller et punir: naissance de la prison* (1975; *Discipline and Punish: The Birth of the Prison*), a monograph on the emergence of the modern prison; three volumes of a history of Western sexuality; and numerous essays.

Foucault was a visiting lecturer at the University of California at Berkeley for several years. He died of a septicemia typical of AIDS in 1984, the fourth volume of his history of sexuality still incomplete.

FOUCAULT'S IDEAS

What types of human beings are there? What is their essence? What is the essence of human history? Of humankind? Contrary to so many of his intellectual predecessors, Foucault sought not to answer these traditional and seemingly straightforward questions but to critically examine them and the responses they had inspired. He directed his most sustained skepticism toward those responses—among them, race, the unity of reason or the psyche, progress, and liberation—that had become commonplaces in Europe and the United States in the 19th century. He argued that such commonplaces informed both Hegelian phenomenology and Marxist materialism. He argued that they also informed the evolutionary biology, physical anthropology, clinical medicine, psychology, sociology, and criminology of the same period. The latter three disciplines are part of what came to be called in French *les sciences humaines*, or "the human sciences."

Several of the philosophers of the Anglo-American positivist tradition, among them Carl Hempel, had faulted the human sciences for failing to achieve the conceptual and methodological rigour of mathematics or physics. Foucault found fault with them as well, but he decisively rejected the positivist tenet that the methods of the pure or natural sciences provided an exclusive standard for arriving at genuine or legitimate knowledge. His critique concentrated instead upon the fundamental point of reference that had grounded and guided inquiry in the human sciences: the concept of "man." The man of this inquiry was a creature purported, like many preceding conceptions, to have a constant essence—indeed, a double essence. On one hand, man was an object, like any other object in the natural world, obedient to the indiscriminate dictates of physical laws. On the other hand, man was a subject, an agent uniquely capable of comprehending and altering his worldly condition in order to become more fully, more essentially, himself. Foucault reviewed the historical record for evidence that such a creature actually had ever existed, but to no avail. Looking for objects, he found only a plurality of subjects whose features varied dramatically with shifts of place and time.

Foucault understood the very possibility of his own critique to be evidence that the concept of man was beginning to loosen its grip on Western thought. Yet a further puzzle remained: How could such an erroneous, such an impossible, figure have been so completely taken for granted for so long? Foucault's solution emphasized that in the emerging nation-states of 17th- and 18th-century Europe, "man" was a conceptual prerequisite for the creation of social institutions and practices that were then necessary to maintain an optimally productive citizenry. With the advent of "man," the notion that human character and experience were immutable gradually gave way to the notion that both body and soul could be manipulated and reformed. The latter notion lent the technologies of modern policing their enduring rationale.

Although this discipline operated on individuals, it was paired with a current of reformism that took not individuals but various human populations as its basic object. The prevailing sensibility of its greatest champions was markedly medical. They scrutinized everything from sexual behaviour to social organization for relative pathology or health. They also sought out the "deviant," but less in order to eradicate it than to keep it in acceptable check. This "bio-politics" of the reformers, according to Foucault, contained the basic principles of the modern welfare state.

For Foucault, domination was not the only outcome of these dynamics. Another was "subjectivation," the historically specific classification and shaping of individual human beings into "subjects" of various kinds—including heroic and ordinary, "normal" and "deviant." The distinction between the two came somewhat late to Foucault, but once he made and refined it he was able to clarify the status of some of his earliest observations and to identify a theme that had been present in all his writings. His understanding of subjectivation, however, changed significantly over the course of two decades, as did the methods he applied to its analysis. Intent on devising a properly specific history of subjects, he initially pressed the analogy between the corpus of statements about subjects produced and presumed true at any given historical moment and the artifacts of some archaeological site or complex. This "archaeology of knowledge" nevertheless had its shortcomings. Among other things, its consideration of both power and power-knowledge was at best partial, if not oblique.

By 1971 Foucault had already demoted "archaeology" in favour of "genealogy," a method that traced the ensemble of historical contingencies, accidents, and illicit relations that made up the ancestry of one or another currently accepted theory or concept in the human sciences. With genealogy, Foucault set out to unearth the artificiality of the dividing line between the putatively illegitimate and its putatively normal and natural opposite. *Discipline and Punish* was his genealogical exposé of the artifices of power-knowledge that had resulted in the naturalization of the "criminal character," and the first volume of *Histoire de la sexualité* (1976; *The History of Sexuality*) was his exposé of the Frankensteinian machinations that had resulted in the naturalization of the dividing line between the "homosexual" and the "heterosexual."

NOAM CHOMSKY

(b. Dec. 7, 1928, Philadelphia, Pa., U.S.)

Noam Chomsky is an American linguist and political activist whose theories of language have revolutionized the field of linguistics and exerted a profound influence on philosophy, psychology, and cognitive science.

Chomsky was introduced to linguistics by his father, a scholar of Hebrew. He studied under the linguist Zellig S. Harris at the University of Pennsylvania, where he earned bachelor's (1949) and master's (1951) degrees. Many elements of his early theories of language appear in his manuscript *Logical Structure of Linguistic Theory* (published 1975), which he wrote while a Junior Fellow at Harvard University in 1951–55. A chapter of this work, "Transformational Analysis," formed his University of Pennsylvania Ph.D. dissertation (1955). After receiving his degree, he joined the faculty of the Massachusetts Institute of Technology (MIT), where he became a full professor in 1961. He was appointed Ferrari P. Ward Professor of Modern Languages and Linguistics in 1966 and Institute Professor in 1976.

In the 1940s and '50s the study of linguistics in the United States was dominated by the school of American structuralism. According to the structuralists, the proper object of study for linguistics is the corpus of sounds of a given language, which they call "primary linguistic data." The task of the linguist is to construct a grammar of the language by applying to the primary linguistic data a series of complex analyses that would isolate the significant units of sound in the language (phonemes) and identify their permissible combinations into words and ultimately sentences. In keeping with their strict empiricism, the structuralists argued that in order to be genuinely scientific the grammar must be mechanically extractable by these analyses from the primary linguistic data and must not include reference to unverifiable and mysterious mental entities such as "meanings." For similar reasons, structuralists proposed or were sympathetic to behaviourist accounts of language learning, in which linguistic knowledge amounts to merely a set of dispositions, or habits, acquired through conditioning and without the aid of any language-specific mental structures.

In contrast to structuralism, Chomsky's approach, as outlined in his first major publication, *Syntactic Structures* (1957), and refined considerably in several works since then, is thoroughly mentalistic, insofar as it takes the proper object of study for linguistics to be the mentally represented grammars that constitute the native speaker's knowledge of his language and the biologically innate "language faculty," or Universal Grammar, that allows the (developmentally normal) language learner as a child to construct a rich, detailed, and accurate grammar of the language to which he is exposed. Children acquire languages in

Noam Chomsky addresses the media during Brazil's World Social Forum in 2002. Vanderlei Almeida/AFP/ Getty Images

relatively little time, with little or no instruction, without apparent difficulty, and on the basis of primary linguistic data that are necessarily incomplete and frequently defective. (Once they reach fluency, children routinely produce sentences they have never heard before, and many of the sentences produced by adults in their environment contain errors of various kinds, such as slurs, false starts, run-on sentences, and so on.)

These facts, according to Chomsky, demonstrate the inadequacy of behaviourist theories of language learning, which typically do not postulate mental structures beyond those representing simple induction and other "general learning strategies." Given the primary linguistic data to which speakers are exposed, it is impossible on behaviourist assumptions to construct a "descriptively adequate" grammar—i.e., a grammar that generates all and only the sentences of the language in question. The ultimate goal of linguistic science for Chomsky is to develop a theory of Universal Grammar that is "explanatorily adequate" in the sense of providing a descriptively adequate grammar for any natural language given exposure to primary linguistic data.

Chomsky's work in linguistics hastened the decline of behaviourism in psychology, prompted a revival of interest in rationalist theories of knowledge in philosophy, and spurred research into the innate rule systems that may underlie other domains of human thought and knowledge.

Chomsky is also known around the world as a political activist, though his views have received little attention in the mass media of the United States. Since the 1960s he has written numerous works and delivered countless lectures and interviews on what he considers the antidemocratic character of corporate power and its insidious effects on U.S. politics and foreign policy, the mass media, and the behaviour of intellectuals.

JÜRGEN HABERMAS

(b. June 18, 1929, Düsseldorf, Ger.)

Jürgen Habermas is the most important German philosopher of the second half of the 20th century. Habermas grew up in Gummersbach, Ger. At age 10 he joined the Hitler Youth, as did many of his contemporaries, and at age 15, during the last months of World War II, he was sent to the Western Front. After the Nazi defeat in May 1945, he completed his secondary education and attended the Universities of Bonn, Göttingen, and Zürich. At Bonn he received a Ph.D. in philosophy in 1954 with a dissertation on Friedrich Schelling. From 1956 to 1959 he worked as Theodor Adorno's first assistant at the Institute for Social Research. Habermas left the institute in 1959 and completed his second doctorate (his habilitation thesis, which qualified him to teach at the university level) in 1961 under the political scientist Wolfgang Abendroth at the University of Marburg. His thesis was published with additions in 1962 as *Strukturwandel der Öffentlichkeit* (*The Structural Transformation of the Public Sphere*).

In 1961 Habermas became a privatdozent (unsalaried professor and lecturer) in Marburg, and in 1962 he was named extraordinary professor (professor without chair) at the University of Heidelberg. He succeeded Max Horkheimer as professor of philosophy and sociology at the Johann Wolfgang Goethe University of Frankfurt am Main (Frankfurt University) in 1964. After 10 years as director of the Max Planck Institute in Starnberg (1971–81), he returned to Frankfurt, where he retired in 1994. Thereafter he taught in the United States at Northwestern University (Evanston, Ill.) and New York University and lectured worldwide.

PHILOSOPHY AND SOCIAL THEORY

In his 1965 inaugural lecture at Frankfurt University, *Erkenntnis und Interesse* (1965; *Knowledge and Human Interests*), and in the book of the same title published three years later, Habermas set forth the foundations of a normative version of critical social theory, the Marxist social theory developed by Horkheimer, Adorno, and other members of the Frankfurt Institute from the 1920s onward. He did this on the basis of a general theory of human interests, according to which different areas of human knowledge and inquiry—e.g., the physical, biological, and social sciences—are expressions of distinct, but equally basic, human interests. These basic interests are in turn unified by reason's overarching pursuit of its own freedom, which is expressed in scholarly disciplines that are critical of unfree modes of social life. In his rethinking of the foundations of early critical social theory, Habermas sought to unite the philosophical traditions of Karl Marx and German idealism with the psychoanalysis of Sigmund Freud and the pragmatism of the American logician and philosopher Charles Sanders Peirce.

Habermas took a linguistic-communicative turn in *Theorie des kommunikativen Handelns* (1981; *The Theory of Communicative Action*). He argued that human interaction in one of its fundamental forms is "communicative" rather than "strategic" in nature, insofar as it is aimed at mutual understanding and agreement rather than at the achievement of the self-interested goals of individuals. Such understanding and agreement, however, are possible only to the extent that the communicative interaction in which individuals take part resists all forms of nonrational coercion. The notion of an "ideal communication community" functions as a guide that can be formally applied both to regulate and to critique concrete speech situations. Using this regulative and critical ideal, individuals would be able to raise, accept, or reject each other's claims to truth, rightness, and sincerity solely on the basis of the "unforced force" of the better argument—i.e., on the basis of reason and evidence—and all participants would be motivated solely by the desire to obtain mutual understanding. Although the ideal communication community is never perfectly realized (which is why Habermas appeals to it as a regulative or critical ideal rather than as a concrete historical community), the projected horizon of unconstrained communicative action within it can serve as a model of free and open public discussion within liberal-democratic societies. Likewise, this type of regulative and critical ideal can serve as a justification of deliberative liberal-democratic political institutions, because it is only within such institutions that unconstrained communicative action is possible.

Liberal democracy is not a guarantee that communicative rationality will flourish, however. Indeed, in modern capitalist societies, social institutions that ideally should be communicative in character—e.g., family, politics, and education—have come to embody a merely "strategic" rationality, according to Habermas. Such institutions are increasingly overrun by economic and bureaucratic forces that are guided not by an ideal of mutual understanding but rather by principles of administrative power and economic efficiency.

Habermas's findings carried wide-ranging normative implications. In *Moralbewusstsein und kommunikatives Handeln* (1983; *Moral Consciousness and Communicative Action*), he elaborated a general theory of "discourse ethics," or "communicative ethics," which concerns the ethical presuppositions of ideal communication that would have to be invoked in an ideal communication community.

Habermas was criticized by both the postmodern left and the neoconservative right for his trust in the power of rational discussion to resolve major domestic and international conflicts. Habermas responded to critics at both ends of the political spectrum by developing a more robust communicative theory of democracy, law, and constitutions in *Faktizität und Geltung* (1992; *Between Facts and Norms*) and other works. In *Zeit der Übergänge* (2001; *Time of Transitions*), he offered global democratic alternatives to wars that employ terrorism as well as to the "war on terrorism."

SIR BERNARD WILLIAMS

(b. Sept. 21, 1929, Westcliff, Essex, Eng.—d. June 10, 2003, Rome, Italy)

Bernard Williams was an English philosopher who is noted especially for his writings on ethics and the history of Western philosophy, both ancient and modern.

Williams was educated at Chigwell School, Essex, and Balliol College, Oxford. During the 1950s he served in the Royal Air Force (1951–53) and was a fellow of All Souls College and New College, Oxford. He was appointed Knightbridge Professor of Philosophy at the University of Cambridge in 1967 and Provost of King's College, Cambridge, in 1979. He was Monroe Deutsch Professor of Philosophy at the University of California, Berkeley, from 1988 to 2003 and White's Professor of Moral Philosophy at Oxford from 1990 to 1996.

In 1955 Williams married Shirley Catlin, who, as Shirley Williams, became a prominent political figure in Britain; in 1993 she was created Baroness Williams of Crosby. In 1974 the marriage was dissolved, and Williams married Patricia Skinner. Williams headed or served on a number of public commissions, notably the Committee on Obscenity and Film Censorship (1977–79), and was a

director of the English National Opera. He was knighted
in 1999.

PHILOSOPHY AS A HUMANISTIC DISCIPLINE

Williams was trained in classics and wrote memorably
about Plato, Aristotle, and Greek moral consciousness,
but he was also one of the most prolific and versatile philosophers of his time. His published works include writings
on René Descartes (1596–1650), Friedrich Nietzsche
(1844–1900), and Ludwig Wittgenstein (1889–1951) and
important papers and books on personal identity, the
relation of morality to human motivation, the idea of
social and political equality, the nature and value of truth,
the significance of death, and the role and limits of
objectivity in science, morality, and human life. He did
not put forward a systematic philosophical theory; indeed,
he was suspicious of systematic theories, particularly in
ethics, because, in his view, they failed to be true to the
contingency, complexity, and individuality of human life.

Williams was recognized for his brilliance even as an
undergraduate. He was trained in philosophy when Oxford
was home to the new movement of linguistic analysis, or
ordinary language philosophy, led by J.L. Austin, but the
breadth of his cultural, historical, and political interests
kept him from becoming an adherent of that school. He
met its standards of clarity of expression and rigour in
argument, but his aims in philosophy went far beyond
conceptual analysis. He regarded philosophy as an effort to
achieve a deeper understanding of human life and the human
point of view in its multiple dimensions. For the same reasons, he also resisted the tendency to regard scientific
knowledge as the model of understanding to which philosophy should aspire at a more abstract level—a tendency
that was strengthened during his lifetime by the growing

Sir Bernard Williams. University of Oxford

influence of the American philosopher W.V.O. Quine and by a shift in the centre of gravity of English-language philosophy from Britain to the United States. Williams held that physical science could aspire to an objectivity and universality that did not make sense for humanistic subjects, and his greatest influence came from his challenge to the ambition of universality and objectivity in ethics, especially as expressed in utilitarianism but also in the tradition established by Immanuel Kant.

THE ABSOLUTE CONCEPTION OF REALITY

In his book *Descartes: The Project of Pure Inquiry* (1978), Williams gave a compelling description of the ideal of objectivity in science, which he called the "absolute conception" of reality. According to this conception, different human perspectives on and representations of the world are the product of interaction between human beings, as constituents of the world, and the world itself as an independently existing reality. Humans cannot apprehend the world except by some form of perception or representation; yet they can recognize, and to some extent identify and try to compensate for, the distortions or limitations that their own point of view and their relation to the rest of reality introduce. The aim of objectivity in science is by this method to approach as closely as possible to the absolute conception—a conception of what is there "anyway," independent of the human point of view. Historical self-consciousness about the contingent elements in this process is compatible with the idea of a single truth toward which humans are trying to make progress.

Williams was cognizant of the doubts that exist regarding whether this ideal is intelligible, let alone attainable, in light of the fact that human thinking must start from some particular historical moment and must use the contingent biological faculties and cultural tools that happen to be at hand. But whatever may be the difficulties in pursuing this ideal, he believed that it makes sense as an ambition. If there is a way things are anyway, then it makes sense to want to know what that way is and to explain the nature of human perceptions in terms of it.

MORALITY AND THE LIMITS OF OBJECTIVITY

Some philosophers, in the tradition of David Hume (1711–76), have denied that there can be objective truth in ethics on the ground that this would have to mean, very implausibly, that moral propositions are true because they represent moral entities or structures that are part of the furniture of the world—moral realities with which humans have some kind of causal interaction, as they do with the physical objects of scientific knowledge. Williams was also doubtful about objectivity in ethics, but his criticism does not depend on this false analogy with science and is more interesting.

Moral judgments, according to Williams, are about what people should do and how they should live; they do not at all purport to represent how things are in the outside world. So, if there is any objectivity in moral judgments, it would have to be sought in a different analogy with scientific objectivity. Objective truth in ethics would have to consist not in ethical entities or properties added to the absolute conception of the external world but in the objective validity of the reasoning that supports certain practical, rather than descriptive, judgments about what people should do and how they should live. The analogy with scientific objectivity would reside in the fact that the way to arrive at such objective and universally valid truth would be to detect and correct for the biases and distortions introduced into one's practical judgment by contingencies of one's personal or parochial perspective. The more distortions one could correct, the closer one would get to the truth.

But it is just this aim, central to the idea of moral objectivity, that Williams thinks is fundamentally misguided. Williams finds something bizarre about the theoretical ambition of discovering a standard for practical judgment that escapes the perspectival peculiarities of the individual point of view. This applies to any ethical theory with a strong basis in impartiality or with a claim to universal validity. Williams's basic point is that, in the practical domain, the ambition of transcending one's own point of view is absurd. If taken seriously, it is likely to be profoundly self-deceived in its application. To Williams, the ambition is akin to that of the person who tries to eliminate from his life all traces of the fact that it is his.

Williams developed this objection through his general view that practical reasons must be "internal" rather than "external": that is, reasons for action must derive from motives that a person already has; they cannot create new motives by themselves, through the force of reason alone. He also defended a limited form of ethical relativism. He believed that, while there can be ethical truth, it is local and historically contingent and based on reasons deriving from people's actual motives and practices, which are not timeless or universal. Consequently, moral judgments cannot be applied to cultures too far removed in time and character from the culture in which they originate.

These arguments appear in *Ethics and the Limits of Philosophy* (1985), *A Critique of Utilitarianism* (1973; in *Utilitarianism: For and Against*), and some of the essays reprinted in *Moral Luck* (1981) and *Making Sense of Humanity* (1995). The debate provoked by Williams's claim that impersonal moral standards undermine the integrity of personal projects and personal relations, which give life its very meaning, was an important part of the moral and political philosophy of the later 20th century. Even philosophers who did not accept Williams's conclusions were in most cases led to recognize the importance of accommodating the personal point of view as a factor in moral theory.

Williams also raised and explored the deep question of whether a person's moral status is immune to "luck," or purely contingent circumstances, as Kant had argued (for Kant, the moral status of an individual depends only on the quality of his will). Williams invented the concept of "moral luck" and offered strong reasons to think that people are morally vulnerable to contingencies beyond their control, a conception he found exemplified in Greek tragedy. Oedipus, for example, is not relieved of guilt for killing his father and marrying his mother by the fact that he did not know at the time that that was what he was doing. Williams's remarkable philosophical-literary-historical work, *Shame and Necessity* (1993), presented these ideas in a rich study of Greek ethical thought.

Williams came to the conclusion that, instead of following the model of natural science, the project of understanding human nature should rely on history, which provides some distance from the perspective of the present without leaving the fullness of the human perspective behind. During the later part of his career, this viewpoint coincided with his admiration for Nietzsche, whose genealogical method was an example of historical self-exploration. In Williams's last book, *Truth and Truthfulness* (2002), he applied these ideas to the importance of truth in the theoretical and practical spheres as well as in political and personal relations.

Williams's major published works, in addition to those mentioned above, include *Morality: An Introduction to Ethics*

(1972); *Problems of the Self: Philosophical Papers* (1973); *In the Beginning Was the Deed: Realism and Moralism in Political Argument* (2005); *The Sense of the Past: Essays in the History of Philosophy* (2005); *Philosophy as a Humanistic Discipline* (2005); and *On Opera* (2006).

JACQUES DERRIDA

(b. July 15, 1930, El Biar, Alg.—d. Oct. 8, 2004, Paris, France)

Jacques Derrida was a French philosopher who developed a technique of philosophical and literary analysis known as deconstruction. His critique of Western philosophy and analyses of the nature of language, writing, and meaning were highly controversial yet immensely influential in much of the intellectual world in the late 20th century.

Derrida was born to Sephardic Jewish parents in French-governed Algeria. Educated in the French tradition, he went to France in 1949, studied at the elite École Normale Supérieure (ENS), and taught philosophy at the Sorbonne (1960–64), the ENS (1964–84), and the École des Hautes Études en Sciences Sociales (1984–99), all in Paris. From the 1960s he published numerous books and essays on an immense range of topics and taught and lectured throughout the world, including at Yale University and the University of California, Irvine, attaining an international celebrity comparable only to that of Jean-Paul Sartre a generation earlier.

Derrida is most celebrated as the principal exponent of deconstruction, a term he coined for the critical examination of the fundamental conceptual distinctions, or "oppositions," inherent in Western philosophy since the time of the ancient Greeks. These oppositions are characteristically "binary" and "hierarchical," involving a pair of terms in which one member of the pair is assumed to be primary or fundamental, the other secondary or derivative. Examples include nature and culture, speech and writing, mind and body, presence and absence, inside and outside, literal and metaphorical, intelligible and sensible, and form and meaning, among many others. To "deconstruct" an opposition is to explore the tensions and contradictions between the hierarchical ordering assumed or asserted in the text and other aspects of the text's meaning, especially those that are indirect or implicit. Such an analysis shows that the opposition is not natural or necessary but a product, or "construction," of the text itself.

The speech/writing opposition, for example, is manifested in texts that treat speech as a more authentic form of language than writing. These texts assume that the speaker's ideas and intentions are directly expressed and immediately "present" in speech, whereas in writing they are comparatively remote or "absent" and thus more easily misunderstood. As Derrida points out, however, speech functions as language only to the extent that it shares characteristics traditionally assigned to writing, such as absence, "difference," and the possibility of misunderstanding. This fact is indicated by philosophical texts themselves, which invariably describe speech in terms of examples and metaphors drawn from writing, even in cases where writing is explicitly claimed to be secondary to speech. Significantly, Derrida does not wish simply to invert the speech/writing opposition—i.e., to show that writing is really prior to speech. As with any deconstructive analysis, the point is to restructure, or "displace," the opposition so as to show that neither term is primary.

The speech/writing opposition derives from a pervasive picture of meaning that equates linguistic meaning with the ideas and intentions in the mind of the speaker or author. Building on theories of the Swiss linguist Ferdinand

Jacques Derrida poses for a photograph in his home near Paris in 2001. Joel Robine/AFP/Getty Images

de Saussure, Derrida coined the term *différance*, meaning both a difference and an act of deferring, to characterize the way in which linguistic meaning is created rather than given. For Derrida as for Saussure, the meaning of a word is a function of the distinctive contrasts it displays with other, related meanings. Because each word depends for its meaning on the meanings of other words, it follows that the meaning of a word is never fully "present" to us, as it would be if meanings were the same as ideas or intentions; instead it is endlessly "deferred" in an infinitely long chain of meanings. Derrida expresses this idea by saying that meaning is created by the "play" of differences between words—a play that is "limitless," "infinite," and "indefinite."

In the 1960s Derrida's work was welcomed in France and elsewhere by thinkers interested in the broad interdisciplinary movement known as structuralism. The structuralists analyzed various cultural phenomena— such as myths, religious rituals, literary narratives, and fashions in dress and adornment—as general systems of signs analogous to natural languages, with their own vocabularies and their own underlying rules and structures, and attempted to develop a metalanguage of terms and concepts in which the various sign systems could be described. Some of Derrida's early work was a critique of major structuralist thinkers such as Saussure, the anthropologist Claude Lévi-Strauss, and the intellectual historian and philosopher Michel Foucault. Derrida was thus seen, especially in the United States, as leading a movement beyond structuralism to "poststructuralism," which was skeptical about the possibility of a general science of meaning.

RICHARD RORTY

(b. Oct. 4, 1931, New York, N.Y., U.S.—d. June 8, 2007, Palo Alto, Calif.)

R ichard Rorty was an American pragmatist philosopher and public intellectual. He is remembered for his wide-ranging critique of the modern conception of philosophy as a quasi-scientific enterprise aimed at reaching certainty and objective truth. In politics he argued against programs of both the left and the right in favour of what he described as a meliorative and reformist "bourgeois liberalism."

The son of nonacademic leftist intellectuals who broke with the American Communist Party in the early 1930s, Rorty attended the University of Chicago and Yale University, where he obtained a Ph.D. in 1956. Following two years in the army, he taught philosophy at Wellesley College (1958–61) and Princeton University (1961–82) before accepting a position in the department of humanities at the University of Virginia. From 1998 until his retirement in 2005, Rorty taught comparative literature at Stanford University.

Rorty's views are somewhat easier to characterize in negative than in positive terms. In epistemology he opposed foundationalism, the view that all knowledge can be grounded, or justified, in a set of basic statements that do not themselves require justification. According to his "epistemological behaviourism," Rorty held that no statement is epistemologically more basic than any other, and no statement is ever justified "finally" but only relative to some circumscribed and contextually determined set of additional statements. In the philosophy of language, Rorty rejected the idea that sentences or beliefs are "true" or "false" in any interesting sense other than being useful or successful within a broad social practice. He also opposed representationism, the view that the main function of language is to represent or picture pieces of an objectively existing reality. Finally, in metaphysics he rejected both realism and antirealism, or idealism, as products of mistaken representationalist assumptions about language.

Because Rorty did not believe in certainty or absolute truth, he did not advocate the philosophical pursuit of such things. Instead, he believed that the role of philosophy is to conduct an intellectual "conversation" between contrasting but equally valid forms of intellectual inquiry—including science, literature, politics, religion, and many others—with the aim of achieving mutual understanding and resolving conflicts. This general view is reflected in Rorty's political works, which consistently defend traditional left-liberalism and criticize newer forms of "cultural leftism" as well as more conservative positions.

Rorty defended himself against charges of relativism and subjectivism by claiming that he rejected the crucial distinctions these doctrines presuppose. His publications include *Philosophy and the Mirror of Nature* (1979), *Consequences of Pragmatism* (1982), and *Contingency, Irony, and Solidarity* (1989).

RICHARD NOZICK

(b. Nov. 16, 1938, Brooklyn, N.Y., U.S.—d. Jan. 23, 2002, Cambridge, Mass.)

The American philosopher Richard Nozick is best known for his rigorous defense of libertarianism in his first major work, *Anarchy, State, and Utopia* (1974). A wide-ranging thinker, Nozick also made important contributions to epistemology, the problem of personal identity, and decision theory.

Nozick was the only child of Max Nozick, a Russian immigrant and businessman, and Sophie Cohen Nozick. After attending public school in Brooklyn, Nozick enrolled at Columbia College, where he earned a bachelor's degree in philosophy in 1959. He received a Ph.D. in philosophy at Princeton University in 1963, having written a dissertation on decision theory under Carl Hempel. He taught at Princeton (1962–65), Harvard University (1965–67), and Rockefeller University (1967–69). In 1969, when he was 30 years old, he returned to Harvard as one of the youngest full professors in the university's history. He remained at Harvard for the remainder of his teaching career.

CONVERSION TO LIBERTARIANISM

During his high school and college years, Nozick was a member of the student New Left and an enthusiastic socialist. At Columbia he helped to found a campus branch of the League for Industrial Democracy, a precursor of the Students for a Democratic Society. While in graduate school he read works by libertarian thinkers such as F.A. Hayek and Ludwig von Mises, and his political views began to change.

His conversion to libertarianism culminated in 1974 with the publication of *Anarchy, State, and Utopia*, a closely argued and highly original defense of the libertarian "minimal state" and a critique of the social-democratic liberalism of his Harvard colleague John Rawls. Immediately hailed by conservative intellectuals, the work became a kind of philosophical manifesto of the New Right, though Nozick himself was not entirely comfortable with this association.

THE MINIMAL STATE

The main purpose of *Anarchy, State, and Utopia* is to show that the minimal state, and only the minimal state, is morally justified. By a minimal state Nozick means a state that functions essentially as a "night watchman," with powers limited to those necessary to protect citizens against violence, theft, and fraud. By arguing that the minimal state is justified, Nozick seeks to refute anarchism, which opposes any state whatsoever. By arguing that no more than the minimal state is justified, Nozick seeks to refute modern forms of liberalism, as well as socialism and other leftist ideologies.

Against anarchism, Nozick claims that a minimal state is justified because it (or something very much like it) would arise spontaneously among people living in a hypothetical "state of nature" through transactions that would not involve the violation of anyone's natural rights. Following the 17th-century English philosopher John Locke, Nozick assumes that everyone possesses the natural rights to life, liberty, and property, including the right to claim as property the fruits or products of one's labour and the right to dispose of one's property as one sees fit (provided that in doing so one does not violate the rights of anyone else). Everyone also has the natural right to punish those who violate or attempt to violate one's own natural rights. Because defending one's natural rights in a state of nature would be difficult for anyone to do on his own, individuals would band together to form "protection associations," in which members would work together to defend each other's rights and to punish rights violators. Eventually, some of these associations would develop into private businesses offering protection and punishment services for a fee.

The great importance that individuals would attach to such services would give the largest protection firms a natural competitive advantage, and eventually only one firm, or a confederation of firms, would control all the protection and punishment business in the community. Because this firm (or confederation of firms) would have a monopoly of force in the territory of the community and because it would protect the rights of everyone living there, it would constitute a minimal state in the libertarian sense. And because the minimal state would come about without violating anyone's natural rights, a state with at least its powers is justified.

Against liberalism and ideologies farther left, Nozick claims that no more than the minimal state is justified, because any state with more extensive powers would violate the natural rights of its citizens. Thus the state should not have the power to control prices or to set a minimum wage, because doing so would violate the natural right of citizens to dispose of their property, including their labour, as they see fit. For similar reasons, the state should not have the power to establish public education or health care through taxes imposed on citizens who may wish to spend their money on private services instead. Indeed, according to Nozick, any mandatory taxation used to fund services or benefits other than those constitutive of the minimal state is unjust, because such taxation amounts to a kind of "forced labour" for the state by those who must pay the tax.

Nozick's vision of legitimate state power thus contrasts markedly with that of Rawls and his followers. Rawls argues that the state should have whatever powers are necessary to ensure that those citizens who are least well-off are as well-off as they can be (though these powers must be consistent with a variety of basic rights and freedoms). This viewpoint is derived from Rawls's theory of justice, one principle of which is that an unequal distribution of wealth and income is acceptable only if those at the bottom are better off than they would be under any other distribution.

Nozick's response to such arguments is to claim that they rest on a false conception of distributive justice. They wrongly define a just distribution in terms of the pattern it exhibits at a given time (e.g., an equal distribution or a distribution that is unequal to a certain extent) or in terms of the historical circumstances surrounding its development (e.g., those who worked the hardest have more) rather than in terms of the nature of the transactions through which the distribution came about. For Nozick, any distribution of "holdings," as he calls them, no matter how unequal, is just if (and only if) it arises from a just distribution through legitimate means. One legitimate means is the appropriation of something that is unowned in circumstances where the acquisition would not disadvantage others. A second means is the voluntary transfer of ownership of holdings to someone else. A third means is the rectification of past injustices in the acquisition or transfer of holdings. According to Nozick, anyone who acquired what he has through these means is morally entitled to it. Thus the "entitlement" theory of justice states that the distribution of holdings in a society is just if (and only if) everyone in that society is entitled to what he has.

Nozick emphasizes that his vision of the minimal state is inclusive and compatible with the existence of smaller communities based on varying theories of justice. A group that wished to form a socialist community governed by an egalitarian theory would be free to do so, as long as it did not force others to join the community against their will. Indeed, every group would enjoy the same freedom to realize its own idea of a good society. In this way, according to Nozick, the minimal state constitutes a "framework for utopia."

Anarchy, State, and Utopia has generated an enormous secondary literature, much of it critical. Unlike Rawls, however, Nozick did not attempt to defend or revise his political views in published work. Nozick's other books include *Philosophical Explanations* (1981), *The Nature of Rationality* (1993), and *Invariances: The Structure of the Objective World* (2001).

SAUL KRIPKE

(b. Nov. 13, 1940, Bay Shore, Long Island, N.Y., U.S.)

Saul Kripke is an American philosopher and logician. From the 1960s he has been one of the most powerful thinkers in Anglo-American (analytic) philosophy.

Kripke began his important work on the semantics of modal logic (the logic of modal notions such as necessity and possibility) while he was still a high-school student in Omaha, Neb. In 1962 he graduated from Harvard with the only nonhonorary degree he ever received, a B.S. in mathematics. He remained at Harvard until 1968, first as a member of the Harvard Society of Fellows and then as a lecturer. During these years he continued a series of publications extending his original results in modal logic; he also published important papers in intuitionistic logic (the logic underlying the mathematical intuitionism of L.E.J. Brouwer), set theory, and the theory of transfinite recursion. Kripke taught logic and philosophy at Rockefeller University from 1968 to 1976 and at Princeton University, as McCosh Professor of Philosophy, from 1976 until his retirement in 1998. He delivered the prestigious John Locke Lectures at the University of Oxford in 1973 and received the Rolf Schock Prize in logic and philosophy, awarded by the Royal Swedish Academy of Sciences, in 2001. In 2003 he was appointed distinguished professor at the City University of New York (CUNY).

NAMING AND NECESSITY

Kripke's most important philosophical publication, *Naming and Necessity* (1980), based on transcripts of three lectures he delivered at Princeton in 1970, changed the course of analytic philosophy. It provided the first cogent account of necessity and possibility as metaphysical concepts, and it distinguished both concepts from the epistemological notions of a posteriori knowledge and a priori knowledge (knowledge acquired through experience and knowledge independent of experience, respectively) and from the linguistic notions of analytic truth and synthetic truth, or truth by virtue of meaning and truth by virtue of fact. In the course of making these distinctions, Kripke revived the ancient doctrine of essentialism, according to which objects possess certain properties necessarily—without them the objects would not exist at all. On the basis of this doctrine and revolutionary new ideas about the meaning and reference of proper names and of common nouns denoting "natural kinds" (such as *heat*, *water*, and *tiger*), he argued forcefully that some propositions are necessarily true but knowable only a posteriori—e.g., "Water is H_2O" and "Heat is mean molecular kinetic energy"—and that some propositions are contingently true (true in some circumstances but not others) but knowable a priori. These arguments overturned the conventional view, inherited from Immanuel Kant (1720–1804), which identified all a priori propositions as necessary and all a posteriori propositions as contingent.

Naming and Necessity also had far-reaching implications regarding the question of whether linguistic meaning and the contents of beliefs and other mental states are partly constituted by social and environmental facts external to the individual. According to Kripke's causal theory of reference, for example, the referent of a given use of a proper name, such as *Aristotle*, is transmitted through an indefinitely long series of earlier uses; this series constitutes a causal-historical chain that is traceable, in principle, to an original, or "baptismal," application. Kripke's view posed a serious challenge to the prevailing "description" theory, which held that the referent of a name is the individual who is picked out by an associated definite description, such as (in the case of Aristotle) *the teacher of Alexander the Great*. Finally, Kripke's work contributed greatly to the decline of ordinary language philosophy and related schools, which held that philosophy is nothing more than the logical analysis of language.

DAVID KELLOGG LEWIS

(b. Sept. 28, 1941, Oberlin, Ohio, U.S. — d. Oct. 14, 2001, Princeton, N.J.)

David Kellogg Lewis was an American philosopher who, at the time of his death, was considered by many to be the leading figure in Anglo-American (analytic) philosophy.

Both Lewis's father and his mother taught government at Oberlin College. Lewis studied philosophy at Swarthmore College (B.A., 1962) and Harvard University, where he received an M.A. in 1964 and a Ph.D. in 1967. His dissertation on linguistic convention, written under the supervision of Willard Van Orman Quine (1908–2000), was published as *Convention: A Philosophical Study* in 1969. Lewis taught at the University of California, Los Angeles, from 1966 to 1970 and thereafter at Princeton University. He died suddenly and unexpectedly at age 60, at the height of his intellectual powers.

In introductory essays written for two collections of his papers, Lewis identified several "recurring themes" that unify his work. Four of these themes are particularly important:

1. There are possible but nonactual things. Nonactual things do not differ from actual things in any fundamentally important way; nonactual human beings, for example, are very much like actual human beings. The largest and most inclusive nonactual things, which are not parts of any larger nonactual things, are nonactual worlds. The actual world, the object that is normally called the cosmos or the universe, and the many nonactual worlds constitute the realm of "possible worlds."

2. Temporal relations are strongly analogous to spatial relations. Just as the far side of the Moon is elsewhere in

space (relative to an observer on Earth), so things in the past or the future are "elsewhere in time" but are no less real for being so. Moreover, relations between actual and nonactual things are strongly analogous to temporal relations and therefore to spatial relations. All things, actual and nonactual, inhabit "logical space," and nonactual things are "elsewhere" in this space but are no less real for being so. Actual human beings correctly call the world they inhabit "actual" because it is the world they inhabit. Nonactual human beings likewise correctly call the worlds they inhabit "actual" for the same reason. The term *actual*, therefore, is strongly analogous to terms like *here* and *now*: in each case the referent of the term varies depending on the context (place, time, or world) in which it is uttered.

3. Physical science, if successful, will provide a complete description of the actual world.

4. Given any possible world in which every inhabitant of that world is in space and time (as is the case in the actual world), everything true about that world and its inhabitants supervenes on—is determined or settled by—the distribution of "local qualities" in space and time in that world. (A local quality is a property or characteristic that can be instantiated at a specific point in space and time. Although it is ultimately up to physics to determine what local qualities there are, two likely candidates are electric charge and temperature.) Theme 3 implies that all local qualities in the actual world are physical qualities. Lewis considered it an open question whether there are non-physical local qualities in other possible worlds.

Lewis regarded his doctrine of nonactual things and worlds as a "philosopher's paradise," and much of his work on particular philosophical problems (in metaphysics, the philosophy of language, the philosophy of mind, and epistemology) presupposed the reality of nonactual things. Few philosophers have accepted this presupposition, however; most have regarded it as simply unbelievable. Nevertheless, almost all philosophers who have studied Lewis's work have concluded that there is very little of it that cannot be detached from his doctrine of the nonactual and restated in terms of what they would consider a more plausible theory. (Lewis, it should be noted, devoted considerable effort to the attempt to show that all theories of the nonactual other than his own are unworkable.) Once so detached, they agree, Lewis's work is uniformly of great value.

PETER (ALBERT DAVID) SINGER

(b. July 6, 1946, Melbourne, Austl.)

Peter Singer, an Australian ethical and political philosopher, is best known for his work in bioethics and his role as one of the intellectual founders of the modern animal rights movement.

Singer's Jewish parents emigrated to Australia from Vienna in 1938 to escape Nazi persecution following the Anschluss. Three of Singer's grandparents were subsequently killed in the Holocaust. Growing up in Melbourne, Singer attended Scotch College and the University of Melbourne, where he earned a B.A. in philosophy and history (1967) and an M.A. in philosophy (1969). In 1969 he entered the University of Oxford, receiving a B.Phil. degree in 1971 and serving as Radcliffe Lecturer in Philosophy at University College from 1971 to 1973. At Oxford his association with a vegetarian student group and his reflection on the morality of his own meat eating led him to adopt vegetarianism. While at Oxford and during a visiting professorship at New York University in

1973–74, he wrote what would become his best-known and most influential work, *Animal Liberation: A New Ethics for Our Treatment of Animals* (1975).

Returning to Australia, he lectured at La Trobe University (1975–76) and was appointed professor of philosophy at Monash University (1977). He also became director of Monash's Centre for Human Bioethics in 1983 and codirector of its Institute for Ethics and Public Policy in 1992. In 1999 he was appointed Ira W. DeCamp Professor of Bioethics in the University Center for Human Values at Princeton University. He became Laureate Professor at the Centre for Applied Philosophy and Public Ethics at the University of Melbourne in 2005.

In keeping with ethical principles that guided his thinking and writing from the 1970s, Singer devoted much of his time and effort (and a considerable portion of his income) to social and political causes, most notably animal rights but also famine and poverty relief, environmentalism, and abortion rights. By the 1990s his intellectual leadership of the increasingly successful animal rights movement and his controversial stands on some bioethical issues had made him one of the world's most widely recognized public intellectuals.

Singer's work in applied ethics and his activism in politics were informed by his utilitarianism, the tradition in ethical philosophy that holds that actions are right or wrong depending on the extent to which they promote happiness or prevent pain. In an influential early article, *Famine, Affluence, and Morality* (1972), occasioned by the catastrophic cyclone in Bangladesh in 1971, he rejected the common prephilosophical assumption that physical proximity is a relevant factor in determining one's moral obligations to others. Regarding the question of whether people in affluent countries have a greater obligation to help those near them than to contribute to famine relief in Bangladesh, he wrote: "It makes no moral difference whether the person I can help is a neighbor's child ten yards from me or a Bengali whose name I shall never know, ten thousand miles away." The only important question, according to Singer, is whether the evil that may be prevented by one's contribution outweighs whatever inconvenience or hardship may be involved in contributing—and for the large majority of people in affluent societies, the answer is clearly yes.

An interesting philosophical implication of Singer's larger argument was that the traditional distinction between duty and charity—between actions that one is obliged to do and actions that it would be good to do even though one is not obliged to do them—was seriously weakened, if not completely undermined. On the utilitarian principles Singer plausibly applied to this case, any action becomes a duty if it will prevent more pain than it causes or cause more happiness than it prevents.

The publication of *Animal Liberation* in 1975 greatly contributed to the growth of the animal rights movement by calling attention to the routine torture and abuse of countless animals in factory farms and in scientific research; at the same time, it generated significant new interest among ethical philosophers in the moral status of nonhuman animals. The most-important philosophical contribution of the book was Singer's penetrating examination of the concept of "speciesism" (which he did not invent): the idea that the species of a being should be relevant to its moral status. Speciesism is rationally unjustified, according to Singer, just as is the comparable notion that race or sex should be relevant to the moral status of a human being. Singer argues that all beings with interests (all beings who are capable of enjoyment or suffering, broadly construed) deserve to have those interests taken into account in one's moral decision making. Furthermore, the kind of consideration a being deserves should depend on the nature of the interests it has (what kinds of enjoyment or suffering it is capable of), not on the species it happens to belong to. To think otherwise is to endorse a prejudice exactly analogous to racism or sexism. Speciesism was extensively explored by ethical philosophers and eventually became a familiar theme in popular discussions of animal rights in a variety of forums.

In numerous books and articles published in the 1980s and after, Singer continued to develop his positions on animal rights and other topics in applied ethical and political philosophy—including stem cell research, infanticide, euthanasia, global environmental concerns, and the political implications of Darwinism—placing them within the context of theoretical developments in utilitarianism.

GLOSSARY

ascetic Someone who is very self-disciplined and denies him- or herself pleasures, usually as a sign of spiritual devotion.

bourgeois Belonging to or typical of the middle class.

deconstruction The critical examination of the fundamental conceptual distinctions, or "oppositions," inherent in Western philosophy.

despotism To rule by absolute power; acting like a tyrant.

dialectic The art of examining the truth or validity of a theory or opinion.

dualism The doctrine that two distinct principles, good and evil, govern the universe.

empiricism The scientific method of going from observation to the formulation of a general principle.

exegesis Critical explanation of text.

existentialism The doctrine that individuals must create their own being according to their situation and environment.

gnostocism A religious movement where followers believe in intuitive spiritual knowledge.

interlocutor Someone who has an official role in a conversation or debate.

junzi Exemplary people.

monistic Reality as a unified whole that acts as the source for all existing things.

nihilism Rejecting all philosophical or ethical principles.

nominalism The school of thought that denies universal concepts such as "father" have any reality apart from the individual things signified by the universal or general term.

orthodoxy The practice of conforming to a preordained set of beliefs.

paradox A statement that seems to contradict itself, but is essentially true.

phenomenology A method of arriving at absolute essences through the analysis of experience in disregard of scientific knowledge.

pogrom The organized persecution of a specific group.

polemic Of or pertaining to controversy.

priggish Making a show of being superior to others.

rationalism The belief that all knowledge and truth consists of what is ascertainable by rational thought.

realism An attitude based on facts and reality, as opposed to emotions or imagining.

sinecure A position that does not have many, or any, duties but still pays a salary or stipend.

stoicism The ability to endure hardship with fortitude.

syllogism A form of reasoning with a major and minor premise, which lead to a conclusion.

tantric Hindu or Buddhist religious literature that contains ritual acts.

teleological Pertaining to the doctrine that natural and historic processes are determined by their ultimate purpose.

temporize To stall, or evade, in order to avoid an argument or postpone a decision.

utilitarianism The doctrine that the moral and political rightness of an action is determined by its usefulness.

vizier An officer in the Muslim government, particularly in the Ottoman Empire.

For Further Reading

Adamson, Peter. *Al-Kindi*. New York, NY: Oxford University Press, 2006.

Ahmed, Arif. *Saul Kripke*. New York, NY: Continuum International Publishing Group, 2007.

Baggini, Julian. *What's It All About? Philosophy and the Meaning of Life*. New York, NY: Oxford University Press, 2004.

Bambrough, Renford, and Creed, J.L. *The Philosophy of Aristotle*. New York, NY: Signet Classics, 2003.

Caputo, John D. *How to Read Kierkegaard*. New York, NY: W.W. Norton, 2008.

Chesterton, G.K. *St. Thomas Aquinas*. Mineola, NY: Dover Publications, 2009.

Chin, Annping. *The Authentic Confucius: A Life of Thought and Politics*. New York, NY: Scribner, 2007.

Clarke, Desmond M. *Descartes: A Biography*. New York, NY: Cambridge University Press, 2006.

Damrosch, Leo. *Jean-Jacques Rousseau: Restless Genius*. New York, NY: Houghton Mifflin, 2005.

Deakin, Michael A. *Hypatia of Alexandria: Mathematician and Martyr*. Amherst, NY: Prometheus Books, 2007.

Diken, Bulent. *Nihilism* (Key Ideas). New York, NY: Routledge, 2009.

Fakhry, Majid. *Al-Farabi, Founder of Islamic Neoplatonism: His Life, Works, and Influence*. Oxford, UK: Oneworld Publications, 2002.

Hampshire, Stuart. *Spinoza and Spinozism*. New York, NY: Oxford University Press, 2005.

Hollingdale, R.J. *Nietsche: The Man and His Philosophy*. New York, NY: Cambridge University Press, 2008.

King, Richard H. *Hannah Arendt and the Uses of History: Imperialism, Nation, Race, and Genocide*. New York, NY: Berghahn Books, 2007.

Kraemer, Joel L. *Maimonides: The Life and World of One of Civilization's Greatest Minds*. New York, NY: Doubleday, 2008.

Long, A.A. *From Epicurus to Epictetus: Studies in Hellenistic and Roman Philosophy*. New York, NY; Oxford University Press, 2006.

Machiavelli, Niccolo. *The Art of War & The Prince*. Radford, VA: Wilder Publications, 2008.

Navia, Luis. *Socrates: A Life Examined*. Amherst, NY; Prometheus Books, 2007.

Panza, Chrisopher, and Gale, Gregory. *Existentialism for Dummies*. Hoboken, NJ: Wiley Publishing, Inc., 2008.

Riedwig, Christopher. *Pythagoras: His Life, Teaching, and Influence*. Ithaca, NY: Cornell University Press, 2008.

Rowley, Hazel. *Tete-a-tete: Simone de Beauvoir and Jean-Paul Sartre*. New York, NY: HarperCollins, 2005.

Royle, Nicholas. *In Memory of Jacques Derrida*. Edinburgh, UK: Edinburgh University Press, 2009.

Russell, Bertrand. *History of Western Philosophy*. London, England: Routledge Classics, 2004.

Saint Augustine. *Confessions*. New York, NY: Oxford University Press, 2009.

Sartre, Jean-Paul. *Between Existentialism and Marxism*. London, England: Verso Publishing, 2008.

Singer, Peter. *The Life You Can Save*. New York, NY: Random House, 2009.

INDEX

A

Abelard, Peter, 100–103
Abendroth, Wolfgang, 317
Abriss der Logistik, 280
Académie Française, 176
Academy (of Plato), 37, 39, 47–48,
    60–61
Academy of Dijon, 183, 184
Academy of Sciences, 167, 197
Adeimantus, 38
Adorno, Theodor Wiesengrund,
    286–287, 317, 318
Advaita Vedanta, 83
Adventures of Ideas, 249
Adversus, mathematicos, 73
Aenesidemus, 73
Aesop's Fables, 211
aesthetic purposiveness, 193
aesthetic theory, 287
Agassiz, Louis, 227
Agathon, 12
Age of Reason, The, 290
Alaric, 77
Alexander IV, 120
Alexander the Great, 47–48, 57
Al-Fārābī, 86–89
al-Ghazālī, 98–100, 105
al-Juwaynī, 98
Al-Kindī, 85–86, 87, 88

"All is one" principle, 26
All Said and Done, 296
Almagest, 79
Almohads, 109
al-Qārābī, 105
America Day by Day, 296
Amida, 115–117
Anabasis, 211
Analects, 21–23, 107
Analysis of Matter, The, 259
Analysis of Mind, The, 259
analytic philosophy, 283
Anarchy, State, and Utopia, 332,
    333, 336
Anaxarchus of Abdera, 57
*Animal Liberation: A New Ethics
    for Our Treatment of Animals*,
    342, 343–344
Anselm of Canterbury, Saint, 11,
    96–98, 149
Anselm of Laon, 101
Antiphon, 38
Antoninus Pius (Titus Aurelius
    Antoninus), 66
Apollonius of Perga, 79
Apology, 29, 32, 33–35, 38–39
Aquinas, Saint Thomas, 9, 96,
    117–122
Arab Students' Organization, 268

Archaeology of Knowledge, The, 310
Arendt, Hannah, 292–294
Arianism, 79, 82
Ariston, 38
Aristotle, 9, 27, 28, 37, 47–54, 71,
    81–82, 85, 86, 89–91, 96, 105,
    113, 119–121, 124, 135, 141,
    144, 151–152, 159, 275, 321, 338
Arithmetica, 79
Arnauld, Antoine, 146
ar-Rāzī, 87, 88
Arrian, 65
atheism, 206, 219
atomic theory of the universe, 35
Augustine, Saint, 11, 74–75, 77–78
Augustus, 63
Augustus I, Ernest, 166
Authoritarian Personality, The, 287
Autobiography, 214
Aurelius, Marcus, 66–69
Austin, J. L., 301, 321
Averroës, 103–105, 113, 120
Avicenna, 89–92, 105
Ayer, Sir A. J., 299–303

B

Bacon, Francis, 12, 134–139, 152
Bacon, Roger, 119
Bair, Deirdre, 296
Bakunin, Mikhail
    Alexandrovich, 222–223
Barnes, Albert C., 262
Barnes Foundation, 262
Basic Laws of Arithmetic, 237
Baudelaire, 290
Beacon Hill, 261
Beauvoir, Simone de, 9, 288, 290,
    295–297
Becket of Canterbury, Thomas, 98

"Beautiful is beautiful, the" 44, 46
Being and Nothingness, 289
Being and Time, 241, 276–278
Benedict XI, 123
Benedict XII, 128
Benedictine monks, 97
Benjamin, Walter, 286
Bentham, Jeremy, 199–200, 211
Bentham, Sir Samuel, 211
Bergson, Henri, 241–244
Berkeley, George, 171–175
Berkeley, Robert, 175
Bernhard, Issak, 195
Between Facts and Norms, 320
Between Past and Future, 294
"Bezels of Wisdom, The," 112
Bhagavadgītā, 93
bhakti, 93–94
Bible, 77, 154, 161, 162, 196, 264
Bill of Rights, English, 159
*Birth of Tragedy from the Spirit of
    Music, The*, 231, 232
Black, Dora, 261–262
*Black-Body Theory and the
    Quantum Discontinuity*, 309
Blackstone, Sir William, 199
block universe, 229
Bloomsbury group, 263
Blücher, Heinrich, 292
Boethius, Anicius Manlius
    Severinus, 80–83
Böhme, Jakob, 265
Bonagratia of Bergamo, 127
Boniface VIII, 123
Bonnet, Charles, 196
"Book of Healing, The," 90
Book of Precepts, 111
Brahma-sūtras, 83, 93
Brahman, 83–84, 92
Braithwaite, R. B., 272

Brentano, Franz, 238, 275
British Academy, 250
British East India Company,
    211, 212
British Museum, 221
Brouwer, L. E. J., 337
Buber, Carl, 264
Buber, Martin, 264–268
Buckmaster, Maria Sarah, 247
Buddha, 21, 57, 70
Buddhism, 21, 69, 84–85, 106,
    114–117, 252–253

C

Caligula, 63
Canterbury University
    College, 285
Cantor, Georg, 255
Caritat, Marie-Jean-Antoine-
    Nicolas de (Marquis de
    Condorcet), 197–198
Carnap, Rudolf, 279–285, 297
Cartesian Circle, 149, 166, 304
Catechism of Positive Religion,
    The, 210
Categories, 48
Catlin, Shirley, 320
Cavendish, Sir Charles, 140
Cavendish, William, 140
Central Questions of Philosophy,
    The, 302
Chamberlain, Neville, 301
Chanut, Hector Pierre, 150
Charles I, 140, 143, 151
Charles II, 143, 153
Charles V, 130
Chassidischen Bücher, 265
Chemins de la liberté, Les, 290
Child and Curriculum, The, 245

Choice Part, 99
Chomsky, Noam, 314–316
Christina, Queen, 150
Chuanxilu, 134
Church of England, 151
Cicero, 81
City College of New York, 262
City of God, 74, 75, 77–78
City University of New York, 337
Civil Wars, English, 151, 152
Clement IV, 120
Clement VI, 128
Clement VII, 130
Clement XI, 98
Clement XII, 169
Clerselier, Claude, 150
Collationes, 124
Collège de France, 243, 310
College of Navarre, 197
Columbia College, 332
Columbia University, 246
Coke, Sir Edward, 135
Commentaries, 199
Commentary on Plato's Republic, 105
Commodus, Lucius Ceionius, 66
Commonplace Book, 1919–1953, 264
Communist Manifesto, The, 218,
    220–221
Communist Party, 206, 219,
    290–291, 301, 330
"Comprehensive Mirror for Aid
    in Government," 107
Comte, Auguste, 209–211
Comte, Louis, 209
Condorcet, Marquis de (Marie-
    Jean-Antoine-Nicolas de
    Caritat), 197–198
Conference on Jewish
    Relations, 292
Confessions, 74, 75, 77, 183

Confucianism, 19, 21, 54–55, 106, 108, 133–134, 252–253
Confucius, 14, 19–24, 54–55, 107
Conics, 79
Consequences of Pragmatism, 332
Considerations on Representative Government, 214
Considérations sur les causes de la grandeur des Romains et de leur décadence, 177
Consolation of Philosophy, 80–81
Constitution, U.S., 151, 156, 178
Contingency, Irony, and Solidarity, 332
Contribution to the Critique of Political Economy, A, 221
"Contributions to the Theory of the Calculus of Variations," 238
Conventions: A Philosophical Study, 339
Cooper, Lord Anthony Ashley, 152
Copernican Revolution, The, 308–309
Cornell University, 306
Corsair, The, 217
Counsel for Kings, 100
Counter-Reformation, 146
Cours de philosophie positive, 210
"Course of Positive Philosophy," 210
Crates of Thebes, 60
Creative Evolution, 243
Crises of the Republic, 294
Critica, La, 250–251
Critique de la raison dialectique, 291
"Critique of Aesthetic Judgment," 193
Critique of Judgment, 193–194
Critique of Practical Reason, 192–193

Critique of Pure Reason, 189–192
"Critique of Teleological Judgment," 193
Critique of Utilitarianism, A, 325
Croce, Benedetto, 250–252
Cromwell, Oliver, 143, 151
Cudworth, Ralph, 159
Cynicism, 60
Cyril, 80
Cyropaedia, 130

D

Daniel, 266, 267
Daoism, 55–57, 106–107, 133
Darwin, Charles, 225, 344
Darwinism, 344
De Antiquissima Italorum Sapientia, 169
De Casibus Perplexis, 165
De Cive, 141, 142
Declaration of Independence, U.S., 156
Declaration of the Rights of Man and of the Citizen, 157, 178
De consolatione philosophiae, 80–81
deconstruction, 327–330
De Corpore, 141
Dedekind, Richard, 255
Défense de L'Espirit de lois, 178
De interpretatione, 48, 124
De l'esprit des loix, 177
Deliverer from Error, The, 99
Democritus, 10, 35–37, 59
De Nostri Temporis Studiorum Ratione, 168
De praedicamentis, 124
Derrida, Jacques, 327–330
Descartes, René, 9–10, 140, 143–150, 152, 159, 162, 164, 169, 304, 321, 323

Descartes: The Project of Pure
  Inquiry, 323
Descriptive Sociology, 224
De sophisticis elenchis, 124
Dessau, Menachem Mendel, 195
Destitio, Teresa, 168
Devereux, Robert, 135
Dewey, John, 244–247
Dialectic of Enlightenment, 287
Dialogues Concerning Natural
  Religion, 182
Diderot, Denis, 183
Dilthey, Wilhelm, 226–227, 275
Diophantus of Alexandria, 79
Discipline and Punish: The Birth of
  the Prison, 310, 313
Discourse, 148
Discourse Addressed to Magistrates
  and Men in Authority, A, 174
Discourse on the Origin of
  Inequality, 184, 186, 187
Discourse on the Sciences and the
  Arts, A, 183–184
Discourses, 65
Discourses on Livy, 129
Doctor Club, 219
"Doctrine of Elements," 192
"Doctrine of Judgment in
  Psychologism: A Critical-
  Positive Contribution in
  Logic, The," 276
Dohm, Christian Wilhelm
  von, 196
Duns Scotus, John, 122–125, 276

E

École Normale Supérieure, 288,
  310, 327
École Polytechnique, 209, 210

Economist, The, 224
Edinburgh Review, The, 211
efficient cause, 51
Eichmann, Adolf, 294
Eichmann in Jerusalem, 294
Einstein, Albert, 249
eirôneia, 31
Either/Or, 216
Eleaticism, 26
Elements, 163
Elements of Law, Natural and
  Politic, The, 141
Elements of Theology, 163
Elizabeth, Queen, 135
Émile, 187
Empiricism, 150, 153, 171, 179,
  240, 280–282, 284–286,
  297–298, 300, 304, 315
Empiricism and the Philosophy of
  Mind, 304
Encheiridion, 65
"Encyclopedia of the
  Philosophical Sciences in
  Outline," 204–205
Encyclopédie, 178, 183, 187
Engels, Friedrich, 219, 220, 222
Enlightenment, 13, 47, 151, 160,
  178, 197–198, 218, 287
Enneads, 71–72
Enquiry Concerning Human
  Understanding, An, 180–182
Enquiry Concerning the Principles
  of Morals, 180
Enquiry Concerning the Principles
  of Natural Knowledge, 249
Epictetus, 65–66, 68
Epicurus, 57, 59–60, 64
epistemology, 12, 192, 240, 259,
  297, 331, 337
Erkenntnis, 280

Erst Philosophie, 240
Esperanto, 284
Essai sur le goût, 178
*Essay Concerning Human
  Understanding, An*, 153,
  157–159
Essay on Taste, 178
Essay on the Calendar, 111
Essays and Treatises, 182
Essays in Radical Empiricism, 229
*Essays on Some Unsettled Questions
  of Political Economy*, 212
*Essay Towards a New Theory of
  Vision, An*, 173
Essence of Christianity, The, 219
Essentials, 99
Essential Tension, The, 309
"eternal feminine" myth, 295
Ethica, 153
ethical intuitionists, 263
Ethics, 161, 163–164
*Ethics and the Limits of
  Philosophy*, 325
Ethics of Ambiguity, The, 296
Eton College, 299
Euclid, 158, 163
Eudemian Ethics, 52, 54
Existentialism, 11, 13, 206, 214,
  241, 275, 276, 287, 290, 295
*Existentialism and
  Humanism*, 290
Experience and Education, 246

F

Falconer, Sir David, 179
falsifiability criterion, 286
Famine, Affluence, and Morality,
  342–343
"Fantôme de Staline, Le," 291

Farewell to Sartre, A, 296
Fascism, 235, 251–252, 287, 301
Faustina, Annia Galeria, 66
Fear and Trembling, 216–217
feminism, 295, 296
Fermat, Pierre de, 79
Feuerbach, Ludwig, 219
Fides quaerens intellectum, 97
Filmer, Sir Robert, 154
Finch, Edith, 262
First Principles, 224, 225
Flaubert, 291
Flaubert, Gustave, 291
Force of Circumstance, 296
*Formal and Transcendental
  Logic*, 240
forms, theory of, 43–47
Forster, Anne, 174
Forster-Nietzsche, Elisabeth,
  235–236
Förster, Bernhard, 235
Forster, E. M., 263
Foucault, Michel, 309–314, 330
*Foundations for a Metaphysics of
  Pure Process*, 305
Foundations of Arithmetic, The, 237,
  255, 270
*Foundations of Empirical
  Knowledge, The*, 300
Fountain of Life, 95–96
Four Noble Truths, 70
Fragment on Government, A, 199
Francis of Assisi, 121
Franco-German War, 222
Franco-Prussian War, 231
Frasier's Magazine, 214
Frederick, John, 166
Frederick the Great, 195
Frege, Alexander, 236
Frege, Auguste, 236

Frege, Friedrich Ludwig Gottlob, 236–238, 255–256, 270, 279
French Revolution, 157, 182, 197–198
Freud, Sigmund, 207, 286, 291, 318
Friars Preachers, 118
Friedrich Wilhelm IV, 230
functionalism, 227, 305

G

Gakushuin University, 253
Gassendi, Pierre, 146
Gast, Peter, 232
Gay Science, The, 232
General Medicine, 104
Genet, Jean, 290
George III, 188
Gibbens, Alice H., 228
Giles of Ligny, 123
Girton College, 261
Glaucon, 38
Glorious Revolution, 151, 154
Gnosticism, 64
Godenshō, 115
Godin, Guillaume Pierre, 124
"golden rule," 24
Gonsalvus Hispanus, 123–124
Gotha Program, 223
Govinda, 83
gradual ascent, 138–139
Graham, Sheilah, 303
Greek Skepticism, 57, 72
Gregory X, 122
Grouchy, Sophie de, 197
Grundgesetze der Arithmetik, 237–238
Guicciardini, Francesco, 130
Guide for the Perplexed, The, 108, 112

Guillaume de Champeaux, 100
Guy's Hospital, 274

H

Habermas, Jürgen, 317–320
Hadrian, 66
hagiographies, 115
Harper, William Rainey, 246
Harris, Zellig S., 314
Harvard Medical School, 228
Harvard University, 227, 249, 283, 297, 306, 308, 314, 332, 333, 337, 339
Hasidism, 265
Hayek, F. A., 333
Hebreo, León, 96
Hebrew University, 266
Hegel, Georg Wilhelm Friedrich, 200–206, 207, 214, 219, 220, 244–245, 263, 311
Heidegger, Martin, 241, 275–279, 292, 294
Hellenism, 81
Hell-Fire Club, 174
Héloïse, 100, 101, 103
Hempel, Carl, 311, 332
Henry IV, 144
Heracleitus, 10, 25–26
Hermarchus, 60
hermeneutics, 275
Hermias, 47–48
Herodotus, 211
Hinduism, 84, 92
Histoire générale de la Chine, 107
historical consciousness, 227
History, 182
History of Sexuality, The, 313
History of Western Philosophy, A, 262

Hitler, Adolf, 235–236, 241, 278
Hobbes, Thomas, 14, 139–143,
 146, 176, 205
Hōjō Takiyoshi, 252
Ho Kepos, 59
Horkheimer, Max, 287, 317, 318
Hugo, Victor, 292
Human, All-Too-Human, 232
Human Condition, The, 293–294
human flourishing, 39
humanism, 120, 138, 250, 275,
 290, 321, 323, 327
*Human Knowledge: Its Scope and
 Limits*, 262
Hume, David, 13, 179–182, 188,
 216, 280, 286, 324
Hume, Joseph, 179
Husserl, Edmund, 238–241,
 275–277, 288
Hypatia, 79–80
Hypotyposes, 73

I

Iamblichus, 79
I and Thou, 264, 267–268
ibn Aknin, Joseph, 112
Ibn al-'Arabī, 112–114
Ibn Gabirol, 95–96
ibn Shoshan, Judah, 109
Ich und Du, 264, 267–268
Idealism, 188, 190, 203, 206,
 263, 318
*Ideas, General Introduction to Pure
 Phenomenology*, 240
Idiot de la famille, L', 291
Idomeneus, 60
Iliad, 143
*Imagination: A Psychological
 Critique*, 288

Imperial College of Science and
 Technology, 248
*Inconsistency—or Incoherence—of
 the Philosophers, The*, 99
indeterminacy of translation,
 298–299
Index Librorum Prohibitorum, 178
individuation, 124, 225–226, 265
Industrial Revolution, 220
Institute for Advanced
 Study, 285
Institute for Social Research,
 286, 317
Institutio theologica, 163
"Instructions for Practical
 Living," 134
Interlingua, 284
*International Encyclopedia of
 Unified Science*, 283
International Working Men's
 Association, 222
"Interpreter of Desires,
 The," 113
*In the Beginning Was the Deed:
 Realism and Moralism in
 Political Argument*, 327
*Introduction to Mathematical
 Philosophy, An*, 259
*Introduction to Mathematics,
 An*, 248
Introduction to Metaphysics, 279
*Introduction to Symbolic Logic and
 Its Applications*, 280
*Introduction to the Principles of
 Morals and Legislation, An*,
 199–200
*Invariances: The Structure of the
 Objective World*, 336
Iron in the Soul, 290
Isagoge, 124

Italian Institute for Historical Studies, 252
"I think, therefore I am," 10, 148–149

J

Jainism, 84
James, Henry, 227–230
James, William, 227–230, 245
James I, 135, 140
James II, 154
Jans, Helena, 146
"Jerusalem, or on Religious Power and Judaism," 196
"Jew, The," 265
jihad, 105
Jinsi Lu, 107
Jōdo Shinshū, 114
Johann Wolfgang Goethe University, 286, 317
John Hopkins University, 244
John XXII, 127–128
Josephus, 62
Jude, Der, 265
Juden, Die, 195
Julius II, 129
junzi fellowship, 23
Justin I, 82
Just Mean in Belief, The, 99

K

Kabbalism, 96
Kant, Immanuel, 188–194, 201, 203, 205, 207, 217, 218, 240, 263, 276, 305, 323, 326
Kapital, Das, 222
Kashf al-Manāhij, 104
Keynes, John, 263

Kierkegaard, Michael Pedersen, 214
Kierkegaard, Søren, 11, 214–218, 275
Kilkenny College, 171
Kitab ash-shifa, 90
Kitarō, Nishida, 252–253
Knights Templar, 125
Knowledge and Human Interests, 318
Kongfuzi/Kongzi, 19
Kort verhandeling van God, de mensch en deszelfs welstand, 161
Kripe, Saul, 336–338
Kuhn, Thomas S., 308–309
Kyōgyōshinshō, 116
Kyoto Imperial University, 253

L

Laërtius, Diogenes, 35
Lamian War, 59
language game, 274
Language, Truth, and Logic, 299–302
La Peyrère, Isaac, 160–161
Lartigue, Jeanne de, 175
Lassalle, Ferdinand, 223
Lavater, J. C., 196
Lawrence Scientific School, 227
Laws, 32
"Laws of Jerusalem," 111
Lawson, Nigel, 303
Lawson, Vanessa, 303
League for Industrial Democracy, 333
League of Nations, 278
Lebre vom Urteil im Psychologismus: Ein kritisch-positiver Beitrag zur Logik, Die, 276

Lees, Renee, 302
Leibniz, Gottfried Wilhelm,
    165–168
Lessing, Gotthold Ephraim,
    195, 197
"Letters on Feeling," 195
Letter to Monsieur d'Alembert on
    the Theatre, 187
Lettres persames, 176
Leucippus, 35
Levasseur, Thérèse, 184, 188
Leviathan, 139, 141–143
Lévi-Strauss, Claude, 330
Lewis, David Kellogg, 339–341
libertarianism, 332–336
Life of Castruccio Castracani of
    Lucca, The, 129–130
Life of David Hume, Esquire,
    Written by Himself, The, 182
Life of the Mind, The, 294
Li Tong, 106
Littré, Maximilien, 210
Locke, John, 12, 150–160, 195, 334
Logical Empiricism, 280–282, 284
Logical Foundations of
    Probability, 285
"Logical Investigations," 239
Logical Positivism, 279–280,
    297, 299
logical purposiveness, 193
Logical Structure of Linguistic
    Theory, 314
Logical Structure of the World:
    Pseudoproblems in Philosophy,
    The, 281
Logical Syntax of Language,
    The, 284
Logic of Scientific Discovery,
    The, 285
Logik der Forschung, 285

logische Aufbau der Welt, Der, 281
Logos, 25, 63, 96, 121
Lombard, Peter, 126
London and Westminster Review,
    The, 211
London School of Economics, 285
Long March, The, 296
Longuet, Jenny, 223
Lotze, R. H., 226
Louis IV, 127
Louis XIII, 145
Louis XIV, 176
Louis XVI, 198
Lu Jiuyuan, 106
Lunyu, 107
Lutterell, John, 126–127
Lu Xiangshan, 106, 134
Lycée Henri IV, 242, 288
Lyceum, 39, 48

M

Mach, Ernst, 280
Machiavelli, Niccolò, 14, 128–133
Madhyamika, 69
Madhyamika-sastra, 70
Madness and Civilization: A
    History of Insanity in the Age
    of Reason, 310
"Madness and Unreason: A
    History of Madness in the
    Classical Age," 310
Magna moralia, 52
Magnus, Albertus, 119
Mahayana Buddhism, 84
Mailla, J. A. M. Moyriac de, 107
Maimonides, Moses, 108–112,
    162–163
Malebranche, Nicolas, 167
Making Sense of Humanity, 325

Mandarins, The, 296
Manichaeism, 75
Manual, 65
Marburg University, 276, 292, 317
Martensen, H. L., 218
Marx, Karl, 206, 218–223, 286, 291, 311, 318
Mary II, 154, 159
Masham, Damaris, 159–160
Massachusetts Institute of Technology, 306, 308, 314
Massin, Caroline, 210
material cause, 51
Matter and Memory, 243
Max Planck Institute, 317
McCarthy, Mary, 294
Meaning and Necessity, 284
Mecca, 99, 113–114
"Meccan Revelations, The," 112
Medici, Giulio de', 129–130
Meditationes de Cognitione, Veritate et Ideis, 167
Meditations, 66, 67–69, 146, 148–150
Memoirs of a Dutiful Daughter, 296
Mencius, 54–55
Mendelssohn, Moses, 194–197
Men in Dark Times, 294
Mersenne, Marin, 140–141, 145, 150
Metaphysics, 51
Metrodorus, 60
Michael of Cesena, 127
Middle Academy, 57
Mill, James, 211
Mill, John Stuart, 210, 211–214, 284
Millot ha-Higgayon, 111
Mind, 263
Mises, Ludwig von, 333
Mishna, 111

Mishne Torah, 111
Molesworth, Sir William, 211
Monadologia, 168
monadology, 167
Montesquieu, Baron de la Brède et de (Charles-Louis de Secondat), 175–178
Moore, G.E., 255, 263–264
Moral Consciousness and Communicative Action, 319
Morality: An Introduction to Ethics, 326
Moral Luck, 325–326
"Morning Hours," 197
Morrell, Lady Ottoline, 260
Morris, Charles W., 283
Mozart, Wolfgang Amadeus, 269
Mussolini, Benito, 251
Mydorge, Claude, 145
Mynster, J. P., 218

N

Nagarjuna, 69–71
Naming and Necessity, 337–338
Nanhua zhenjing, 56
Nathan the Wise, 195
Naturalism and Ontology, 305
natural philosophy, 50
natural selection, 225
"Nature of Judgment, The," 263
Nature of Rationality, The, 336
Nausea, 288
Nausiphanes, 59
Nazi Party, 266, 278–279, 286, 292, 294, 317, 341
Negative Dialectics, 287
neo-Confucianism, 133–134
neo-Kantianism, 276

Neoplatonism, 69, 70, 79–80, 86, 89, 90, 95, 96, 124, 163
Neuburger, Louise, 242
Neurath, Otto, 283
neuroasthenia, 228
New Academy, 57
New Atlantis, The, 139
New Eloise, The, 188
New Republic, The, 246–247
New School for Social Research, 292
Newton, Isaac, 309
New York University, 317, 341–342
Niche for Lights, The, 99
Nicholas of Cusa, 265
Nichomachean Ethics, 52, 54
Nichomachus, 47
Nietzsche, Carl Ludwig, 230
Nietzsche, Freidrich, 13, 217, 230–236, 265, 275, 321, 326
nihilism, 70, 234, 265
nirvana, 69, 70
Nishida Yasunori, 252
Nobel Prize for Literature, 242, 243, 254, 262, 287
nominalism, 125, 136
Nonconformist, The, 224
Northwestern University, 317
Novum Organum, 135, 138
Nozick, Max, 332
Nozick, Robert, 332–336
Nozick, Sophie Cohen, 332

O

Oberlin College, 297, 339
Objections and Replies, 150
objektive Logik, Die, 204

Ockham, William of, 125–128
"Ockham's razor," 126–127
Odyssey, 143
Oedipus, 326
Old Age, 296
Olsen, Regine, 215
Olybrius, 81
Olympius, 72
"On Denoting," 259
On Liberty, 214
On Nature, 26
On Opera, 327
"On Perplexing Cases," 165
On Revolution, 294
"On the Civil Improvement of the Jews," 196
On the Concept of Irony, with Constant Reference to Socrates, 215
"On the Concept of Number: Psychological Analyses," 239
On the Good, 43
On the Special Laws, 63
ontology, 10, 275, 297, 299, 305
On Violence, 294
Open Society and Its Enemies, The, 286
"opium of the people," religion as, 220
Order of Merit, 250, 262
Order of Things, The, 310
Ordinatio, 124, 127
Organon, 81
Origins of Totalitarianism, 293
Our Knowledge of the External World, 259
"Outline and Digest of the General Mirror," 107
Outlines, 222

Outlines of Pyrrhonism, 73
Overbeck, Franz, 235

P

paganism, 78, 79–80, 88, 103
Paraclete, 103
Parerga und Paralipomena, 209
Paris Commune, 222
Parmenides, 26–27, 38, 44–45
Patriarcha, 154
Peano, Giuseppe, 237
Peirce, Charles Sanders, 318
Pericles, 38
Perictione, 38
Peripatetic doctrines, 89
Persian Letters, 176
Pesnel, Marie-Françoise de, 175
Petrarch, 133
Phaedo, 44, 196
"Phaedo, or on the Immortality
    of the Soul," 195
Phaenarete, 29
Phänomenologie, 206
phenomenology, 203–204, 206,
    238, 239–241, 275–277, 288, 311
Phenomenology of Mind, The,
    203–204
Philip II, 48
Philip IV, 123, 125
Philo Judaeus, 62–65
"Philosophical Essays," 253
*Philosophical Essays Concerning
    Human Understanding*, 180
Philosophical Explanations, 336
Philosophical Investigations,
    273–274
Philosophical Papers, 264
Philosophical Perspectives, 305

"Philosophical Speeches," 195
Philosophical Studies, 264
*Philosophy and the Mirror of
    Nature*, 332
*Philosophy and the Scientific Image
    of Man*, 304
*Philosophy as a Humanistic
    Discipline*, 327
*Philosophy of Logical Atomism,
    The*, 259
Philosophy of Modern Music, 287
Philosophy of Right, The, 205
Philosophy of Science, 282
"Philosophy of the Spirit,"
    250–251
physicalism, 282
Physics, 50–52
Pico della Mirandola,
    Giovanni, 171
Plato, 9, 12, 21, 26, 27, 29, 31–34,
    37–39, 41–47, 61, 64, 68–69,
    71, 81, 85, 89, 105, 159, 186,
    196, 207, 217, 257, 261, 275, 321
Platonism, 64, 68, 78, 81–82, 100
Plotinus, 71–72, 79, 90, 96
Popish Plot, 153
Popper, Sir Karl, 285–286
Porphyry, 71–72, 124
Poseidon, 38
positivism, 209, 234, 311
*Postscript to the Logic of Scientific
    Discovery*, 286
poststructuralism, 330
Pouilly, Jean de, 125
Poverty of Historicism, The, 286
practical propositions, 49
Prae-Adamitae, 160
Pragmatism, 227, 229, 244–245,
    283, 330, 332

Pressburg, Henrietta, 218
Prime of Life, The, 296
Prince, The, 128–129, 130, 132–133
Prince Maurice, 145
Princeton University, 286,
  305–306, 308, 331, 332, 337,
  339, 342
Principes de la nature et de la Grace fondés en raison, 168
Principe, Il, 128–129, 130, 132–133
Principia Ethica, 263
Principia Mathematica, 247, 248,
  257, 259, 260
Principia Philosophiae, 150, 162
Principles of Mathematics, The,
  248, 255–256, 270
Principles of Philosophy, 150, 162
Principles of Political Economy, 212
Principles of Psychology, The, 224,
  228, 245
Principles of Sociology, The, 224
Prior Analytics, 48
probability theory, 285
Problem of Knowledge, The, 301–302
Problem of Method, The, 291
Problems of the Self: Philosophical Papers, 327
process philosophy, 241–242
Proclus, 163
progressive education, 246
Proper Sphere of Government, The, 224
Proposal for the better Supplying of Churches, A, 173
Proslogium, 97
Proust, Marcel, 242
Psyche, 230
psychic harmony, 42
Psychology of Imagination, The,
  288–289

Ptolemy, 79, 309
Puritanism, 151, 152
Pyrrhonism, 57, 73–74
Pyrrhon of Elis, 13, 57
Pythagoras, 10–11, 17, 60, 256,
  257, 261
Pythagorean theorem, 10–11, 17

Q

Quaestiones in Metaphysicam Aristotelis, 124
Querist, The, 174
Quine, Willard Van Orman, 283,
  284, 297–299, 323, 339
Qur'ān, 86, 104

R

Rāmānuja, 92–94
Ramsey, Frank, 272
Rationalism, 160, 169, 192, 240, 251
Rawls, John, 305–308, 330, 335, 336
Rawls, William Lee, 305
Realism, 190, 206, 263, 327
Records of the Historian, 21
rectification, politics as, 23–24
Reden über das Judentum, 267
Reflections on Knowledge, Truth, and Ideas, 167
Reflections on the Causes of the Grandeur and Declension of the Romans, 177
"Reflections on Things at Hand," 107
Reformation, 47
Reform Bill of 1832, 205
Reform Bill of 1867, 222
"Refutation of Idealism, The," 263
Reichenbach, Hans, 280
relativity, theory of, 278

Renaissance, 47, 128, 171
Renati des Cartes Principiorum Philosophiae, 162
René Descartes's Principles of Philosophy, 162
Reprieve, The, 290
Republic, 12, 38, 41–43
Research Project on Social Discrimination, 287
Responsibility and Judgment, 294
Restoration, 143
"Revival of the Religious Sciences, The," 98
Rickert, Heinrich, 275–276
Ritschl, Friedrich Wilhelm, 230, 231
Robespierre, Maximilien, 198
Rockefeller University, 332, 337
Rodin, Auguste, 10
Rohde, Erwin, 230
Roman Empire, 66, 78
Roots of Reference, The, 299
Rorty, Richard, 330–332
Roscelin of Compiègne, 100
Rousseau, Jean-Jacques, 13–14, 182–188
Royal Athenaeum, 210
Royal Society, 152, 165, 176, 250
Royal Swedish Academy of Sciences, 337
Rufus, Musonius, 65
Rufus, William II, 98
Russell, Bertrand, 237–238, 247–248, 254–262, 263, 270, 283, 302
Ryle, Gilbert, 299, 301

S

Saint Genet, 290
Śaṅkara, 83–85

Sartre, Jean-Paul, 9, 11, 276, 287–292, 295, 296, 327
Sartrian Socialism, 291
Saussure, Ferdinand de, 328–330
Savonarola, Girolamo, 129
Sayfad-Dawlah, 87
Schelling, Friedrich, 317
Schlick, Moritz, 272, 280
Scholasticism, 96, 117, 122, 127
School and Society, The, 245
Schopenhauer, Arthur, 9, 206–209, 230, 232
Schopenhauer, Heinrich Floris, 207
Science and Metaphysics, 305
Science and the Modern World, 249
"Science of Logic," 204, 206
Science, Perception, and Reality, 305
scientific materialism, 249
Scienza nuova, 169–170
Search for a Method, 291
Secondat, Charles-Louis de, 175–178
Secondat, Jacques de, 175
Second Sex, The, 295, 296
Sellars, Roy, 303
Sellars, Wilfrid, 303–305
Sense of the Past: Essays in the History of Philosophy, The, 327
Sentences, 126
Seventh Day, The, 268
Sextus Empiricus, 57, 72–74
Shame and Necessity, 326
She Came to Stay, 295–296
Shinran, 114–117
Short Treatise on God, Man and His Well-Being, 161
Shujing, 23
Sickness unto Death, 215

Siger of Brabant, 120
Simone de Beauvoir: A Biography, 296
Singer, Peter (Albert David), 341–344
Siris, 174–175
Sivaguru, 83
Six-Day War, 268
Skepticism, 13, 57, 72–73, 138, 179, 302
Sketch for a Historical Picture of the Progress of the Human Mind, 198
Sketch for a Theory of the Emotions, 288
Skinner, Patricia, 320
sober intoxication, 64
Social Contract, The, 186–187
Socialism, 212, 219, 261, 278–279, 283, 291, 333
Social Statics, 224, 225
Socrates, 9, 12, 21, 26, 27, 28–35, 37, 38–39, 41–42, 44–47, 51, 63, 195, 215, 275
Socratic method, 12, 31–33
Soderini, Piero, 129
Solger, Karl, 206
Some Main Problems of Philosophy, 263
Some Problems of Philosophy, 229
Song Confucianism, 106
Sophist, 44
Sophroniscus, 29
Sorbonne, 288, 295, 327
speciesism, 343–344
Spence, Patricia "Peter," 261–262
Spencer, Herbert, 223–226
Spencer, Rev. Thomas, 224

Spencer, William George, 224
Spinoza, Baruch, 11
Spinoza, Benedict de, 96, 160–164, 197
"Spirit of Christianity and Its Fate, The," 201, 203
Spirit of Laws, The, 175, 177–178
Stanford University, 331
Steinschneider, Malvine, 238
Stilpon of Megara, 60
Stoa Poikile, 60–61
Stoicism, 60–62, 65, 66, 68
structuralism, 330
Structural Transformation of the Public Sphere, The, 317
Structure of Scientific Revolutions, The, 308
Students for a Democratic Society, 333
Stump, Anna Abell, 305
Stumpf, Carl, 238
"Subjective Synthesis," 210
subjektive Logik, Die, 204
Suda Lexicon, 79
Sufism, 98–99, 113
"survival of the fittest," 223, 225
Swarthmore College, 339
Sydenham, Thomas, 152
syllogism, 48–50, 104
Symmachus, Quintus Aurelius Memmius, 81
Symposium, 44, 64
Synesius of Cyrene, 79
Syntactic Structures, 315
Synthetic Philosophy, The, 224
syphilis, 235
Système nouveau, 167
System of Logic, A, 212
System of Positive Policy, 210

T

Tahāfut al-Tahāfut, 104

"Talks on Judaism," 267

Talmud, 111

Tarski, Alfred, 283, 297

Taylor, Henry Osborn, 249

Temps Modernes, Le, 290–291, 295

"Testability and Meaning,"
    282–283

Theaetetus, 29

Théodicée, 168

Theodoric, 81–82

Theodosius I, 78, 79

Theologia, 101, 103

"Theology of Aristotle," 85

Theon, 79

Theories of Surplus Value, 222

Theory of Communicative Action,
    The, 318–319

theory of descriptions, 259

Theory of Justice, A, 306

theory of relativity, 278

Thinker, The, 10

Thirteen Articles of Faith, 111

Thirty Tyrants, 38

Thirty Years' War, 150, 165

Thomism, 117

Thoughts on Parliamentary
    Reform, 214

Three Dialogues between Hylas and
    Philonous, 173

Three Essays, Moral and
    Political, 180

Three Essays on Religion, 214

Thus Spoke Zarathustra, 234–235

Time and Free Will: An Essay on the
    Immediate Data of
    Consciousness, 242–243

Time of My Life, The, 299

Time of Transitions, 320

Timon of Phlius, 57

Tongjian gangmu, 107

topology, general, 166

"Torah Reviewed, The," 111

"Toward the Critique of the
    Hegelian Philosophy of
    Right," 220

Tractatus de Intellectus
    Emendatione, 161–162

Tractatus de primo principio, 124

Tractatus Logico-Philosophicus,
    260, 271–273

Tractatus Theologoico-Politicus,
    161–163

"Transcendental Aesthetic," 191

"Transcendental Analytic," 191

"Transcendental Dialectic," 191

Treatise Concerning the Principles of
    Human Knowledge, Part I, 173

Treatise on Human Nature, A,
    179–180

"Treatise on Logical
    Terminology," 111

Treatise on the Emendation of the
    Intellect, 161

Treatise on Universal Algebra, 247

Trinity College, 171–172,
    247–248, 254, 261, 262, 263,
    270, 272

Troglodytes, 176

Troubled Sleep, 290

True Pure Land School,
    114–116, 252

Truth and Truthfulness, 326

Two Sources of Morality and
    Religion, The, 243

Two Treatises of Government, 154

U

Übermensch, 235
Universal Grammar, 315–316
University College, London,
  301–302, 341
University of Basel, 231
University of Berlin, 207, 219,
  226, 238, 265
University of Bonn, 218–219,
  230, 317
University of Bordeaux, 175
University of Buffalo, 303
University of California,
  Berkeley, 287, 308, 311, 320
University of California,
  Irvine, 327
University of California, Los
  Angeles, 262, 285, 339
University of Cambridge, 224,
  254, 270, 274, 302, 320
University of Chicago, 244, 246,
  262, 283, 292, 330
University of Clermont-
  Ferrand, 310
University of Copenhagen, 214
University of Edinburgh, 229
University of Frankfurt, 286, 287,
  317, 318
University of Freiburg, 240, 275,
  276, 277, 278, 279, 292
University of Göttingen, 207,
  239, 317
University of Halle, 238–239
University of Heidelberg, 292, 317
University of Iowa, 304
University of Jena, 207, 236, 279
University of Leipzig, 230, 231,
  238, 265

University of Lille, 310
University of Michigan, 244, 303
University of Minnesota, 244, 304
University of Naples, 168
University of Oxford, 261, 286,
  299, 302, 303, 320, 321, 337, 341
University of Paris, Vincennes, 310
University of Pennsylvania, 314
University of Pittsburgh, 304
University of Tunis, 310
University of Vermont, 244
University of Vienna, 238, 265,
  280, 285
University of Virginia, 331
University of Zürich, 265, 317
Untimely Meditations, 232
Utilitarianism, 199, 211, 214, 306,
  325, 342, 344
Utilitarianism, 214
Utilitarianism: For and Against, 325

V

Vanini, Lucilio, 146
Variations on Kantian Themes, 305
*Varieties of Religious Experience,
  The*, 229
verifiability principle, 300
verificationist theory of
  meaning, 300
Verulam, Baron, 135
Verus, Marcus Aelius Aurelius,
  66–67
Very Easy Death, A, 296
Vico, Giambattista, 168–171
Victoria, Queen, 254
Vienna, 265
Vienna Circle, 272, 280, 283, 285,
  297, 299–300

"Vindication of the Jews," 196
Vishnu, 92
Void, the, 35–37
Voltaire, 218

W

Wade, Evelyn Willoughby, 247
Wagner, Richard, 230, 232
Waismann, Friedrich, 272
Wallace, Alfred Russel, 225
Walpole, Sir Robert, 174
Wang Yangming, 133–134
Watt, G. F., 214
Weierstrass, Karl, 255
Wellesley College, 331
Wells, Dee, 303
Westminster, The, 211
What Is Metaphysics?, 277
Whigs, 152
Whitehead, Alfred, 247
Whitehead, Alfred North,
   247–250, 257
"Why I Am Not a Christian," 261
William the Conqueror, 98
William II, 154
Williams, Sir Bernard, 320–327
Will to Believe and Other Essays in
   Popular Philosophy, The, 228
Winckler, Paula, 265
Wittgenstein, Karl, 269
Wittgenstein, Leopoldine, 269
Wittgenstein, Ludwig, 260,
   269–274, 300, 301, 321
Woolf, Virginia, 263

Word and Object, 299
"Words and Things," 310
World as Will and Idea, The,
   207, 209
World War I, 240, 251, 261, 270,
   272, 274
World War II, 251, 274, 279, 287,
   288, 290, 296, 309, 317

X

Xanthippe, 29
Xenophon, 31, 130, 211
Xiang of Lu, Duke, 19

Y

Yale University, 304, 327, 330
Yekutiel, 95
Young Hegelians, 219

Z

Zen Buddhism, 253
Zeno of Citium, 60–62
Zeno of Elea, 27–28
Zenran, 116
Zhang Zai, 107
Zhou, 56
Zhou Dunyi, 107
Zhuangzi, 55–57
Zhu Xi, 105–108, 133
Zionism, 265, 267
Zisi, 54
Zizhi tongjian, 107